JEWS AND ARABS

JEWS AND ARABS

Their Contacts Through the Ages

S. D. GOITEIN

Schocken Books • *New York*

Library of Congress Catalog Card Number: 55-7968
Manufactured in the United States of America

CONTENTS

A book on the relationships between Jews and Arabs through the ages needs no justification. These relationships have been so influential on the destinies of the two peoples and, to some extent, on the general course of history, that they deserve study in their own right. In addition, their knowledge is conducive to a better understanding of the problems facing the Middle East in our own days.

There is no textbook on either Jewish or Arab history that would provide an adequate picture of these contacts which stretch over many hundreds of years and touch on almost every aspect of culture. Much of the material is scattered in innumerable publications: partly it had to be culled directly from still untapped and unpublished sources.

When Mr. S. Schocken, who already had published my Yemenite anthology, *Tales from the Land of Sheba,* asked me to write a book on the history of the social and cultural contacts between Jews and Arabs, I responded with enthusiasm. I had worked in this field for almost thirty years: First, in connection with large scale researches into Muslim religious literature and historiography; secondly, during my study of the Oriental Jewish communities, in particular the Yemenites, the most genuine Jews living among the most genuine Arabs; finally, owing to my work on the *Geniza,* medieval documents, written in Hebrew characters, but mostly in the Arabic language. These studies, many of which were of a specialized nature and were published in different languages, needed integration and summarizing. The writing of a book of the character described offered an ideal opportunity.

Jews and Arabs was written in 1954 and published in 1955. It grew out of a series of lectures. The personal tone of a lecturer addressing an audience has been preserved throughout. When depletion of the stock made a new edition necessary, it was decided to publish it in paperback, for the book has been widely used in colleges and universities. Since *Jews and Arabs* deals with social and cultural relationships to the exclusion of political and military issues, there was no need for drastic changes or additions. The Introduction and the concluding section, which emphasized the importance of the subject in connection with present relations between Israel and her neighbors, have been omitted. There is no longer any need for such emphasis. A few inaccuracies and flaws have been corrected. A number of omissions have been remedied. Parts of Chapter Eight had to be rewritten, because certain trends in contemporary Arabic literature have become more pronounced today than could have been anticipated ten years ago. On the other hand, Chapter Four, "The Jewish Tradition in Islam," has not been touched. A slight modification of the author's views about the Jewish companions of the Prophet of Islam is explained in his forthcoming volume *Studies in Islamic History and Institutions.*

In conclusion, the author wishes to express his gratitude to the learned and unbiased reviewers of the first edition. To their remarks must be credited what improvement may be apparent in this new version.

S. D. GOITEIN

JEWS AND ARABS

1

1. A *Historical Survey of Jewish-Arab Relations*.

The Middle East was the cradle of human civilization and the place of origin of the three monotheistic religions. However, from approximately 750 B.C. onwards, the free creative nations of the Middle East were crushed and atomized by the steamrollers of conquering empires: Assyrians, Neo-Babylonians, ancient Persians, Macedonians and Romans. Even the Arab conquest of the Middle East did not lead to the formation of new and enduring national states. For reasons explained in the concluding chapter, the Arabs, while impressing their language and religion on large sections of the Middle East, soon submerged themselves in its ancient subject population and were ruled from about 900 A.D. on by foreign soldier castes, mostly of Central Asian and Caucasian origin. For centuries the Arab-speaking countries have had the character of a colonial area, governed neither by, nor for, the local population.

Although great colonial empires have their advantages, as a whole the history of the Middle East under its various foreign rulers was a sad one. It is with this heritage of long suffering that the present states of the Middle East have to cope. Poverty, illiteracy and fanaticism are still rampant. In our generation, however, a fundamental change is taking place.

Inaugurated by the great Turkish revolution after the First World War, followed by the change of dynasty and system in Iran, and completed by the reemergence of the Arabs and the coming of Israel, a new era has begun for that part of the Middle East. Again, as in its ancient and most creative period, self-conscious, self-governing and autonomous nations have been making their appearance. The very foundation of the state of Israel is symbolic in this respect. Israel, together with its northern neighbor, Lebanon, which harbors the descendants of the Phoenicians, one of the most gifted and enterprising peoples of antiquity, marks the return of those classical times, when free peoples created the variegated culture of the Middle East.

As soon as a people called the Arabs makes its appearance in history, it has a connection of some kind with Israel. The very first Arab known to us by name and date, Gindibu (which means locust), is mentioned as a member of an alliance against an Assyrian invader, in which King Ahab of Israel figures at the head of 10,000 foot-soldiers and 2,000 war chariots, while the Arab sheik heads 1,000 camel riders. This—the battle of Karkar in Syria—which took place in the year 853 B.C. is not mentioned in the Bible and not, of course, in Arabic sources, because Arab history in the proper sense of the term begins only much later with the founding of the Arab religion, Islam, just as Jewish history really begins only with Moses, the founder of the Jewish creed.

The Arabs had some knowledge of their forefathers one or two centuries before the beginnings of Islam, just as the Book of Genesis has preserved a number of the traditions prevalent in Israel concerning their racial ancestors prior to the formation of their religion and nationhood. However, the Muslim Arabs were fully aware of the fact that in remote antiquity there had existed a number of Arab peoples of which they knew nothing at all. They rightly spoke of *al'Arab al-ba'ida*, "the Arabs who had disappeared," a telling designation for all these ancient Arab peoples, who had made their appearance in the borderlands of the countries of ancient civilization—Syria, Iraq and Yemen—and were absorbed by the higher civilizations of their environment.

As a striking example of such an ancient Arab people, I might mention the Nabataeans, who were the immediate eastern neighbors of the Jewish people during the fateful centuries of Maccabean, Herodian and Roman rule, and who had very close relations with the Jews, both friendly and hostile. These Nabataeans had originally been an Arab people, but adopted the Aramaic language, which at that time was spoken throughout the lands of the Fertile Crescent, including Palestine (and in which to the present day the *Kaddish*, one of the most holy and most familiar prayers of the synagogue, is still recited). In addition to their linguistic assimilation, these Nabataeans settled down; and so completely were they submerged in the predominant civilization that, some centuries later, the word "Nabati," Nabataean, signified in the language of the Muslim Arabs an Aramaic-speaking peasant.

In any case, although it is not mentioned in Muslim-Arabic sources for the reasons just explained, close relations existed between Israel and the Arab peoples from the ninth century B.C. on, and numerous references to Arabs are found in the later books of the Bible, in Flavius Josephus and in particular in the vast literature of the Jews which developed in the first centuries of the Christian era, the Talmud and the *Midrash*.

Furthermore, if we do not confine our survey to the peoples actually called Arabs, but include under this designation peoples showing the typical traits of real Arabs, i.e., camel-breeders, raiders and merchants engaged in foreign trade, then we can trace back the relations between Israel and peoples of this description to an even earlier date; for the tribes of Ishmael and Midian, who were typically Arab in character, and who appear in the stories of Joseph, Moses and Gideon, are regarded in the Bible as descendants of Abraham, which makes them the closest kin of Israel. Some prominent American orientalists have even described Israel itself as an Arab tribe, and an English Arabist suggests that the ancestors of Israel originate from the ancient land of Sheba in South Arabia. (This would mean that the present-day exodus from Yemen is only a repetition of an event which took place about 4,000 years ago.)

In the following chapter we shall have occasion to discuss these and other theories about the common origins of Israel and the Arabs. In any case, it is evident that the relations between the two peoples go back to the most remote times. However, they became striking and of the highest historical significance only in the age of the Prophet Muhammad, about 1,350 years ago, when Judaism, and a segment of the Jewish people then living in Arabia, stood beside the cradle of the Muslim religion and Arab statehood.

Concerning the fateful events and developments which took place at that time, during the three most decisive decades of oriental history (about 615 and 645 A.D.), not a single contemporary account has come down to us from Jewish sources. While we learn about Jewish-Arab relations in ancient times solely from Jewish and other non-Arab sources, we derive all our knowledge concerning these relations in the time of Muhammad and the subsequent early period of Islam either from explicit statements or the inner evidence contained in Arab-Muslim books. Nevertheless, even this one-sided source of information shows fully the great importance of Judaism both for the development of religious, moral and legal conceptions in the Koran, the sacred book of the Muslims, in early Islam, and for the formation of the young Muslim community and state.

It has often been stressed by prominent scholars, for example, Theodor Noeldeke, the great German orientalist, that Islam was far more akin to Judaism, in its basic ideas, as well as in the details regulating the lives of its believers, than Christianity, despite the closer "family relations" between Christianity and its mother-religion. This opinion, although requiring some qualifications, is basically true; the Muslim religious law in particular, which is the very core of Islam (as the *Halakha* is of Judaism) bears a most astonishing resemblance to the Jewish religious law, its older sister. To what extent these phenomena betray parallel developments or are borrowed will be discussed in Chapter 5. In any case, they did not fail to exercise a deep influence on Jewish-Arab relations in Islamic times.

With the great Arab conquests following the rise of Islam, which converted all the countries between Spain and Persia into a single territory dominated by the new religion, and soon after by the Arabic language as well, the majority of the Jewish people of that time came under Arab rule. Thus began the long and great period of Jewish-Arab symbiosis. The Jewish historians of the nineteenth century, as in the case of Graetz (the author of a classic ten-volume history of the Jews), who were deeply embittered by the contrast between the enlightened ideas of that century and the denial of civic rights to Jews in many European countries, pointed out most emphatically that the legal and actual position of the Jews during the Middle Ages was much better in Muslim-Arab countries than in Christian Europe; and the "Golden Age" of Judaism in Muslim Spain has become a phrase which has found its way even into the most popular accounts of Jewish history.

As we shall see, there is some exaggeration in these assertions. However, there can be no doubt that the legal status of the Jewish religion under Islam, particularly during its early period when the Arabs were still predominant, was very much better than their situation in the Byzantine Empire, which ruled over many countries occupied later on by the Arabs. In addition to a more favorable legal status, the Jewish people in early Islamic times enjoyed a complete economic and social revival, to which, however, the Arab contribution was indirect.

At the time of the Muslim-Arab conquest, the majority of the Jews were still engaged in agriculture and manual labor. Farmers, however, had a wretched time under Arab rule, and the remnants of the ancient agricultural peoples in the Middle East died out, that is, they lost their identity, in Islamic times. The Jewish people, too, so to say, died as an agricultural people during the seventh and eighth centuries, but, unlike other ancient populations, returned to life as a nation of merchants and artisans.

This transformation was due to the great "bourgeois revolution" of the ninth century (which has not yet been sufficiently investigated). Due to this revolution, the civilization of the Middle East during early medieval times was characterized by its commerce, industry and bureaucratic organization, at a time when western Europe was mainly agricultural and was dominated by knights and feudal lords. The Jews took their full share in this great Middle-Eastern mercantile civilization, in particular from the tenth to the thirteenth centuries; and it was at that time and in that part of the world that Judaism itself received its final shape.

There, under Arab-Muslim influence, Jewish thought and philosophy and even Jewish law and religious practice were systematized and finally formulated. Even the Hebrew language developed its grammar and vocabulary on the model of the Arab language. The revival of Hebrew in our own times would be entirely unthinkable without the services rendered to it by Arabic in various ways a thousand years ago. Arabic itself became a Jewish language and, unlike Latin in Europe, was employed by Jews for all secular and religious purposes, with the sole exception of the synagogue service.

The intermingling of Jewish and Arab life can best be demonstrated by the fact that the Jews in Arab countries had their full share in the appalling decline of those countries in the later Middle Ages, and the following centuries. As early as 1377 Ibn Khaldun, the great Tunisian sociologist and philosopher of history, wrote:

> The realm of the Arabs has been wiped out completely; the power now rests in the hand of non-Arabs, such as the Turks in the East . . . and the Franks (European) in the North.

This state of affairs remained unchanged unto our time. At the beginning of the First World War, not a single independent Arab state was in existence, and the world at large—the majority of statesmen not excluded—was not aware that an Arab nation existed at all. Concurrently, the Jews in Arabic-speaking countries, who at one time had formed both the majority of the Jewish people and its social and spiritual pivot, simply faded out of Jewish history. They were almost forgotten by the bulk of the nation, which was now concentrated in the Christian countries, taking its full part in their stupendous development in modern times. There remained Jews in all the Arabic-speaking territories (with the sole exception of northern Arabia), but their number was relatively small—less than ten per cent of the total Jewish population of the world. The Jewish-Arab symbiosis had lost its historical importance.

All this changed completely when, during the last three generations, the erection of a National Home for the Jewish people was conceived and realized in Palestine—a country which originally was regarded as a part of the Ottoman-Turkish Empire and which could, therefore, simply be acquired by means of a Charter from the Turkish Sultan. The endeavors of Theodore Herzl, the founder of the Zionist organization, to obtain such a charter are characteristic of the situation around 1900, when Arabic nationalism was not yet born. However, Palestine eventually proved to be in the very heart of a new Arab world emerging from the ashes of that Ottoman Empire at the end of World War I.

Thus, after the prolonged connection of ninety per cent of the Jewish people with Europe and Western civilization, the revival of Jewish statehood, although in the main the outcome of this connection with Europe, was taking place in the center of an awakening East. This East—it is true—is itself deeply indebted for its revival to the West, but still sees in antagonism to Europe the essential content of its newly created national life. *Sirr min asrar Allah*—"a secret of God's secrets"—this is how Ibn Khaldun would have described this unique situation.

The State of Israel, which is the direct result of a great romantic longing for a return to the East, a longing expressed in a famous piece of nineteenth century Hebrew literature, Feierberg's novel *Le'an* (*Whither*), finds itself, or at least is regarded, as the spearhead of the West in the midst of a still hostile Eastern world.

Not only that, but the oriental Jews living in Arabic-speaking countries who had been completely lost sight of by the majority of the Jewish people, are again in the foreground. Whoever knew or cared anything about the Jews of Yemen, Iraq or Libya? At present, however, after their mass immigration into Israel, they constitute one of the major assets and problems of the new State.

Into Israel, which is a society of a completely Western pattern, the East has intruded in the form of the huge influx of co-religionists from Arab and oriental countries. In addition, Israel has a very considerable Arab minority, so that we have here the interesting phenomenon of Arabs living in a Jewish environment.

These two facts combined compel Israel to tackle in a most concentrated form, a problem which today confronts the world at large: whether the culture of the West is strong enough to amalgamate the gigantic masses of the Eastern peoples—from Morocco to Indonesia and the Philippines—who have already adopted not only Western techniques, but also many Western patterns of thought, into one basic global civilization.

Israel is engaged today in the same task—on a comparatively small scale, it is true, but in a most intensive form. Israel thus has become the laboratory for the world. It has to do the job, whether it likes it or not. Israel, simultaneously a Western society planted in an Eastern environment, and an Eastern intruder into a Western structure, has this problem: the East to which, on the one hand it has come and by which, on the other hand, it is invaded, is mainly represented by the Arabs, with whom it had so long a history in common.

Two peoples which had been in close contact with one another for thousands of years—sometimes as different nations, sometimes as different religions, sometimes even as different civilizations—are now confronting each other in a totally new and a most complex situation.

To sum up: the long history of Jewish-Arab relations consists of four main periods óf unequal length.

The first, which might be fittingly called "pre-history," stretches over two thousand or more years and divides itself into two parts: the dim, but important, age of common origins of the two peoples —and the 1,400 years of recorded contacts from King Ahab down to the many references to the Arabs in talmudic literature, contacts which were interesting in many respects, but not of very great historical consequence.

Then came the second and, in the past, most important, period of creative Jewish-Arab symbiosis lasting about 800 years, during the first half of which Muslim religion and Arab nationhood took form under Jewish impact, while in the second half traditional Judaism received its final shape under Muslim-Arab influence.

During the third period, extending over 600 years, approximately from 1300 to 1900, Arabs faded out from world history, and Oriental Jews from Jewish history.

The last stage of Jewish-Arab relations, the twentieth century, is one of a new confrontation. The Westernized Jewish people is again connected with the original scene of its history, the Orient, while the Arabs, although revived under Western impact and with Western help, still are inclined to oppose the West and with it Israel as its closest representative. The State of Israel itself, however, has become through the influx of huge masses of immigrants from Muslim countries far more "oriental" in its character than the present-day Jewish people at large.

These four stages in the history of Jewish-Arab relations may be illustrated by the following table:

The History of Jewish-Arab Relations

I. PREHISTORY 1500 B.C.–500 A.D.	a. *Common Origins* *Myths:* Semitic Race. Israel an Arab Tribe *Facts:* Common social patterns ("Primitive Democracy") and religious tradition. "Cousins." b. *Recorded Contacts as from 853 B.C.* 1. Biblical period 2. Maccabean, Herodian and Roman periods 3. Talmudic times
II. CREATIVE SYMBIOSIS 500–1300	a. The origin and early development of Islam in its Jewish environment. "Islam an Arab recast of Israel's religion." b. The influence of Islam on Jewish thought and that of Arab language and literature on Hebrew.
III. FADING OUT 1300–1900	a. Of Arabs from World History b. Of Oriental Jews from Jewish History c. The common heritage of suffering

2.   *The State of Israel in its Arab Environment.*

Indeed, the contrast between Israel and most of its neighbors appears, at present, to be very pointed. The majority of its inhabitants have themselves come from Europe or are the children of such immigrants. The European character of the new State is even more pronounced, if one takes into account its political and spiritual leadership. As far as I know, of the Ministers of State only one is of non-European extraction; and of the members of the Supreme Court of Justice or of the full professors at the Hebrew University of Jerusalem not a single one. In other walks of life, the situation is not very much different, if, for example, one examines the leading writers of the older generation, the doctors or the engineers.

The fact that the new State of Israel is the result of a huge migration movement, which itself was caused by a tremendous spiritual and social upheaval, accounts largely—although not solely—for the unique character of its society.

Israel is essentially a society without classes. No remnants of

feudalism, no aristocracy of safely entrenched families, no plutoc-
racy of industrial trusts or business concerns, not even a rule of
a small bureaucracy as in totalitarian states, are to be found in
Israel. It is true that the Labor Party (*Mapai*) and the General
Federation of Labor (*Histadrut*) wield very great power, but they
do not represent a single class; in fact, it is the free and frequent
transition from one walk of life to another, even in the same families, that is the truest indication of the social freedom which char-
acterizes Israel. It is quite natural to find sons—even only sons—of
university professors taking up manual work as members of a Kib-
butz (a communal settlement), while a bus driver may occupy a
flat which is the envy of a successful industrialist. The social equality and equity prevailing in Israel is best illustrated by its rigid
austerity regime and the great privations incurred for the sake of
the new immigrants by all Israelites.

If we now turn for comparison to the adjacent Arab states, we
must be careful, of course, to avoid generalizations. There is a very
marked difference between the social structure of Egypt and Lebanon and even between those of Iraq and Syria. And even Egyptian
society which struck the foreign observer (only a few years ago as
in the past) as a real "house of bondage," is not devoid of democratic traits, both traditional, deriving mainly from the Islamic
notion of equality before God, and modern, caused by the influx
of many contemporary social ideas.

However, after all due allowance has been made, one must concede that there is still great social inequality in the countries in
Israel's vicinity. Millions live in great poverty, while others enjoy
undeserved and often misused riches. The "Arab Socialism" of
Abd en-Nasser's Egypt is an impressive experiment. However, anyone familiar with the country will concede that personal freedom
is very severely curtailed. To be sure, formal slavery seems not to
exist any more even on the Arabian peninsula. However, many
people in the Arab states are dependent upon others to a degree
unworthy of free men.

As an illustration of this fact, I would like to describe a little
scene which I witnessed in the receiving camp of Hashid near
Aden in November 1949. The scene occurred between two Yemen-

ites, one an Israeli, a man who had lived in Palestine long enough to become socially naturalized, and the other an immigrant who had arrived at the camp only a few days previously.

The Israeli Yemenite, an attendant working in the camp, of course mixed on terms of complete equality with everyone else there, with the director of the camp, the chief doctor and with a university professor. One day I was standing near him when an immigrant Yemenite ran up to him and in a fraction of a second threw himself down on the ground before the attendant, kissing his feet and embracing his legs, while making some trivial request. The mere physical aspect was quite remarkable. Throwing oneself down on the ground with such force without getting hurt showed that the man must have had long practice in such matters. Yemen is, of course, one of the more backward Arab countries; still, that unforgettable little scene illustrates a tremendous contrast.

There is another domain in which there is a most striking difference between Israel and its neighbors. I refer to the attitude towards sex. Of Israel it is as true as of the United States that it is a "Woman's Paradise." The equality of the sexes is expressed not only in the institutions of the new State, for example, in the law granting equal rights to women, which was passed in the Knesset, Israel's Parliament, on July 17, 1951, but also in the fact of complete co-education, with the exception of some of the most orthodox schools, or of compulsory military service for girls for the full term of two years (a feature, I am informed, which is peculiar to Israel). Equality is a fact to be observed in the daily life of ordinary people, in the natural companionship of boys and girls working together, found in a religious communal settlement as everywhere else in Israel.

On the other hand, in the countries adjacent to Israel, two great traditions have left behind them a contrary attitude: the one, which I would call the Muslim-Arab tradition of warriors and religious men, is contemptuous of the sex which is regarded as weak and imperfect and excludes it rigorously from public life; the other tradition, which is mainly Persian, to a certain extent also Greek, and found chiefly in Iran and Egypt, but is not lacking in the countries of the Levant, regards friendship—and more than friendship—between members of the male sex alone as the acme of civilization.

Both traditions create a deep gulf between the Arabs and the modern *Yishuv* (the Jewish population) of Israel. During the mandatory period, when mass arrests in connection with the disturbances were rather frequent, Jews and Arabs lived closely side by side and so had opportunities to observe each other's social behavior.

In a book on life in prison called *Behind the Walls*, a former leader of Jewish activists points out that the Arab looked with outright contempt at the free mingling of sexes in the Jewish society of Palestine, while the young Jews naturally could see in certain phenomena of Arab society nothing but sexual aberrations. As a matter of fact, in this respect, as in many others, Arab society is undergoing marked changes, and it seems that much of the nervous, unbalanced state of mind of the present urban population in the Arab East is due to the overthrow, in theory more than in practice, of old-established notions and habits with regard to the relations between the sexes.

There are many other fields in which the contrast between Israel and its neighbors is most striking—for instance, the case of religion. One may be dissatisfied with the present state of religion in Israel. One thing, however, is certain. Nobody in Israel pays lip service to religion. You may be an orthodox Jew, a free-lance seeker of God, have a romantic attitude toward Judaism as the most precious treasure of the national past, or be altogether opposed to any religion. Whatever the case, one professes what one believes and acts accordingly.

The situation in adjacent countries is totally different. It is, of course, extremely difficult, if not impossible, to assess what the Muslim religion really means today to the various diverse sections of the Arab population. That is why there are so many books bearing the titles *Whither Islam?* or *Islam Today* or *Modern Trends in Islam*. There can, however, be no doubt that there is a wide gap between what is really believed and practiced by many people today and between what they profess publicly.

Dr. John Van Ess, a great American philanthropist and sincere friend of the Arabs, who lived and worked for forty years in Basra, begins his last article before his recent death with the following words: "Only very few young men pray today in the Near East." I am unable to check the correctness of this statement. Naturally Dr. Van Ess had more opportunities to observe young Muslims than I have; in any case, it is correct to assume that many young men in Arab countries do not pray today, but —they would fervently deny that they did not conform to orthodox Islamic practice, or did not regard Islam as the most perfect spiritual system that has ever existed.

There is something sound in this outward adherence to Islam. It is another most interesting instance of the interplay between modern *Nationalism and Religion*—a problem so admirably expounded in Professor Salo W. Baron's book bearing the same title. We have here a sort of self-assertion against Western domination; religion being the primary heritage of the Arab past, it is extolled to the skies by those who have no use for it in their own lives. However, this discrepancy between belief and profession also has its serious drawbacks and constitutes one of the many reasons for the unrest prevailing at present among large sections of the Arab intelligentsia.

This clinging to appearances, which we have seen to be characteristic of the contemporary Arabs, is in general a trait which makes them so different from the Israelis, in particular from the younger generation, the famous *sabras*. The *sabras* are notorious for their complete disregard of form and formality. Good manners and politeness are suspect. On the other hand, the whole social life of the Arabs is dominated by a carefully observed etiquette. An Arab would address you politely, even if he felt like insulting you, while the young men of Israel are sometimes rude, even where they have every reason to be polite.

The utter dislike of these young people for outward show is best proved by the fact that they hate talking about ideals, the more they are engaged in realizing them. Zionism, as everyone in Israel knows, means in their slang, "idle talk," just as "prophecy," by the way, came to mean "lies" in the later parts of the Bible. The Israeli students can't stand talk about the "mission of Judaism" and the like, and the notion of the "Chosen People" drives them to distraction. They pay no attention whatsoever to form in either speech or writing.

Contrariwise, in the adjacent countries, they still prefer to use flowery superlatives—"the spirituality of the East as opposed to the materialism of the West," "the Mission of Islam," "the noble Arab Race," "social justice," and other subjects which often have little bearing on real life; and a good, or even an elaborate, style is still an ideal.

I must confess that I wish very much that we had more form in Israel—in thinking, in behavior and in oral and written expression. In addition, non-profession of ideals, although a natural reaction against decades of Zionist propaganda, should not go on indefinitely. In any case, the greatest conceivable contrast in all these matters exists between Israel and the surrounding Arab society.

The list of antagonisms between Israel and her neighbors could easily be increased, even if one excluded, as we have, aspects of politics and strategy. Under these circumstances, it may be asked whether these divergences are inherent in the characters and conditions of existence of the two peoples, and, therefore, likely to be permanent, or whether they simply indicate different stages of development and, therefore, are bound to disappear.

If one assumes the possibility of the gradual or imminent disappearance of differences, there arises another question: in which direction will the rapprochement take place? Will Israel society become more like the Arab or vice versa, or will both develop in a third direction?

It is evident that there does not exist a single, clear-cut answer to these questions. However, it is possible to provide the objective material needed for such an answer. For this purpose one should clarify the facts of the past and discuss their relevance to the problems of the present.

This is what we are trying to do in this book.

First, the common origins of the two peoples will be discussed.

Secondly, it will be asked why the history of the two peoples has taken such different courses, despite their extensive common background.

Thirdly, the direct relations and mutual influences will be considered.

Finally, the coincidence of the Jewish and Arab revivals in our own time will be appraised.

2

THE TRUTH ABOUT THE COMMON

ORIGINS OF THE PEOPLE OF ISRAEL

AND THE ARABS

Nine out of ten educated Americans or Europeans, when asked about the affinities of Jews and Arabs, would reply: of course both belong to the Semitic race.

What are the facts about the Semitic race? First, the word "Semitic" is a comparatively recent invention. It was coined by a German scholar in the year 1781 to denote a group of closely related languages, of which Hebrew and Arabic were then the best known.

The affinities among Hebrew, Arabic and Aramaic had been recognized and discussed by Jewish scholars as early as the tenth century. In the sixteenth century, European scholars also learned about the languages of Abyssinia (or Ethiopia, *Kush* in biblical Hebrew), which belong to the same group.

The term Semitic is, of course, derived from Shem, one of the three sons of Noah, the patriarch whose name is familiar to everyone through the biblical story of The Flood. However, this name is not compatible even with the facts given in the Bible. For instance, in the Bible Hebrew is rightly called *Sefath Kena'an*, the language of Canaan, because the Israelites knew very well that it had been spoken by the inhabitants of Palestine even before the tribes of Israel had conquered the country, a fact, incidentally, which has been established by archeological evidence.

But both Canaan and Kush, the forefather of the Ethiopians, are regarded in the Bible—not without reason—as descendants of Ham, another son of Noah's, and not of Shem. Thus, according to the Bible, Hebrew would be a "Hamitic" and not a "Semitic" language. We see that the term Semitic was a mere artificial creation coined for the convenience of grouping languages without any reference to the historical connections between the peoples speaking them, let alone their anthropological and racial origin.

Unfortunately, however, in the nineteenth century, under the influence of the romantic approach to the ideas of language, nation and soil, the purely linguistic term "Semites" came to denote something quite different: a *race* with very conspicuous physical, psychological and social peculiarities. Books were written about the positive or negative (mostly, of course, the latter) characteristics of the Semitic race by scholars who generalized as a rule from what they knew or thought they knew about Arab or Hebrew literature and history, and forgot to ask themselves whether such a thing as a Semitic race had ever existed at all.

To give just one instance: the famous scholar, Ernest Renan, described the Semites as a race without imagination, a desert people with an abstract mentality—an assertion which he sought to prove by the fact that the Semites developed no mythology, while the Indo-Germanic peoples of Greece or India, for example, possessed most exuberant legends about the deeds and loves of their gods and heroes.

However, excavations have brought to light a most extensive mythological literature written in Semitic languages, not only in Babylonia and Assyria, but also in the neighborhood of Palestine, at Ras Shamra in Northern Syria. As a matter of fact, numerous traces of mythology are to be found in the Bible and also in early Arabic literature, although in this respect there may be some differences between Israel, the Arabs and some other peoples on the one hand, and the Babylonians and the people of Ras Shamra on the other.

In general, the assumption that all the peoples who spoke a Semitic language had a common racial origin with distinctive

physical and sociological characteristics has no scientific foundation whatsoever. We know the outward appearance of the ancient
peoples who spoke Semitic dialects from their pictures, as well as
from bodies found in excavations; and they were as different from
each other anthropologically as any people could possibly be.
Their economic and social conditions differed even more widely.
What they had in common in literature or religious ideas can be
proved to be the outcome of a long process of cultural integration.
The diffusion of a language is a most complicated affair, which
must be investigated separately in each case. The fact that Negroes
in the United States of America talk and think exactly like other
Americans does not prove that their forefathers and the English
once formed a single race. Similarly, it is wrong to make such an
assumption with respect to the many peoples who are known to
have spoken or to speak a Semitic language.

Generalizations serve no good purpose; and, as the tragic misuse
of the term "Semites" during the last eighty years has shown,
such superficial pseudo-scientific labels may even do great harm.
Therefore, in discussing the common origins of Israel and the
Arabs we should disregard the nebulous notion about a Semitic
race altogether.

While the pseudo-scientific myth of the Semitic race has no
basis in reality, there is much more to the popular belief that Jews
and Arabs are close relatives, "cousins," because they were descended from the brothers Isaac and Ishmael, the sons of Abraham.
To be sure, there is no record in the Bible showing that Ishmael
was the forefather of the "Arabs."

Ishmael obviously was a very ancient tribe which vanished soon
from history, and therefore the word Ishmaeli came to be used,
even in the Bible, as a common noun denoting a desert people of
camel-breeders who engaged in raids or overland transport. Thus,
for example, the Midianites, whom Gideon fought, are called Ish-
maelis (Judges 8:24). This also possibly accounts for the strange
fact that Joseph was sold, apparently twice, to both Midianites
and Ishmaelites (the word Ishmaelite being used in that context

perhaps not as a proper but as a common noun) (see Genesis 37:25, 28, 36).

It is, therefore, not surprising that when, during the period of the Second Temple, the Jewish people had many dealings with Arab tribes (we have already mentioned the Nabataeans), the term Ishmaeli was extended to them and so used in early Christian and talmudic literature.

The Arabs are called "cousins," *dodanim* (from *dod*, uncle) of Israel in various ancient Jewish sources, all this as a pun on the name of the Arab tribe Dedanim, mentioned in Isaiah 21:13. The Jewish notion that the Arabs are Ishmaelites and hence the descendants of Ishmael, the son of Abraham, was taken over by the Arabs themselves. At a later stage in Muhammad's career he made this a cornerstone of his new creed. In chapter 2, verse 125, of the Koran, Muhammad has Ishmael help his father, Abraham, convert the *Ka'ba* of Mecca into a shrine of the true religion, thus making Abraham, the presumed physical ancestor of the Arabs, also the founder of Islam, their religion.

The idea that Jews and Arabs are "cousins" through Ishmael and Isaac, the sons of Abraham, was not an indigenous tradition, either in the Bible or among the ancient Arabs. However, as it was accepted as a fact in the whole of Jewish literature since the time of the Second Commonwealth, and as it was incorporated by Muhammad into the Holy Book of Islam itself, this idea of close relationship was accepted by the two peoples throughout the long period of their symbiosis in Islamic times. As we shall see presently, that idea was not without relation to facts.

However, before we can proceed to discuss these facts, we must dispel two other scientific myths connected with the idea of the Semitic race. I would not take the trouble to discuss these theories had they not been propounded by two fine American scholars, each notable in his own field.

I refer to Professor James A. Montgomery's book, *Arabia and the Bible* (Philadelphia 1934), and Duncan Black Macdonald's *The Hebrew Literary Genius* (Princeton University Press 1933). I have reviewed both these books at length under the heading of

"The Alleged Arabic Origin of Israel and its Religion" (*Zion*, Jerusalem 1937), where I discussed also Professor D. S. Margoliouth's Schweich Lecture on *The Relations between Arabs and Israelites prior to the rise of Islam* (London 1924). These books alike assume first that Arabia was the common homeland of the Semites, who in successive waves occupied the adjacent fertile countries; and, secondly, that Israel was nothing but an Arab tribe; the literary traditions of the Hebrews—even their religious ideas, being designated as Arabic. I do not propose to dwell on the first point. As I do not believe in the existence of a Semitic race, I naturally do not care to look for a common homeland of its various branches.

The question as to where the old Babylonians, Assyrians, Aramaeans, Phoenicians and the various other peoples who spoke Semitic languages came from lies in the domain of those expert in ancient Middle-Eastern history. However, as far as I can see, the theory of the successive migrations of Semitic peoples emerging from the Arabian Peninsula, although repeated even in schoolbooks, is not corroborated by a single historical record; it is a mere theory derived by a false analogy from the conquest of the Middle East by the Muslim Arabs.

Since that event was unique, no analogy can be drawn from it. There exist ancient records of the appearance of Arabian tribes on the fringe of the desert or of the forced settlement of units from Northern Arabia in the cultivated area. As an example of the latter I might mention the transfer of Arabs to Samaria in Palestine by an Assyrian king after the destruction of the kingdom of Israel. Under these circumstances is it not most improbable that the much more important events of the successive conquests of wide areas like Babylonia, Assyria, or Phoenicia by tribes coming out of the Arabian Peninsula should have gone unrecorded?

However, I should like to confine myself to the discussion of the second theory which can best be styled as "the Pan-Arabistic approach" to the history of Israel and its thought. This approach has a very old ancestry. The great Jewish commentators of the Bible and the Talmud in the Middle Ages made free use of the Arab language and even of Arab institutions and *realia*. In their wake followed modern biblical research, beginning with the Dutch and other Protestant scholars of the eighteenth century.

This trend reached its peak in the second half of the nineteenth century, when it became the fashion to describe the forefathers of Israel as Bedouins as they had been known either from ancient Arabic literature or from the descriptions of modern travellers in Arabia like Burckhardt or Doughty.

Two great names must be mentioned in this connection: Wellhausen, the famous exponent of biblical criticism and Israelite history, wrote no less than seven books on the ancient Arabs, both of pre-Islamic and of early Islamic times. He did so, as he himself once remarked, in order to determine "the wild stock on which the twig of the Israelite prophetism was grafted," the presumption being that the ancient Arabs would provide the best illustration for the life of Israel before it was subjected to the impact of the monotheist religion. A similar attitude was taken up by the Scotsman Robertson Smith, the very names of whose books *Kinship and Marriage in Ancient Arabia* (1885) and *Lectures on the Religion*—note: religion, not religions!—*of the Semites* indicate the trend of his thought.

Hugo Winckler, the German scholar, who, more than any other man, was responsible for diffusing the idea of the successive migrations of Semites trooping out of Arabia, severely criticized the work of both Wellhausen and Robertson Smith. He pointed out —and in this he was preceded by the great Arab historian Ibn Khaldun (whom we have already mentioned)—that the Bedouins are everywhere dependent on the neighboring civilization; it was therefore unscientific to depict the life of Israel, which was dependent on the civilization of the ancient East, according to the customs and beliefs of the Arab tribes in the age of Muhammad or in our times being surrounded by entirely different civilizations. However, it is hardly necessary to point out that Winckler, too, regarded Israel as a Bedouin tribe which emerged from the Arabian desert.

In the years following the First World War, no considerable

new discoveries were made with regard to the relations between ancient Israel and Arabia. However, Arabia itself emerged from its long obscurity and was suddenly brought to the attention of the Western mind by the events of the war and the post-war period and by a whole flood of books on the subject, some of which were of very high quality. It suffices to mention names like Lawrence, Philby, Bertram Thomas or Alois Musil (the Czech scholar, whose books were published in America in English translation after the war). It was this revival of Arabia and its renewed importance which led to what I have just called "the Pan-Arabistic approach" to the Bible and the ancient history of Israel.

What is there to be said about this theory which regards Israel as an Arab tribe coming out of the Arabian desert and Israel's religion as the creation of an Arab mind? This theory is nothing but a series of misconceptions. The sooner we get rid of it the better we shall be able to evaluate the actual common background of Israel and the Arabs.

The people of Israel, as soon as we can recognize it from concrete historical accounts—say from the time of the Judges onwards —is an entirely agricultural people whose whole life, both secular and religious, was centered in agriculture. But, we are told, Israel's organization in tribal units betrays a Bedouin origin. Here we have the first fallacy. Tribal grouping, that is, according to units which believe themselves to be linked together by ties of blood or by special covenants, is not confined to Bedouins or even to nomads; it is found today even in an agricultural country as intensively cultivated as Yemen, and it existed there thousands of years ago, as the evidence of the Sabaean and other South Arabian inscriptions proves. Tribal organization is therefore no indication of Bedouin origin.

The stories about the Patriarchs who wandered about between towns like Bethel, Hebron and Beersheba are another favorite topic with our Pan-Arabists. Abraham, they say, is a typical Arab sheik. Here we have another misconception. There is a very substantial difference between sheep- and cattle-raising semi-nomads, wandering about like the Patriarchs and occasionally taking to agriculture *inside* the sedentary area (as reported in the Book of Genesis), and between the camel-breeding Bedouins—*bedou* in Arabic means "outside"—who live far out in the desert, where alone good camels can be raised. There is not a single reference in the Bible which would indicate that the Israelites at any time were camel-breeding Bedouins or that they emigrated from Arabia. However, one might argue, does not the Pentateuch itself teach us that Israel's religion was born in the desert, and do not the Prophets regard Israel's desert period as their ideal? Here is the third mistake.

Israel's sojourn in the desert is described everywhere in the Bible as a short *interval* between prolonged residence in Egypt and the conquest (or reconquest) of Canaan, as a trial for a people *not* accustomed to desert life. It was the time of God's love for Israel because it went after Him into the desert, the land that was not sown (Jeremiah 2:2): "the land of great drought" (Hosea 13:5), a most repugnant situation for an agricultural people.

In refutation of this, it might of course be said that the express statements of the Pentateuch and the Prophets reflect later thoughts, and that we must rely on the internal evidence of the Bible in drawing conclusions on the origins of the people of Israel. However, it is precisely the internal evidence deriving from comparisons of the Arab and biblical *literatures* which shows how different the origins of the two peoples must have been.

Arabic classical literature, like the Bible, was written down almost entirely in sedentary environments—mainly in Iraq and Syria, by authors from families who had lived for many generations in towns or who were not Arabs at all; but its every page betrays the origin of its people in the Arabian desert. The vocabulary, the metaphors, the similes, the very themes of their poetry teem with reference to camel-breeding tent life in Arabia. Nothing of that kind is to be found in the Bible, where everything breathes the fragrance of the Palestinian soil, and reflects the life of farmers and shepherds.

The "Pan-Arabist" theory has not, in fact, found many followers among serious Bible scholars. I should like to point out that in a recent survey of the present stage of Bible research, *The Old Testament and Modern Study: A Generation of Discovery and Research* (Oxford 1951) or in the latest comprehensive textbooks on the history of Israel (Martin Noth, *Geschichte Israels*, Goettingen 1950), as far as I can see, not a single reference is made to Israel's alleged origin in Arabia. As we shall see, the great affinities between Israel and the Arabs are to be explained otherwise.

Ancient Israel, as it appears to us in the Bible, and the original Arabs, as we are able to discern their nature through the medium of the early Muslim literature, show very distinctive affinities which make them akin to each other and different from the great civilizations which surrounded and influenced them. There were very definite common traits in the social traditions and the moral attitudes of the two peoples. These common traits can best be described as those of a *primitive democracy*.

Against the background of the civilization of the ancient Orient, which crystallized chiefly in the mighty kingdoms of Mesopotamia, Egypt and Asia Minor; and in contrast to the neighboring early medieval civilizations of Byzantium and Sassanid Persia, Israel and the Arabs present the type of a society which is characterized by the absence of privileged castes and classes, by the absence of enforced obedience to a strong authority, by undefined but nonetheless very powerful agencies for the formation and expression of public opinion, by freedom of speech, and by a high respect for human life, dignity and freedom.

Now, primitive democracies of various types have existed in many parts of the world, e.g., in Mesopotamia. In addition, we must bear in mind that the ancient East, as it is revealed to us by continuous new discoveries, was most diversified not only linguistically and ethnically, but also in its social organization.

One thing, however, is certain: Israel and the Arabs alone preserved their primitive democracy, and the moral attitude implied by it, at the decisive hour in their history: when both peoples became the bearers of religions which were destined to mold the development of a great part of the human race.

There is no need to go into detail. In Israel and among the

Arabs, as everywhere else in the world, some people were rich and fortunate, while others were poor and miserable. But neither in Israel nor in Arabia were there privileged classes differentiated from others by *law*, as represented, for example in the otherwise progressive Code of Hammurabi, by the castes of the *amelum* and *mushkenum*, usually translated as seignor and peasant. The very *lex talionis*, which demands "a life for a life," irrespective of the class of murderer or victim, implies that all are equal before the law, "riches and poverty are incidental and transient; but one man's life can be of no greater value than another's" (John Garstrang, *Solomon's Heritage*, London 1934, p. 200.)

But what about slavery? This is a most important point, for both Hebrews and Arabs kept slaves, and the verb "to be a slave," and "to serve," denotes in the languages of both peoples the relation between man and God. Ernest Renan stressed this detail very strongly, contrasting the alleged servile spirit of the Semites with the love of freedom prevailing among the Indo-Europeans.

Unfortunately, Renan's conception, although already refuted seventy years ago by Robertson Smith, still looms large in the minds of scholars and laymen. When Professor Mordecai Kaplan, in his *The Future of the American Jew*, repeatedly speaks of the new American conception of God as opposed to that of the oriental despot, to whom servile submission is due, he echoes the old Renan.

Now, slavery in the ancient East is a very complicated subject. But, when we confine ourselves to the status of slaves in Israel and in Arabia, a comparatively consistent and univocal institution emerges. There, slaves were not the wretched, sweating beasts of the American plantations, or the Roman *latifundia*, or the potteries of Athens; they were members of the household with more independent status at times than sons or younger brothers.

Eliezer, the servant of Abraham, is a good example of such status. He was styled "the son of the house" and was expected to inherit his master's property in the absence of a natural heir (Genesis 15:3); after a son was born, he looked after him just as an elder brother would do (24:3 ff.). Similar relationships are reported in ancient Arabic sources and in the accounts of well-informed trustworthy travellers in Arabia like Doughty. Freya Stark in her book, *The Southern Gates of Arabia,* relates "that each boy is given a slave of his own age and that they grow up as good friends together." This practice, which is known to have existed in ancient Arabia, has its counterpart in present-day South Africa, where, of course, no formal slavery exists.

It should be noted that the Prophets of Israel often complained about the treatment of the poor, the widow, the orphan or the stranger, but there is not a single reference to ill-treatment of slaves in their writings, while in a famous passage in Job (31:13–15), the slave is recognized to have the same human rights as his master. The family attachment of the Jewish slave is best expressed in a statement from Italy in the tenth century A.D. to the effect that a master may recite the *Kaddish* prayer for the soul of his slave, something done as a rule only for very close relatives.

Therefore, when an Arab or Jew prayed, "I am Thy servant, the son of Thy handmaid" (Psalm 116:16), he meant to say, "I am a most intimate member of your household"—the notion of sonship (which is fairly frequent in Hebrew, but very rare in Arab sources) is eschewed as implying procreation and sexual relations. When Moses is given the honorary title of "the servant of God" this is to be understood in the sense described in Numbers (12:7), "my servant Moses, who is faithful in all my house"—signifying one who knows all the wishes of his master and carries them out faithfully.

To sum up: the institution of slavery, which Israel and the Arabs had in common with the neighboring civilizations, took on among these two peoples a specific character which may be explained by the close relationship between them.

A similar statement may be made regarding the status of women. This much-discussed subject is even more complicated than that of slavery. There are very marked differences in this respect between Israel and the Arabs, but also some striking similarities.

A very typical example of such similarities is a certain form of participation by women in public life. Both in Israel and in ancient (and to some extent modern) Arabia, women, although not taking part directly in public discussions and decisions, voiced public opinion in poems or other utterances, which were at times assumed to derive from supernatural inspiration. The women of ancient Arabia were famous not only for their dirges and songs of praise, but in particular for their satirical poems, which largely served the same function as the press of today.

Muhammad, who carefully avoided bloodshed among populations which he thought capable of being otherwise won over, is reported twice to have ordered the execution of such female satirists, who were greatly dreaded by even such a powerful man as the head of the new Muslim State. This makes it clear why King Saul was so upset when the "dancing women" in their songs of triumph ascribed, or, as the Bible says, "gave" to David the slaying of ten thousands and to him only thousands, or why Barak refused to wage war against Sisera unless Deborah would accompany him. The biting satires of the woman judge, some of which were later included in the so-called Song of Deborah (Judges 5) were a most effective means of activating the languid tribes. Prophetesses were consulted or dreaded, up to the very end of the Old-Israelite prophetism, if we may judge from the examples of Hulda, who was approached by King Josiah, and Noadya, who was obviously a great nuisance to Nehemiah, the Governor of Judea in Persian times, even though he was an energetic and rather ruthless man (Nehemiah 6:14).

The Jewish women of Yemen today, whose comment on public events takes the form of poetic—mainly satirical—utterances, no doubt follow a local tradition which, moreover, some of them still carry on even in Israel. There they compose verses, in Arabic of course, on such amusing topics as canned foods or female soldiers, or—funniest of all—the public elections.

I have called the Arab-Israel democracies primitive, because they did not develop fixed and permanent public bodies representing the State, like Athens or the United States of America. For that, however, they were not less vigorous. When Gideon said, "Not I shall rule over you . . . the Lord shall rule over you," he expressed the true attitude of Israel. Even a reputedly bad King like Ahab could not get rid of an adversary without a routine court procedure, as the famous case of Naboth shows. When King Hezekiah or King Josiah of Judea wished to introduce reforms they had to consult the people and enter into solemn covenants with them. In a later age Nehemiah, although officially installed as governor by the King of Persia, did the same thing. Similarly, the Arabs in pre-Islamic times, as we have seen, were a community which had no ruling authorities. During the first century of Islam, when the Arab element was still predominant, the Caliphate bore a definitely democratic character. The incessant domestic wars, which led to the downfall of the "Arab Kingdom," also testify to the indomitable spirit of independence which was as characteristic of the ancient Arabs as of the ancient Jews.

In addition to the general characteristics common to the two peoples, there are many special traits which reveal a close relationship between them. I should like to give just one example. A very important concept in the religion of ancient Israel was that of the "God of the Fathers," an unnamed God revered by a family or clan, because He had appeared to and helped their ancestors. Thus, the Bible speaks of "The God of Abraham," the "God of Isaac," etc. This notion, which became so significant in Israel's religion, has an exact parallel in the gods of the Fathers mentioned centuries later in the inscriptions of the Nabateans, who, as we have already seen, were originally an Arab people.

It may be asked, where did this great resemblance between the two peoples stem from? It would be hazardous to attribute it to similar economic conditions, since Israel was a thoroughly agricultural nation whose forefathers had been at most semi-nomads in a region of ancient civilization, while Northern Arabia was the home of Bedouins and traders. It would seem that the answer to this question is to be sought in the aboriginal affinity alluded to in the Bible.

According to Genesis (21:20–21, 25:1–6, 12–18), Abraham, the ancestor of Israel, was not only the father of Ishmael, but also of Midian and many other tribes living in North Arabia, and even of Sheba, a tribe most probably connected with the old country of Sheba in Southern Arabia. Genesis reports that Abraham sent these sons into the countries of the East, after giving them presents, thus leaving Isaac the sole heir of the Land of Canaan.

These reports seem to signify the following:

(a) The people of Israel felt themselves closely akin to those tribes of Northern Arabia or even of Southern Arabia.

(b) The secession of those tribes from the Abrahamite stem was envisaged as follows: Abraham migrated with his men from Mesopotamia to Palestine (obviously some great catastrophe had occurred there; as we know from the history of Zionism, the mere word "go" (Genesis 12:1) is seldom sufficient impetus for migration).

In Palestine at that time there was no room for "sitting together." Some branches of the Abrahamites, such as Lot and Esau-Edom, therefore moved on to the arable areas east and south of Palestine, while others, the Ishmael-Midian tribes, followed the great caravan routes which led from Beersheba eastward and southward into the Arabian Peninsula. There they mixed, as Israel did elsewhere, with other peoples, and became typical traders and raiders, just as they were portrayed in the Bible. Obviously, it was the domestication of the camel—a very important achievement made in the latter part of the second millennium B.C.—which created a separate Arab people.

We have, of course, no means whatsoever of determining the historical facts of these population movements. However, no other migrations would be compatible with the tradition preserved in the Bible; and they may well account for the astounding affinities between Israel and the Arabs, which are an indubitable fact.

3

WHY HAS THE HISTORY OF THE TWO PEOPLES TAKEN SUCH DIFFERENT COURSES?

In the previous chapter an aboriginal affinity between Israel and the Arabs has been assumed because of the great similarity of social patterns and outlooks during their classical periods. This affinity is even more strikingly demonstrated by what could be called the *common motif* in the history of the two peoples, the absolutely unique fact that in both cases a basically national religion was ultimately transferred to many other peoples.

As far as Israel is concerned, there is no need for elaborate explanations. The Old Testament, which comprises the remains of a national literature and the record of a national history, has become a holy book for one half of mankind, while the greater part of the New Testament is also very strongly tinged with local color.

A similar process took place in Islam. Muhammad wanted to create a holy book for the Arabs, an "Arabic Koran," as he said himself, and the so-called "Muslim sciences," i.e., the body of knowledge an educated Muslim is expected to acquire, has always comprised the Arabic language and the history of Muhammad and his pious successors together with the oral traditions attributed to them.

The connection between the Muslim religion and Arab nationhood is best demonstrated nowadays by the writings of Pakistan Muslims, who find their spiritual antecedents not in their own

country but in the deserts of Arabia, or by the very strange fact
that it could be seriously proposed that Arabic be adopted as the
official language of that vast Indian republic.

Of course, the migration of religions from one people to another
is a very common occurrence in human history. The wide diffusion of Indian Buddhism in Central Asia, China, Japan and
Ceylon, or of Iranian Manichaeism in both the West and the
East are telling examples of this phenomenon. However, in all
these and similar cases we do not find that close relationship between a religion and the national traditions of a people, which is
characteristic of the religions of Israel and Islam.

There seems to be a definite connection between this unique
fact and the common social pattern of Arab and Israel society,
which was described in the previous chapter as a primitive democracy. For a society which does not recognize class privileges and
which places a high estimate on the sanctity of life and the rights
of the individual, is best suited to serve as a basis for a religion
which, despite its national affiliations, is essentially universal in
character.

Why, then, with such similar antecedents, has the history of the
two peoples taken such different courses? At the root of most of
the differences between the histories of Israel and the Arabs lies the
simple fact that Jewish religion was the original one and took
1200 years to achieve the final shape that served as the basis for
both Christianity and Islam, while Muhammad's religion could
rely on a completely worked out system which was developed and
accepted by the Arabs in the course of a single generation.

As many pages of the Bible, Flavius Josephus and the Talmud
show, the development of Israel's religion was a long and painful
process of inner struggle often with denationalizing effects, and of
incessant clashes with its environment while, for the Arabs, Islam
was the very cement of their swiftly acquired state and nationhood. I need hardly say that I have no intention of belittling the
originality of the Muslim Prophet or of denying Israel's profound
indebtedness to the great civilizations of the ancient East One
thing, however, is abundantly clear: Israel's religion developed

out of the strongest possible opposition to all that preceded and all that surrounded it.

This idea is expressed very tellingly in Leviticus: "After the doings of the land of Egypt, wherein ye dwelt, ye shall not do; and after the doings of the land of Canaan, whither I bring you, ye shall not do" (Leviticus 18:3). This was necessarily the typical attitude of Israel's religion, while Muhammad, on the contrary, found most convincing proof of the truth of his message in its complete conformity with the older religions, or, as he himself put it, "what had already been known by the wise men of Israel" (Koran 26:197).

In a recent French-Algerian publication, Islam has been characterized as a Judaism with universalistic tendencies. There is some truth in this definition. However, the difference between the two is due not to basically opposed tenets, but to the absolutely different conditions of their origins. With regard to religion, the Arabs were in the position of fortunate heirs; or, as a saying attributed to Muhammad has it: "Islam received all the sweetness of religion, while its predecessors had to struggle for it bitterly": *lakum alhelu walahum almurr*. From this basic premise practically all the rest follows.

First of all, there was, so to speak, a profound difference between the histories of the two peoples in timing. Israel began to develop its unique religion at the very dawn of its history, when it was still nothing but a small people. Islam came to the Arabs as an almost complete system, at the time when they already had behind them a history of over 1500 years and had occupied not only the whole Peninsula of Arabia, but also penetrated into the neighboring countries of Southern Persia, Iraq, Syria and Egypt.

We find Arabs making their appearance in Northern Syria as early as the ninth century B.C., and from that time on continuous reference is made to Arabs by historical sources in various languages. True, most of these Arabs, who penetrated into the borderlands of the cultivated area, were absorbed by the higher civilizations of their environment. The Nabataeans have served us as a typical instance of that process. However, these losses were more than made good during the centuries preceding the rise of Islam, when Arabia occupied the favorable position of a neutral country prospering as a commercial mediator between the East and the West, the Roman Empire and the Persian kingdom, which were engaged in incessant warfare for seven hundred years.

Another very important historical process occurred in pre-Islamic times to which, however, the history books have not yet paid due attention. For various reasons, the old kingdoms of highly civilized Southern Arabia (of which the State of Sheba is best known to the West, thanks to its queen of biblical fame) disintegrated in the centuries preceding the rise of Islam, and its populations became Arabicized.

This tremendous fact greatly enhanced both the numerical strength and the spiritual faculties of the Arabs; for without that process of the Arabization of the Land of Sheba and the adjacent countries, which was completed shortly before the rise of Islam, both the Arab conquests and the stupendous inner development of Islam would have been unthinkable. True, these various Arab tribes did not yet form an organized national body. On the other hand, they were not developed enough to constitute themselves as different nations, as were the tiny tribes of Syria and Palestine in ancient times.

These pre-Islamic Arab tribes spoke quite different dialects; they had, however, a literary language in common, the language of poetry as well as the inter-tribal language of commerce. Each tribe and locality had its own gods and cults. These, however, were not very well developed, having no elaborate services or priesthoods with vested interests, while there were some holy shrines, like that of Mecca, and some famous fairs, like that at Ukaz, which were frequented by many different tribes in the so-called holy months, during which warfare was forbidden.

All these factors combined to make it comparatively easy for Muhammad and his followers to overcome local resistance and to unite all the Arab tribes into one State, one religion, and one nation. The result was that they immediately became the most formidable force in the whole Middle East.

How different was the position when Israel's religion came into being! As we learn from the inscriptions of the Phoenician towns or of Mesha, King of Moab, and others, the languages of the various peoples of Southern Syria and Palestine were almost identical. The finds at Ras Shamra show that the language spoken in the second millennium B.C. in Northern Syria was somewhat different. On the other hand, a comparison of Ras Shamra documents and the Hebrew Bible reveals a very strong common tradition. In addition, the stories about Balaam and the traditions which grew up around Elijah, Elisha and Jeremiah teach us that the institution of prophecy was not confined to the boundaries of a particular people. However, all these tiny tribes of Syria and Palestine had developed into settled nations with fully established autonomous States and elaborate religious cults backed by organized clerical bodies.

Professor A. J. Toynbee suggested in his monumental *A Study of History* the idea of a *Syriac* civilization which, in his opinion, is to be credited with three great achievements: the invention or adaptation for practical use of the alphabetical script; the development of seafaring which led to the discovery of the Atlantic Ocean, and, greatest of all, the creation of monotheism. However, the trouble is that such a civilization has never existed. The various peoples to whom Toynbee attributes these achievements never consciously united for one continuous cultural or political effort, as the Greeks or the Arabs were able to do later on. Israel's religion came into being too early, when it was still too small a people, or—what amounts to the same thing—it came too *late*, i.e., when Israel and the peoples related to it had already developed into fixed national and religious entities.

This is why the prophecy of Isaiah on world peace could not be realized even among the peoples of Palestine and Syria who were so closely related to one another linguistically and in many other respects.

So far we have seen how Israel's priority in religious creation worked against it in the field of national achievement. There were other extremely important factors which made Israel's history and religion so different from that of its Arab "cousins." Of the highest importance in this respect was the diverse economic and social background of the two peoples. As we have already had an opportunity to observe, Israel had always been an essentially agricultural nation, while from the outset the Arabs were traders and nomads.

Commerce and travel teach men the arts of propaganda and advertisement, while cultivation of the soil, although it may deepen a man's inner life, inclines him to become contained and even parochial. Proselytes in considerable number made their appearance in Israel only after the days of the Babylonian Captivity, that is, only after a segment of the Jewish people there had taken to commerce and, as we know from documentary evidence, some large Jewish commercial firms had come into being.

The tremendous expansion of Judaism at the time of the Second Temple was certainly not unconnected with the part—however limited—that the Jews were then taking in world trade.

On the other hand, Muhammad was born in a flourishing caravan city, and he and all his companions, the future caliphs and generals of the Muslim State, were merchants engaged in the great transport trade between the Roman and Persian Empires and Southern Arabia. As already mentioned, Arab nomads penetrated into the cultivated area and superseded the decimated population of two rotten empires. Not less important were the commercial activities of the caravan traders of Mecca and other Arab towns. Before the Arabs appeared in the towns of Syria, Egypt or Mesopotamia as conquerors, they had been there as merchants or as escorts of caravans, and the technique acquired in handling customers proved most useful in diffusing the new faith. I refer not only to the numerous commercial ideas and expressions found in the Koran—a phenomenon to which Professor Charles C. Torrey has devoted a whole book, but to the astounding adaptability and flexibility displayed both by Muhammad while shaping and preaching his religion, and by his early successors.

Contrariwise, the ancient Israelites had no ideal other than that each man should sit under his own vine and fig tree. When they came into contact with foreign peoples or ideas, they were inclined to be intransigent, demanding complete and unconditional acceptance of their religious and ethical ideals. Such an attitude may have been inevitable in the case of a unique religion, which had to hold its own against all the rest of the world, but it was not very well suited to the requirements of religious propaganda or national expansion.

The basic difference in the social backgrounds of Israel and the Arabs makes itself felt not only in the *diffusion* of their religions, but also in their *content* and character.

The Jewish calendar with its Festivals which celebrated the ingathering of the proceeds from livestock, the fields, the orchard and the vineyard, the Jubilee year and many other things connected with the cultivation of the soil, is thoroughly agricultural.

The Muslim year, which is a lunar year without intercalation (that is, without adaptation to the cycle of the seasons) has no relations whatsoever to the circle of the year. The month of fasting may fall either during the shortest days of the winter or the longest days of the summer—a circumstance that proved most embarrassing to early Muslim traders in Finland and Sweden who found that they had sometimes to fast twenty-three hours a day for a whole month.

The Sabbath, the weekly rest day, "this greatest gift of Judaism to the world," is sometimes inconvenient for the farmer, particularly when seasonal work is at its heaviest. It is therefore expressly laid down (in Exodus 34:21): "In ploughing time and during the harvest ye shall rest." But the Sabbath was primarily created so "that thine ox and thine ass may rest, and the son of thy handmaid and the stranger may be refreshed" (Exodus 23:12), that is, all agricultural workers should enjoy one day's full rest.

Muhammad was thoroughly familiar with the Jewish Sabbath, but he categorically refused to accept its main purpose as a day of rest, and retained only its other aspect, that of a day of public assembly and prayer (which, by the way, probably made a stronger impression on foreigners). Muhammad's Arab followers had no use for a day of rest. The Bedouin—because he did not work regularly even on weekdays—and the merchants—because a weekly break in their large-scale transport was unpracticable. These economic and social implications, rather than theological arguments, would seem to account for the fact that Islam, unlike Christianity, has never accepted the religious idea of a weekly day of rest.

The contrast between the Israel and the Arab forms of society is evident chiefly in their respective *laws*. The primitive farmer is deeply attached to his possessions, and regards selling them as a disaster (Ezekiel 7:12: "the buyer will not rejoice, nor the seller mourn"). That is why, when he parts with anything, he insists on an extremely formalistic and strict procedure. It makes a very great difference to him whether he sells a plot of land or a cow or a piece of cloth woven by his wife. For each type of transaction a specific procedure, in actual or symbolic transfer of property, must be followed. Anyone having even the slightest acquaintance with talmudic law knows how large such formalities loom in the discussions of the Jewish lawyers of old. The abstract idea of contract is unknown to them and consequently there is no word for it in ancient Hebrew.

For the commercially minded Arab, however, everything is merchandise, and a simple procedure of "offer and acceptance" constitutes a legal contract by means of which, in principle, any kind of property may be transferred. To be sure, when Muslim law came into being, Jewish law was already fairly well developed, and it may have influenced Muslim jurisprudence in some aspects of its law of contract. However, even if this were true—which is not certain—it would not diminish the great difference in the basic attitude in the two religious laws towards the transfer of property.

Even more conspicuous is the dissimilarity between the system of inheritance in Islam and Judaism. A farmer endeavors as far as possible to keep his estate intact. Therefore, in Jewish law (as in that of many other agricultural peoples) the share of the firstborn son is twice as large as that of the other sons—with the result that the eldest son receives the whole estate and the others only small compensation for themselves. The daughters are married off by their brothers, but do not inherit the land jointly with them. If there is no son, a daughter inherits the whole estate—on the assumption that she will have no difficulty in finding a man to run it for her.

The Muslim law of inheritance does not recognize primogeniture and in most cases splits up the inherited fortune into such small shares, that only cash or a herd of camels—but not a piece of land of normal size—can be divided up under such an arrangement. Daughters always have a part in the estate, but even an only daughter never inherits more than half of an estate. This law of inheritance which, in my opinion, was based on the model of the division of spoils in tribal warfare, although very impracticable for sedentary populations, is still in force in most Muslim countries.

The social unit of the camel-breeders is the tribe or clan, the yearly wanderings from summer to winter pastures necessitating a comparatively large group for defense and other purposes. The natural social unit of the farmer is the family—father, mother, sons, servants and hired seasonal laborers. Collective farming as the basis of social grouping has long existed in various parts of the world, but not, so far as we know, in ancient Israel. There we always find the family, or, as it is called in Hebrew, "The House"— the household presided over by the pater familias—as the unit which runs the farm.

This economic-social antithesis may account partly—but certainly not solely—for the profound difference in the attitude toward the family among the Jews and the Arabs. As we learn from the stories in Genesis and other parts of the Bible, and even observe today, the attachment between parents and children or between man and wife is very strong, perhaps almost a little too sentimental, in the genuinely Jewish family. This is in many respects a great asset—and it may even be said that the model of family affection shown, for example, in the story of Joseph, had considerable educational influence on the world at large.

On the other hand, the too intensive concentration of affection on the smallest social group, the family, no doubt had a somewhat adverse influence on Jewish history because it weakened the impulse to serve the community as a whole.

In ancient Arabic poetry and narrative literature there are moving passages on the relations among the various members of a family, and eloquent sayings on the subject may be culled from the Koran and the so-called oral traditions of early Islam. There is no need to point out, however, that it is a far cry from the family life in pre-Islamic and early Islamic times to that in later sedentary Arabic-speaking societies, such as those so admirably described 120 years ago by E. W. Lane in his book on *The Manners and Customs of the Modern Egyptians* or in our own day by Mr. K. Daghestani in his *Étude sociologique sur la famille musulmane contemporaine en Syrie.*

However, when all due allowance has been made for the diversity of human nature in general and of Muslim Arab society in particular, one is bound to admit that, with respect to family life, Jewish and Arab religion and society have been entirely different from each other. When we think about Israel in this regard, there immediately comes to mind a vision of the intimate family table praised in Psalm 128, and the idea expressed in two complementary sayings in rabbinical literature: that "the family table atones for sins" and that "the mother of the family atones for the whole household just as the altar in the Temple made atonement for the world."

On the Arab side, one would immediately think of the *Liwan*, the large reception hall which is a characteristic feature of oriental houses, crowded with brothers and uncles and cousins of different degrees of kinship. Here we have an animated, but dignified, gathering of men, all proud of their membership in a large and often powerful family or clan. This clan attachment is a very important factor in Arab history. Even today, sons, brothers, nephews and cousins of the ruling monarch hold posts as ministers and governors in the Arab States of Saudiya and Yemen.

A similar tendency to family rule is evident in the history of the two greatest Arab dynasties, the Umayyads and the Abbasids. On the other hand, the strong tribal feeling which prevails in Arab society often worked against national unity, and the semi-feudal family rule found in many Arab countries today can hardly be regarded as a blessing.

In conclusion, we shall consider an antithesis between Israel and the Arabs which, although lying in the fields of linguistics and literature, was, in my mind, one of the main reasons why the history of the two peoples has taken such unlike courses.

I refer to the fact that the Arabs have always been fervently attached to their language, and have laid the strongest emphasis on elegant and even artificially refined expression, the cult of language being almost the sole content of their original civilization. The Jews, however, always concentrated on ideas, never clung closely to their national language and paid very little attention to form, in particular to elegance and delicacy of expression.

The result was that the Arabs, in their almost fanatical devotion to their much-studied tongue, imposed it, almost inadvertently, on most of the peoples living between the Atlantic Ocean and the mountains of Iran, while the Jews readily gave up their own language and frequently exchanged one language for another.

During the Middle Ages these contrary attitudes toward language were of no great consequence. The Jews did not cease to be regarded as one people everywhere, although they were known to speak a number of different languages, while the Arabic-speaking townspeople—called "Moors" by European travellers of the later Middle Ages—would never have dreamt of identifying themselves with the original Arabs, the desert-dwellers, who alone at that time were called "Arabs."

However, in the twentieth century, when language became almost the only certain criterion of nationalism, the Arabs, without lifting a finger, despite geographical, political and social divisions, were accepted as one of the large nations of the world, while Israel, after a history of over 3,500 years, had to begin all over again. Even now its newly re-instated national language, modern Hebrew, is something of a barrier between the Jewish State and the majority of the Jewish people, which at present is concentrated in the English-speaking countries.

This different attitude toward language on the part of the two peoples and its historical significance requires further elucidation.

Ancient Muslim writers frequently pointed out that, just as the

Greeks had a natural gift for science and philosophy, the Chinese for minor arts and industries, and other peoples for other branches of human activity, so the ancient Arabs were endowed with a peculiar talent for oral expression and poetry. There can be no doubt that classical Arabic, with its extremely elaborate grammatical forms and its rich vocabulary, is a unique creation. It is, therefore, only natural that its creators should have clung to it tenaciously, the more so as the Bedouin, owing to the precarious life of the desert, tends to seek stability in tradition and fixed forms.

There are many reasons which account for the rapid and wide diffusion of the Arabic language. We shall have an opportunity to return to some of them in the course of this chapter. To my mind, however, the most basic reason of all was that the Arabs' sincere enthusiasm for their precious inheritance so infected the peoples which came under their rule that they strove with all their might to speak, or at least to write, pure classical Arabic.

It was not religion which caused the Koran to be read everywhere —with insignificant and temporary exceptions—in the Arabic original. The Hebrew Bible was translated by the Jews themselves and for their own use into Aramaic, Greek, Arabic and many other tongues. It was only the devotion of the Arabs to their language which made it unthinkable for them that their Holy Book should be read in any vernacular except their own.

The Arabs have earned a most abundant reward for their staunch allegiance to their language. On the other hand, it must be admitted that the language cult, the exaggerated emphasis on outward forms of expressions, had a detrimental influence on the spiritual development of all the Arabic-speaking peoples. One senses this in their literature and not only in the periods of decadence which set in very early, epigonism being essentially inherent in this formalistic and tradition-bound world. The effect is already clearly discernible in that most classical creation of the Arab spirit, pre-Islamic and early Islamic poetry, which was regarded until recently as the unsurpassed model for all works of literary art.

Personally I have a weakness for ancient Arabic poetry. I believe that any unprejudiced person will admit that it contains some noble ideas and some fine observations. On the other hand, in proportion to the stupendous amount of material preserved, it strikes one as particularly poor in motifs and literary forms in the higher sense, and largely devoid of genuine feeling.

All the efforts of the poets are concentrated on elegant idioms, bold comparisons, unusual metaphors and the like. Arabic poetry may be compared to an ornament which may take the form of a plant or even of an animal, but does so not for the sake of representation but in order to turn it into an ingenious, arbitrary and abstract form.

This remoteness of poetical creation from real life, together with its rigid traditionalism, was probably one of the causes of the terrible spiritual stagnation from which the Arab world has not yet fully recovered to this day.

How different was the Hebrew literary genius! Only a small fraction of ancient Hebrew literature has been preserved, but how rich it is in motifs and how close to life! There is no ostentatious display of art; the entire attention is concentrated on genuine feeling and ideas. If we have compared Arabic poetry with an ornament, we may liken Hebrew creation only to a living man himself.

However, the lack of fixed literary forms as well as of a theory of poetical art had the consequence that biblical literature found practically no imitators even in Israel itself, while the artificial verse-making of the ancient Arabs found a tremendous following even beyond the scope of the Arabic language. The development of Hebrew poetry along Arab lines in the Middle Ages is only one example of this. In literature—as in life—it is often not the higher values, but the more impressive forms, which prevail.

We have seen why the histories of Israel and the Arabs, despite a large common background and despite the common "leitmotif" of their existence, have taken very different courses. In the succeeding chapters we shall try to show how these two worlds acted on each other when they were forced into a very intimate symbiosis.

4

THE JEWISH TRADITION IN ISLAM

In a famous saying attributed to Muhammad in the most authoritative collections of so-called Muslim oral traditions, he is reported to have described the relation of Islam to the older religions in this way: "You will follow the traditions of those who preceded you span by span and cubit by cubit—so closely that you will go after them even if they creep into the hole of a lizard."

There is nothing surprising in the saying except perhaps that it is so picturesque. It is, however, remarkable that a prominent Egyptian Muslim writer—A. M. Aqqad—used it as the basis of an article published in the widely read Arab monthly, *Al-Kitab* (October 1946). It indicates that the questions with which we shall deal in the following chapters are freely discussed today even in a Muslim country.

The early biographers of Muhammad regarded it as a sign of God's providence that the town al-Medina, the seat of the first Muslim community, harbored so large a Jewish population which, by its example and influence, was able to prepare its Arab neighbors for the acceptance of a monotheistic religion. It was indeed a unique coincidence that at so crucial a juncture in Arab history there were many Jewish settlements spread throughout Arabia.

It is idle to speculate about the beginnings of the Jewish settlements in the Arabian peninsula. When I stood in the ancient graveyard of the Jewish community of Aden—from which tombstones 700 or 800 years old had been taken away to museums—and looked toward the natural harbor where ships of local design were still being built, it occurred to me that King Solomon's ships, not very different from those I saw there, might have anchored nearby. Perhaps they laid the foundation for the first Jewish community on what is regarded as Arab soil. The prophet Joel makes definite allusions to Jewish trade with the Land of Sheba, and there are, of course, many legends, both Jewish and Arab, about the origins of the Jewish community in Arabia. Nor is there any lack of scientific conjecture—the modern form of legend—on the subject.

Archaeological evidence puts us on firmer ground. In the great necropolis of Beth She'arim, Palestine, excavated by Benjamin Mazar, there was discovered a room, dating from approximately 200 A.D., which was reserved for Jews from Himyar in South Arabia. Himyarite inscriptions found in Yemen prove that some pre-Islamic kings of that country had indeed embraced Judaism, as was asserted by Muslim historians. Through the discoveries and publications of Gonzague Ryckmans of Louvain, Belgium, we are particularly well informed about Dhu Nuwas As'ar, the last Jewish king of Himyar. The inscriptions referring to this king depict him as a monotheist who called his God Rahman, the All-Merciful, as was then Jewish custom. At that time, the local shrines were still venerated in a way reminiscent of Muhammad's allegiance to the sanctuary of the Ka'ba of his native Mecca. In these judaizing Himyarite inscriptions we also find, for the first time on Arab soil, the idea of a Holy War waged for the diffusion of the true religion.

Thus Jews must have settled in Yemen at the latest in the second century A.D. This agrees with the results of British and American excavations conducted in the former British protectorate of Aden which indicate that Hellenistic civilization had an overwhelming influence on ancient South Arabia. The Jewish settlers in Yemen constituted only a small group among the many merchants who traded between the Mediterranean and the incense-growing lands of Southern Arabia and India. It is, no doubt, due to this fact that the craftsmanship of the Yemenite Jews to this day shows certain definite Hellenistic traits.

That Jews were present in *Northern* Arabia is proved by the existence of Jewish tombstones on ancient sites halfway between al-Medina and Palestine. These date to an even earlier period, the years before and after the destruction of the Second Temple. The settlements must have been of considerable importance, for the Jewish law had to make special regulations for them.

One of these is particularly interesting. In view of the essentially agricultural character of the Jewish people, Jewish law assumed that everyone possessed land. The rights of a wife in case of the death of her husband or of divorce were, therefore, safeguarded by assigning to her a portion of the land belonging to the husband.

In Arabia, however, according to a Palestinian authority of the third century, camels and incense served the same purpose. Thus we see in that period most of the Arabian Jews were merchants. However, in Muhammad's time, about 300 years later, we find them organized into compact agricultural units engaged mainly in the cultivation of dates.

It is not difficult to explain this change. As often happened in Jewish commercial history, a flourishing trade was taken over by another, larger group. The emergence of Mecca as a great commercial center may not be unconnected with the decline of Jewish trade in Arabia, while it may be surmised that severe persecution of the Jewish religion by the Byzantines caused the Jewish date-growers of the Jordan Valley to emigrate to Arabia and to carry on their former occupation there. This would explain why some of these Jews, when they were expelled from Arabia by Muhammad, made their way back to Jericho.

I would like to dwell on one important point. The Muslim historiographers describe the two main Jewish tribes—or congregations—in al-Medina as *Kohanim*, "priests." As the late Professor S. Klein has shown, towns exclusively or mainly inhabited by priests were common many centuries after the destruction of the Temple, because the elaborate laws of priestly purity could be more readily observed in compact communities. It was long ago suggested that al-Medina, which means "town" in Aramaic, had been called so by its first Jewish settlers, in contrast to the nearby Wadi-al-Qura, "the valley of the villages," which was also inhabited by Jews.

Similarly, up to the present-day mass emigration from Yemen, many families of *Kohanim* lived in San'a, the capital, and other towns, but none in the nearby villages. Some *Midrashim* refer expressly to the flight of priests into Arabia. All this taken together leads us to accept the testimony of the Muslim writers that al-Medina, the main scene of Muhammad's activities, was originally a priestly town, a community of *Kohanim,* of which very considerable remnants were still extant in the Prophet's time.

It must not be inferred from this fact that the Jews of al-Medina were very observant or learned. Does not the Talmud say about the *Kohanim* of Meshan in Southern Babylonia, the main seat of Jewish learning, that they never observed the biblical law forbidding a priest to marry a divorced woman?

On the other hand, what has been said here about al-Medina bears upon the often discussed question as to whether the Arabian Jews were immigrants from Palestine and other Jewish centers or aboriginal inhabitants of Arabia converted to Judaism.

In attempting to answer this question it is useful to compare the Yemenites, the modern descendants of the Arabian Jews, with the Falashas, the black Jews of Abyssinia (who were brought to the attention of the English-speaking public by Professor Wolf Leslau's *Falasha Anthology,* published recently by Yale University Press). The Yemenites are in every respect ordinary Jews who have always taken their full share in the development of the Jewish religion, so full a share indeed that some believe the Yemenites to be the most Jewish of all Jews, while the Falashas, although no doubt once converted to Judaism, have retained or assimilated elements that are peculiar to a non-Jewish population.

In Arabia, as elsewhere, Judaism made converts. The Arabic poems ascribed to the famous as-Samau'al and other pre-Islamic Jewish poets do not differ in language or spirit from those of their pagan contemporaries. This fact, however, was probably due to assimilation rather than to the racial origin of the poets in question.

The most eloquent testimony to the Jewish character of the Israelite communities of Arabia, however, is found in the Koran itself, which makes repeated reference to their rabbis and learned men, who read and expounded the Torah and were held in the highest esteem by the community for their scholarship; they were called *rabbaniun wa'ahbar*, the latter word being an arabized form of *Haver*, "Fellow," a title current in Palestine.

The Koran refers repeatedly to the Sabbath as a day of rest, and to the Jewish dietary and other laws, and it contains so many legends and theological ideas found in talmudic literature that we are able to draw a picture of the spiritual life of the Jews with whom Muhammad must have come into contact.

Of course, one cannot expect this picture to be exact or complete, for the exposition in the Koran of the tenets and the rites of the new religion itself is very far from being comprehensive, systematic, or even unambiguous. In particular, it is not expressly stated in the Koran whether the Jewish community in Arabia in Muhammad's time formed one compact religious denomination or contained some dissenting group or groups, or whether that community as a whole adapted some sectarian deviation from the Judaism known to us from talmudic literature.

I should like to illustrate this problem by some examples. One of Muhammad's considerable merits was the reform of marriage and the amelioration of the position of Arab women. Muhammad adopted the biblical laws concerning forbidden marriages.

As is well known, marriage with a niece constituted a point of controversy between orthodox Judaism, which allowed it, and Jewish sects, both before and after Muhammad, which regarded it as forbidden, for example, the Karaites and the so-called "Covenanters of Damascus," who were closely connected with the authors of the newly found Dead Sea Scrolls. Muhammad might, of course, also have learned about the prohibition of the marriage with one's niece from some Christian source.

The driving force in Muhammad's preaching at the beginning of his career was the dread of the imminent Last Judgment, which he described in the most vivid terms. Much of this material can be traced back to Jewish sources. To give just one illustration: the Koran says (16:77) that "Resurrection will come as in the twinkling of an eye." This was recited three times a day by the Jews who prayed the *Shemone Esre*, the daily prayer according to the Palestinian ritual.

But the talmudic piety in general was obviously inspired more by the idea of permanent reward in a future life than by the fear of the impending Doomsday. There existed, however, in earlier times, Jewish groups of another religious type, whose rich apocryphal literature is pervaded, like Muhammad's preaching, by genuine apprehension that the end of the physical world is imminent.

It may be that a Jewish group of that type lived in Arabia, which would explain the many appropriations from Jewish literature found in Muhammad's earliest preachings on the Last Judgment.

Furthermore, in the Prophet's later disputes with the Jews we find what might be called a "Karaitic tendency," an insistence on the written word of the Bible alone, and exhortations against "human" additions or circumventions. The biblical prohibition against taking interest on loans which, according to Muhammad, was disregarded by the Arabian Jews—just as the similar koranic prohibition was circumvented by his own followers—may serve as an illustration of such "Karaitic tendency."

There are allusions in the Koran to the fact that, while the majority of the Jews absolutely refused to join the new creed, some of them acknowledged Muhammad as a prophet. It is not unlikely that what we have called the "Karaitic tendency" in the Koran is due to such converts.

Finally, in the Holy Book of Islam there are found unmistakably Jewish *Midrashim* which so far have not been traced in Hebrew literature. It was explained in the previous chapter that Muhammad did not incorporate into his new religion the idea or the practice of a day of rest. Therefore, if we find in the Koran legends praising Jews for observing the Sabbath or rebuking them for not doing so, these legends can stem only from a Jewish source.

There is an engaging tale in the Koran about a Jewish seashore village to which fish came only on Saturdays—as long as the people observed the Sabbath—because the fish, of course, knew very well that Jews cannot do without fish on the Sabbath. According to another story, Sabbath-breakers were transformed into monkeys. Both legends may be of local origin, as monkeys are very common in Southern Arabia (while there are none in Palestine), and the

Red Sea harbor, Elath, in Muhammad's time was inhabited by Jewish fishermen. Taken together with other *Midrashim* appearing in the Koran but not from other sources, they may indicate some divergent Jewish tradition.

All this leads us to the great question: which religion, or which sect, served Muhammad as his immediate model, or, since the Koran alludes in various places to persons who instructed the Prophet, who were these teachers?

A somewhat uneven literature has grown up around this question. The best single contribution in this field, to my mind, is the book of that excellent Swedish scholar, Tor Andrae, *The Origin of Islam and Christianity*, published in German in 1926. Of recent publications, Professor A. Jeffery's *The Foreign Vocabulary of the Koran*, 1938, is most useful, while Professor J. Obermann's "Islamic Origins" in *The Arab Heritage* (Princeton University Press 1944) shows that a fresh scrutiny of the question is apt to bring out some forgotten aspects. My article on the Koran in the *Encyclopedia Judaica* might serve as a critical survey of the literature up to 1930.

Why is it so difficult to find a solution to this problem? The main reasons are these:

The Koran contains a huge mass of material which can be traced to both Jewish and Christian sources. This is true not only of biblical and apocryphal literature with which Muhammad might have been acquainted through both Christian and Jewish channels, but it also holds good for elements from the Jewish liturgy and lore which had found their way into Christian circles very early. They could have been independently developed from similar premises; for example, the phrase, "the day of resurrection will come in the twinkling of an eye," which, as we have seen, occurs in the daily Jewish prayers according to the Palestinian ritual, is also used by a famous Christian preacher.

On the other hand, the Koran contains many things which, as far as we know at present, are clearly either of Jewish or Christian origin. On the Christian side, we have an additional difficulty. What Muhammad has to say about Christ and things Christian is not applicable to any of the many Christian denominations and sects of pre-Islamic times.

Furthermore, there seems to have been a third "tradition," neither Christian explicitly nor Jewish, which may have influenced Muhammad (although personally I am not so certain about this as Tor Andrae or those before and after him who held this assumption). For Muhammad believed that, beginning with Noah and Abraham, he was preceded by a long succession of prophets sent to various peoples, including some Arab tribes, all of whom were equally true and all of whom preached essentially the same faith— a belief which enabled him to proclaim himself a prophet.

To my mind, this idea could easily have developed, especially for missionary purposes, out of the ordinary Jewish—and possibly also Christian—tendency to portray the patriarchs and other figures in biblical narratives as holy men if not prophets, all preaching the same long-established tenets of creed and behavior. In any case, some prominent scholars, puzzled by the variety and incongruity of the material brought together in the Koran and impressed by the fact that the "prophetology" of the Koran bore some likeness to the succession of "prophets of truth," recognized by Judaeo-Christian gnostic sects, believed that they had found the solution to the problem by assuming that Muhammad's immediate model was a Judaeo-Christian sect such as the Ebionites (a sect whose name was derived from the Hebrew word *Evion*, a poor man), or, rather, a later, gnostic development of that trend, the Elkesaites.

It is on this basis that Harnack, the great authority on early Christianity, denies the possibility that the recognized Christian churches could have had any influence on Muhammad. "Islam," he says, "is a recast of the Jewish religion on Arab soil, after the Jewish religion itself had been recast by a gnostic Judaizing Christianity" (*Dogmengeschichte* II, pp. 553-7).

However, this view, although taken up again in detail by H. J. Schoeps, a German-Jewish professor of the History of Religion, in his recent book, *Theologie und Geschichte des Judenchristentums*, 1949, cannot be maintained. For, as Tor Andrae has shown most convincingly—and as an unprejudiced reading of the Koran shows—

Muhammad's preaching does not contain any really gnostic ideas and, in general, reveals a religious attitude quite different from those esoteric circles; but this precludes the possibility that the Elkesaites or a similar sect might have served him as an immediate model.

Tor Andrae's own, penetrating but somewhat lengthy, exposition may be summarized as follows:

(a) Muhammad drew his main and immediate inspiration from the piety of the Christian monastic world with its continuous waiting upon the Lord and His judgment, its prayers, vigils and fasting.

(b) No single Christian denomination could have served as a model to the Prophet, because he obviously drew indiscriminately from all or most of those with whom he could have come into contact.

(c) The idea about the succession of the prophets of truth must have come to him from a different source.

(d) In the latter half of his career, in al-Medina, Muhammad was considerably influenced by Jewish thought and ways of life.

(e) Muhammad's own spirituality, with its uncompromising monotheism, had in it much of the spirit of Judaism.

However, Andrae's conclusions require some qualification.

(1) The assumption that Muhammad, at the beginning of his prophetic career, was mainly, if not exclusively, inspired by Christians of various denominations, including Judaeo-Christians, seems to be absolutely precluded by the simple fact that there is no reference whatsoever to the figure (even name) of Christ and anything else specifically Christian in the earlier parts of the Koran, the very parts which teem with narratives about holy men from the Old Testament and from Arab antiquity.

According to Noeldeke's *Introduction to the Quran*, which arranges the chapters of the Koran in chronological order, stories about Christ and other New Testament figures appear for the first time in *Sura* (chapter 19), which is the 58th out of 114 chapters according to Noeldeke's chronology. Not only that, but in the 90 chapters of the Holy Book, which were composed in Mecca, the name of Christ occurs only in four, in two of which his name only is mentioned, so that one gets the impression that Muhammad made a specific study of the Christian narratives and dogmas only at a very late stage of his activities.

It cannot be argued that all the Christian or Judaeo-Christian preachers of the various denominations who might have inspired Muhammad before he decided to become a prophet, purposely left out everything connected with the New Testament stories. The assumption of such silent agreement among so many people is very unlikely in itself. And why should they have done so? Does not the Koran show that it was precisely the narratives which made a deep impression on Muhammad and his audience? And what would have appealed to them more than the beautiful stories about Christ, and what would have been more in conformity with Muhammad's early preaching than the proclamations of the Baptist and of Christ that the Hour had come?

In short, Muhammad as a native of a flourishing caravan-city had no doubt met Christians before he became a prophet. But the mentors alluded to in the Koran from whom he actually received the material for his new religion could not have been professing Christians.

Later on, when—as would be natural for a man engaged in a religious mission—he began to inquire about other religions, he obtained a knowledge of the Christian faith which, though imperfect and confused, he immediately included in his own book. That this knowledge was acquired only gradually is best shown by the fact that the very name of Christ (in Arabic, *al-Masih*, Messiah) became known to Muhammad—or at all events, was mentioned by him—only after he migrated to al-Medina.

(2) Moses, on the other hand, is the predominant figure in the Koran. I would not like to lay too much stress on the quantitative aspect, although it is impressive enough; compared to Jesus, who is mentioned only four times in the Koran during the Meccan, that is, the formative, period of Muhammad's career, Moses' name occurs there over a hundred times. Much more important is the fact that the stories about Moses are not confined to certain chapters, but pervade the whole Koran and the idea of Moses, the

Prophet with a Book, possessed Muhammad to such an extent that he immediately proceeded to produce a divine book of his own.

It seems beyond doubt that during the earlier period of his career, Muhammad knew about only one such prophet, Moses, and therefore regarded himself as his direct successor. Thus, he says (46:12): "Before this book there was Moses' book . . . and this book confirms it in the Arabic language." In the same chapter (v. 30), the *Jinn* (the invisible spirits) who attend the reading of the Koran say: "We have heard a book which came down from Heaven after Moses to confirm its predecessor." And when Muhammad swears in one of the oldest *Suras* by Mount Sinai and by holy Mecca, his own town, the same idea seems to underlie his oath.

(3) During the period in which specifically Christian traits do not yet appear in the Koran, there are numerous details which can be traced back to Jewish literature. This fact has often been discussed, beginning with Abraham Geiger's famous thesis on the subject, which appeared in 1833, down to Obermann's "Islamic Origins" which I have quoted above. Therefore it seems reasonable to assume that in his early years Muhammad had close contact with Jews who were not very different from those portrayed in the talmudic literature.

(4) The Koran contains many words and expressions which are of undoubtedly Christian origin. To give just two examples, one of the Devil's names is *Iblis*, from the Greek Diabolos (the English word "devil" is derived from the same word; the English leave out the end of the original Greek word, and the Arabs its beginning); and, what is even more important, *al-Qiyama*, "Resurrection," which occurs very frequently, is Christian. Even biblical names like Elias for Elijah, or Suleiman for Solomon, reveal an unmistakable Christian origin.

It was, however, natural that after Arabia had been surrounded and invaded by Christian peoples for hundreds of years, its language should have absorbed many Christian words.

(5) The Koran also took over literary forms so far found only in Christian literature. As far back as thirty years ago I showed in my Ph.D. thesis that in his middle Meccan period Muhammad used

to conclude each story about a prophet with a blessing on the prophet (e.g., chaps. 37 and 19). This literary device is found in Syriac religious poems (*Memre*). Even more important is the fact that the general trend of Muhammad's ascetic, pietistic religiosity with its dominant note of dread of the imminent Day of Judgment, seems to be more akin to monastic piety than to rabbinic Judaism.

(6) The way out of the difficulty created by this apparently contradictory evidence seems to be the simple assumption that the group of Jews who, we may suppose, influenced Muhammad's beginnings, although they were basically ordinary Orthodox Jews, had themselves come under the influence of monastic piety and adopted some of its practices and possibly also some of its literature.

Anyone acquainted with modern research in Jewish history will find nothing strange in this assumption. As F. Baer, Professor of Jewish history at the Hebrew University, Jerusalem, has shown (*Zion*, vol. 3, 6-7), at the very time of the Crusades, when the sufferings of the Jews at the hands of Christians were still a vivid memory, the pious Jews of Germany, the famous Hasidei Ashkenaz, were influenced by the preachings of the Christian monks, while the contemporary Jewish pietistic movement in the East, headed by Abraham, the son of Maimonides, avowedly emulated the Muslim mystics and even adopted some of their practices, for example, the practice of frequent prostrations.

(7) To be sure, most or all of the ingredients of monastic pietism which found their way into the Koran, were already present in some form in early Judaism: "Vigils" are mentioned several times in the Book of Psalms and played a very important role in the life of the community in the Dead Sea Scrolls. In talmudic times, however, *study* at night took the place of the nightly prayer. Prostrations were a very characteristic feature of Jewish prayer up to the second century. Later, this practice was discouraged precisely because it was so conspicuously preached by the monks. However, the Jewish group which influenced Muhammad could hardly have been a direct offshoot of some older sect—as, for example, the community associated with the Dead Sea Scrolls—because if it were,

it would not have had those close affinities to talmudic literature to which the Koran bears such eloquent testimony.

(8) The solution I venture to propose for the question concerning the identity of Muhammad's mentors seems also to be the most plausible explanation of the undiluted and uncompromising attitude on monotheism maintained by the Prophet from the very beginning of his mission. This cannot be explained by his natural disposition or mood, but could have been due only to a very strong influence by monotheists of such description, namely, Jews.

(9) I do not believe that all the Arabian Jews of Muhammad's time were of the type I have just mentioned. On the contrary, the majority of the Jews of Medina, with whom Muhammad had so many dealings in the second part of his career, seem to have been more like the ordinary talmudic Jews. Whether the group I have already described bore a distinct name, cannot of course be determined. If it has, one would suggest, in view of the great number of references to Moses in the Koran, a name connected with that Prophet, such as *Bene Moshe*, the followers of Moses. There seems to be some allusions to it in the later part of the Meccan section of the Koran, when Muhammad had already made his first study of the Christian faith.

Thus, after proclaiming himself the Prophet of the Gentiles, he continues: "Among the followers of Moses there is one people who lead others with the Truth and with it they judge" (*Sura* 7, v. 59). I do not, of course, wish to press this point or to state definitely that this group was also responsible for what I have called certain "Karaitic tendencies" in the Koran, although I am inclined to believe that this was indeed the case.

In conclusion, I wish to say this: Whether the solution I have proposed here for the problem of the origin of Islam is accepted or not, one thing is beyond doubt: the battle which Muhammad so gloriously and so easily won over his Arab compatriots, had been decided many centuries before on the hills of Judaea.

The intrinsic values of the belief in one God, the Creator of the world and designer of human destiny, the God of Justice and Mercy, before whom everyone, high and low, bears personal responsibility, came to Muhammad, as he never ceased to emphasize, from Israel.

The Koran is the Holy Book of Islam and its fundamental source in every respect. However, just as the Jewish religion developed very much after the conclusion of the biblical period and created a literature many times as comprehensive as the Hebrew Bible, thus Islam changed enormously after the death of the Arab Prophet, until it became an extremely elaborate system of ideas, institutions, customs and writings. A comparison between classical Islam and Judaism is extremely revealing. For if, as we have seen above, there is a very close connection between Muhammad's creation, the Koran, and the religion of Israel, there is an even more amazing affinity between the fully developed systems of the two religions. Apart from many aspects of religious law and literature common to the two religions—a fact which can hardly be due to chance—all the main characteristic features of their systems are identical, or almost identical.

(1) Islam, like Judaism, is a religion of *Halakha*, in Arabic *Shari'a*, that is, a God-given law which regulates minutely all aspects of life: law, worship, ethics and social etiquette. *Halakha-Shari'a* is the very essence and core of both religions.

(2) This religious law is based on the Oral Tradition called in Arabic *Hadith* and in Hebrew by words of identical meaning which authoritatively interprets and supplements the written law, in Arabic *Kitab* and in Hebrew *Tora she-bikhtav*, which is the same word.

(3) The Oral Tradition falls into two parts, one legal in the widest sense of the word and the other moral. In both Muslim and Jewish literature they assume the same form of loosely connected maxims and short anecdotes.

(4) Although the Muslims had a State when they created their religious law, and although they had contact with the organized Christian churches, their *Shari'a*, like the Jewish *Halakha*, was developed by a completely free and unorganized republic of scholars; rulers in ancient Islam might make decisions with regard

to special cases, but they never created or officially promulgated laws. Nor did Islam ever have a hierarchy of religious dignitaries who decided questions while sitting in official synods or councils, as was the practice in the Christian churches.

(5) In both Judaism and Islam the religious law took its final shape in the form of different Schools or Rites, which originally represented the most widely accepted decisions or usages of one country like the Jewish rites of Babylonia and Palestine or the Muslim rites of al-Medina and Iraq, with the conception common to both religions that these Schools or Rites were all equally orthodox.

(6) The logical reasoning applied to the development of the religious law is largely identical in Islam and Judaism. This is not a mere coincidence inherent in the nature of things; but, as some of the terms used show, must be based on direct connections.

(7) The study even of purely legal matters is regarded in both religions as worship. The holy men of Islam and Judaism are not priests or monks, but students of the divinely revealed Law. In later Islam antagonism developed between the lawyers and the saints who were inclined to mysticism. However, in the formative years of Islam the two were identical. This, by the way, would explain why the early pietistic Muslim literature contains many sayings found also in the writings of the rabbis.

In view of the facts just enumerated, one must consider the following points:

(a) that Judaism was a fully developed system at the time when the Arab Muslims made their first conquests;

(b) that, as recent research has shown, Muslim religious law developed mainly in Iraq, the chief center of Jewish studies;

(c) that Islam by its very nature was prone to learn from other religions;

(d) that Muhammad's uncompromising monotheism must have impelled at least some of his believers to seek instruction from equally strict monotheists.

In view of these, one is led to assume that the influence of Judaism on early Islam must have been very considerable, if not decisive. This question is extremely complicated, and an analysis of more technical details would be required to discuss it fully. However, the basic fact of the important rôle of Judaism in the development of post-koranic Islam cannot be denied. In chapter VII we shall learn that Islam amply repaid Judaism. There, also, some aspects of Jewish religious law and lore which may have influenced Islam will be treated.

5

THE ACTUAL AND LEGAL POSITION
OF THE JEWS UNDER ARAB ISLAM

Because of the Arab conquests, which started almost immediately after the establishment of the Muslim community in al-Medina and continued for over a hundred years, the great majority of the Jewish people and most of the Christian communities of Western Asia, North Africa and Spain came under Muslim rule. Although the legend of the spread of the Islamic religion by fire and sword has long ago been proved untrue, it goes without saying that so great and extensive a war, waged mainly by Bedouin hordes, must have been a terrible shock to the populations affected. There is archaeological evidence of burned synagogues, and there can be no doubt that there were great losses of property, life and freedom (through enslavement).

On the other hand, it is certain that the Muslim conquest meant for the Jews a great improvement in their situation in various respects: first, they ceased to be an outcast community persecuted by the ruling church and became part of a vast class of subjects with a special status; for, as we shall presently see, Muslim public law made no distinction between Jews and Christians; secondly, the actual provisions which regulated the legal status of so large a part of the population were by the very force of circumstance less oppressive than those intended by the Byzantine rulers especially for the Jews; finally, when the once mighty Empires of Persia and the Byzantines were vanquished, there were good prospects for other changes as well—in particular, for the messianic restoration of the Jewish people.

It is therefore not surprising that everywhere, and especially in Palestine, Syria and Spain, the Jews actively helped the Muslim conquerors and were regarded by them as their allies.

Very different was the situation of the Jews in Northern Arabia; there they had the ill-luck to live in compact settlements in the very heart of the newly formed Muslim community. This fact proved to be a great stimulus to the development of Islam during Muhammad's second great period, that of al-Medina, but it was not conducive to the creation of friendly Jewish-Arab relations.

In a treatise against Christians by the famous Muslim writer, al-Jahiz, who died in 869, the author asks why the Muslims are less favorably disposed toward the Jews than toward the Christians, when the latter, with their belief in the Trinity, are more offensive in their religious tenets and more dangerous as economic rivals.

His answer is most instructive: the Jews, he says, were immediate neighbors of the Muslims in the al-Medina and other places, and hostility between neighbors is as strong and tenacious as that between relatives; for people hate only what they know and are opposed to those who are like them, knowing the weaknesses of those with whom they are in daily contact.

Why then did not the bulk of the Jewish community in Arabia recognize Muhammad as a prophet to the Gentiles, as Muhammad demanded while he was still in Mecca; and as the pietist Jewish group discussed in the previous chapter obviously did. This is the more surprising as at that time, before the pagan rites of the Pilgrimage to Mecca were incorporated into Islam, there was nothing repugnant to the Jewish religion in Muhammad's preaching. Moreover, Muhammad's message to the Arabs was described later on in a widely disseminated Jewish document of the late Umayyad period, as an act of God's mercy, which was tantamount to acknowledging it as a true religion.

To my mind, however, it is precisely Muhammad's connection with a dissenting Jewish group, which impelled the majority of the adherents of the Jewish faith in Arabia to reject Muhammad outright. Judaism was engaged in a continuous battle against sectarianism, both before and after Muhammad, so much that a special prayer denouncing dissenters, *Minim*, was included in the daily services.

The rejection of Muhammad by the majority of the Jews of Arabia is therefore to be interpreted in the light of the internal Jewish struggle between orthodoxy and sectarianism. On the other hand, however, it is only natural that Muhammad could not tolerate as a neighbor a large monotheistic community which categorically denied his claim as a prophet, and probably also ridiculed his inevitable blunders in referring to the biblical narratives and laws (as when he has Pharaoh ask his vizier *Haman*(!) to erect a "Tower of Babel" (28:38)).

There was, however, a more prosaic side to Muhammad's wars against his Jewish neighbors. His Meccan followers were landless emigrants who had to be indemnified for all they had lost when leaving their native city. The Jewish castles and date-palm plantations of Northern Arabia served this purpose all too well. Thus, the ousting of Jews from their land in Northern Arabia was only a repetition of the process whereby, as we assumed in the last chapter, they were crowded out of the great foreign trade of Arabia some centuries previously.

In any case, it is very unfortunate that the struggle, which very specific historical circumstances forced on the Jews and Muhammad, has left its mark on the Holy Book of Islam. To be sure, Muhammad rejected the Christian creed much more vigorously than Judaism, but his actual wars with Jewish communities impelled him to say some very unfavorable things about them, particularly where he remarks that they were more hostile to Islam than the Christians.

Hence it is the more noteworthy that Muslim law makes no distinction whatsoever between Jews and Christians with regard to their legal status under Islam, although the Arabs found that the Jews were severely discriminated against in the Christian countries they conquered, and although they could, had they wished, have found a basis for such discrimination in the Koran. Among others, two reasons seem to account for this remarkable legal situation:

(a) the Jewish help to, and alliance with, the Arabs during their wars of conquest, mentioned previously, and

(b) the fact that Muslim jurisprudence during its formative period had its main center in Iraq or Babylonia, where both Jews and Christians had previously been subjects to the Persian, Zoroastrian kings, and where the head of the large flourishing Jewish community, the *Resh Galutha*, enjoyed an honored position at the Court of the Caliphs.

In general, it was a very important factor in the history of Arab-Jewish symbiosis that Iraq, which was the spiritual and economic center of the Muslim state and shortly afterwards became its political center as well, had a large Jewish community and was also the spiritual and political center of the Jewish world, both before and after the Arab conquest.

It is a most remarkable fact that, while Christianity gradually disappeared in various parts of the Arab Muslim Empire, flourishing Jewish communities survived—and continued to exist. The phenomenon occurred in the furthermost eastern corner of that Empire: in Bukhara in central Asia, which was once a very important center of Christian propaganda; in Yemen in south Arabia, once a Christian bishopric; and, finally, in North Africa, significant as the birthplace and home of St. Augustine, the most famous of all Church Fathers. The disappearance of Christianity and the survival of Judaism in each of these countries was due to particular historical circumstances, which do, however, illustrate the fact that under Arab Islam Jews were not treated differently from members of other non-Muslim religions.

Above it was said, in passing, that the Jewish scholars of the nineteenth century overemphasized the favorable legal and actual position of the Jews (and Christians) in Muslim countries during the Middle Ages. The famous chapter on Muslim tolerance in the second chapter of the great Islamist's, I. Goldziher, classic *Vorlesungen über den Islam* is a striking indication of that trend in Jewish scholarship.

Subsequent research, however, as well as information gathered about the actual position of Jews in the Arab countries in modern times, gradually led to an anticlimax. An article published by Cecil Roth of the University of Oxford in the *Jewish Forum* (1946, pp. 28–33) is a typical example. Roth asserts that Islam was as intolerant as any other religion, and that the Arabs were as much given to outbursts of hatred against foreigners as other peoples.

It is, of course, impossible to give a single answer to a question applying to so many countries and to a religion as complex as Islam. Certain points, however, emerge quite clearly from the mass of evidence at our disposal.

To begin, the Koran itself, the basic source of Muslim religion and law, shows two quite different attitudes with regard to the treatment of non-Muslims. The new Muslim community of al-Medina took shape at a time of incessant wars. Most emphatic incitement to war therefore became a prominent feature in the section of the Holy Book which was promulgated at Medina; and warmongers and preachers of hatred never had great difficulties in finding quotations in it for their purposes. Islam is a militant religion, which makes perpetual war incumbent on the Muslim community until the whole world is subjected to its rule. The conquered nations which had a revealed religion had to pay a special tax and to live in abject subjection to the followers of Islam.

On the other hand, Muhammad never entirely gave up his original belief that all religions contained essentially the same truth. Therefore lovers of peace and cooperation between the various religious communities could find support for their aims in some very liberal verses in the Koran, and something of that large-hearted spirit of early Islam has always been alive in the hearts of many of its followers. Consequently—and this is a very important point—Muslim law guarantees to Jews and Christians the free exercise of their religion provided that it is not offensive to Muslims. An example of offensive conduct in this regard would be the display of a cross or the blowing of a *Shofar* (a ram's horn blown in the synagogue on various occasions) in a Muslim quarter.

During the first century of Muslim rule over the newly conquered countries, the more tolerant aspect of Islam prevailed.
Some scholars are inclined to explain this on the basis that the
then ruling dynasty of the Umayyads was still inspired by pagan
ideals and was therefore free from Muslim fanaticism. This explanation is not borne out by subsequent research. The first
Umayyad, Mu'awiya, was a very clever man, and clever men are
often tolerant. However, it was not so much the personal inclina-
tions of the rulers or the ruling class, but hard facts which made
tolerance a political necessity.

In their vast, newly won kingdom, the Muslims formed a small
minority group which had to depend for its very food, its military security, its finances and administration on the conquered
peoples. Oppressive measures against these, the majority, although
often imposed locally, were, on the whole, not a practical proposi-
tion. In addition, the Muslims had not developed a religious law
worth mentioning.

However, in the second, and in particular the third century
of the Muslim era, when, for many reasons, the Muslims had become the majority and had developed an elaborate religious law,
many humiliating restrictions were imposed upon Christians and
Jews, some of which went back directly to Byzantine anti-Jewish
legislation.

First, infidels were forced to dress differently from Muslims.
This injunction gave rise throughout the centuries to a spate of
often ridiculous laws; for example, some rules forced Jewish women
to wear shoes of different colors, one black and the other white.
The yellow badge for Jews was known in Muslim countries many
centuries before it was introduced into Christian Europe.

There were other restrictions: regarding government posts, the
height of houses or the use of riding animals (a very important
measure, of course, comparable to the prohibition against keeping a
car or travelling in public vehicles invented by the Nazis). In the
only Arab country with non-Muslim inhabitants, which has never
been dominated by a European power, Yemen, all these and other
restrictions have remained in full force up to this day, and, on the

basis of my personal acquaintance with many Yemen Jews, I can vouch that they have had a very adverse effect upon the life and the psychology of the people concerned.

Muslim lawyers exerted all the imagination and ingenuity they possessed on the question of the social isolation and degradation of the non-Muslims and tried constantly to induce the rulers of their time to put their findings into effect. On the other hand, it was often the Muslim lawyers, themselves, who endeavored to check arbitrary rulers from infringing upon the rights of their non-Muslim subjects. An enormous amount of information on this question can be culled from books on Muslim law and Muslim history and, naturally, it is a story of much human misery. I confine myself here to a discussion of some of its more characteristic aspects.

The object against which the religious fanaticism of an excited mob can most easily be directed is the house of worship of another faith. The Christian Roman emperors were much annoyed by the disorder resulting from the attacking and burning of synagogues and sometimes even ordered their reconstruction. After much wavering the Eastern Roman Empire adopted a law which forbade the erection of new synagogues, but guaranteed safety from attack to those already in existence. This law was adopted by the Muslims with regard to the non-Muslim religions prevailing in their countries, which did not, however, protect many a famous church from being converted into a mosque, or others from being damaged or altogether destroyed. Even the Holy Sepulcher, the church in Jerusalem which is reputed to contain the tomb of Jesus, suffered such attacks and at one time was almost completely demolished.

Moreover, under Islam many new cities came into existence, originally as military centers, because the Muslim rulers did not wish their soldiers to be stationed among the local population. These cities were the seats of government and naturally, in the course of time, attracted many Christians and Jews. Soon a great portion of the non-Muslim population was concentrated in such cities. How, under these circumstances, was it possible to observe the law forbidding the erection of new churches and synagogues?

Bagdad, the capital of Iraq (founded in 762), included in its precincts a village bearing a Persian name ("God has given": *Bag*, God; *dad*, has given), which finally stuck to the whole city. Therefore, the lawyers might claim that the churches and synagogues found in Bagdad had been erected prior to the building of the city—although the buildings were obviously new. By no stretch of the imagination, however, could this have been said of some other cities. Nevertheless, the force of circumstance was stronger than the provisions of the law. In addition, the new buildings of the non-Muslim communities normally were of modest dimensions and appearance.

On the other hand, in times of tension, the old law could always be invoked by religious fanatics or by profit-seekers. Thus in 1474, the only synagogue then in existence in Jerusalem was demolished by a mob, led by a fanatic *Kadi* (Muslim religious judge). That *Kadi*, from the point of view of Muslim law, no doubt, was better justified than the Muslim ruler who ordered its reconstruction, for that particular synagogue certainly had not been in existence prior to the conquest of the town by the Muslims. In Yemen, for instance, before the mass exodus of 1949/50, there existed hundreds of tiny Jewish villages. Quite a number of them were very old, older certainly than the surrounding Muslim villages. New synagogues, however, were built all the time; whether such transgression of the law went unpunished depended on the good will of the neighbors. All in all, one sees that an intolerant religious law, although disregarded often and in many places, constitutes a menace, so long as it is in force.

Another discriminatory law, which Islam inherited from the Eastern Roman Church, was the provision, alluded to previously, that "unbelievers" could not hold government posts. The idea behind the law was that government posts confer authority and prestige, neither of which might accrue to non-Muslims.

For many reasons—in particular, an absence of suitable Muslim candidates—many Christians and Jews obtained government posts in Muslim countries, sometimes reaching even the highest positions. Often, however, bloody reactions followed, or the non-

Muslim government servants were forced to adopt the ruling religion. Such a convert to Islam was Jacob Ibn Killis (died 991), the Jewish vizier of the first Fatimid caliph of Cairo, who, according to some sources, was responsible also for the foundation of al-Azhar, the oldest Muslim religious college still in operation. On the other hand, an example of those leading Jewish statesmen who remained faithful to their religion and were killed while in office was Joseph, the son and successor of the famous author and political-military leader, Samuel, the *Nagid* (the head of the Jewish community). Joseph was killed in Granada, Spain, in 1066, and his death was accompanied by a wholesale massacre of the Jewish population.

A special case, also paralleled in Christian legislation, was the prohibition against Muslim use of the services of a Christian or Jewish doctor or pharmacist. The reason offered for this by the Muslim lawyers is the same one that gave rise to the famous "doctors' trials" of 1953 in Soviet Russia, namely, the suspicion that an "unbeliever" may provide medicine injurious to a patient's life.

Another argument in favor of the prohibition reflects the high esteem in which the medical profession was held in Muslim countries: one should not confide one's body to a doctor of another persuasion, because it led possibly to his control of one's soul. A similar prohibition against medical treatment by anyone but an observing Jew, and for the same reasons, is contained in the *Mishneh Torah*, (the codification of Jewish law and lore), of Maimonides, himself a famous doctor. Characteristically enough, in the code ("Manslaughter," chap. XII, 9–10), the provisions against a non-Jewish doctor are less severe than those against a Jewish atheist.

No discriminatory ruling was less observed than this prohibition. Christian and Jewish doctors are known to have been court physicians to caliphs and other Muslim rulers in practically every Muslim country, including Yemen. Many others occupied leading positions in hospitals founded and maintained by Muslim rulers. Reading Arabic sources on the history of medicine, for example, Ibn Abi Usaibia, a colleague of Maimonides's son and successor,

Abraham, one is impressed by the spirit of true fellowship which bound together the doctors of various denominations of that time. It is an indication of the decline of the Muslim world in the later Middle Ages that the agitation of the religious scholars against non-Muslim doctors was endorsed by official government decree.

As we have seen, the laws against the employment of non-Muslims in government service or against the consultation of non-Muslim doctors were socio-religious in character. Naturally, they also had economic repercussions. However, discrimination in the economic field—as in Europe, where the Jews were confined for many centuries to the position of usurers, peddlers and other degrading and precarious professions—was largely unknown in Islam, at least in practice and as far as the central countries of the Muslim world are concerned. It is true that some Muslim law books contain the provision that non-Muslims should not engage in the same commerce as Muslims. This provision was reiterated in a public proclamation as late as 1905 by the Imam, the secular and religious head of the state of Yemen. However, this law was not general Islamic and its application was limited even in Yemen itself.

It is not true—although it has often been stated—that the Jews were not allowed to own or to cultivate land in Yemen. They were not allowed to reclaim virgin soil—for the soil as such was regarded as the common property of the Muslims, but they were fully entitled to buy land and to leave it to their children. I have collected from the immigrants from Yemen a great number of legal deeds proving that many of them possessed land in various parts of that country.

On the other hand, it is true that the most ancient law books of Islam discriminated heavily against non-Muslims in the economic field. The Arab Muslim conquerors were led by the mercantile aristocracy of Mecca, who wished, in addition to their political and social ascendancy, to acquire supremacy in the commercial life of the new empire. In order to destroy non-Muslim competition, Muslim law provided that, while a Muslim merchant had to pay two and one-half per cent of the value of his merchandise at any customs' station, a non-Muslim had to pay five per cent; and the minimum value of a consignment on which duties had to be paid, was forty dinars (the standard gold coin), for a Muslim, but only twenty for an "unbeliever." It is not yet clear, however, how far this provision was carried out and how deeply it affected the commercial activities of the various communities. It would appear that during the Fatimid rule over Egypt and the adjacent countries (969–1171), under which the trade between the Mediterranean world and the Far East and India was most flourishing, there was no such discrimination. At any rate, there is no reference to it in the many documents related to this trade, which will be discussed later. Saladin, the famous Kurdish ruler who followed the Fatimids, was extremely orthodox and renewed many of the ancient discriminatory laws, among them the differential treatment of Muslims and non-Muslims in customs' payments. But under the pressure of European merchants, who frequented the ports of his kingdom, he was forced to change his attitude. It is notable that the edict abolishing the discrimination expressly refers to Jews and Christians, both foreign and local.

The absence of oppressive discriminatory economic legislation in Islam can be judged from the great variety of professions and crafts followed by the Jews in Islamic countries as opposed to the few trades available to them in Medieval Europe. The abject economic and general conditions of the Jewish masses in most Arabic-speaking countries, which have impressed countless visitors in modern times, are the outcome of the *general* decline of these countries, and a corollary of the unfavorable socio-religious position of the non-Muslims.

We may similarly regard the legal situation of non-Muslims under Islam. To be sure, non-Muslims were heavily discriminated against, although there were great differences in this respect among the various law schools. In general, a non-Muslim witness against a Muslim was not accepted, or accepted only with qualifications— which largely deprived him of the protection of the law; the murderer of a non-Muslim was not usually punished in the same way as the murderer of a Muslim, and there were many other minor legal disqualifications. How very unpleasant such a situation can be even in our own day may be learned from a recent publication by André Chouraqui, *La condition juridique de l'Israelite marocain*, Paris 1950, which describes conditions in Morocco, a country which has been a French protectorate since 1912 and where American influence is very strongly felt at present. However, it was not so much express discrimination—bad as that was—but rather the general weakness of the administration of justice, and its disregard for the helpless, which made the legal position of the non-Muslims so precarious. A Muslim historian, who wanted to emphasize the sense of justice of Nur ed-Din Zengi, the famous champion of Islam in its fight against the Crusaders, said of him the following: "Even if the plaintiff was a Jew and the accused his own son, he would do justice to the plaintiff." The assumption is clear that an unprotected member of a second-class community had little chance normally that his case would be properly heard.

Conditions varied in different regions of the Arabic-speaking world and were particularly oppressive where the majority of the population adhered to sectarian Islam. This has been the case in Yemen for the last one thousand years. The inhabitants of central Yemen are Shi'ites, a great branch of the Muslim community, which is also represented in Persia, although by a very much different subsection. The theological tenets of that sect cannot be explained here, but its relations with its non-Muslim population must be discussed, because Yemen is rightly regarded as one of the most "Arabic" of all Arab countries, and the mass exodus by air of the Yemenite Jews to Israel has aroused considerable attention in many quarters.

The Shi'ites of Yemen are characterized by a particularly legalistic attitude toward religion; consequently they attribute great value to the study of religious law. In both respects the Yemenite Jews felt themselves akin to their environment and therefore accepted many discriminatory laws affecting them with more equanimity than might be anticipated.

It is a Shi'ite law, for example, that any dishes touched by a non-

Muslim become unclean and have to be smashed. Far from seeing this injunction as an insult to himself, the Yemenite Jew regarded it as a dietary law and adapted himself to the circumstances. His professions as traveling craftsman often forced him to take food in Muslim houses. He would carry with him the indispensable coffee cup in a little basket fastened by a strap of leather to his bag of tools. In any shop of Yemenite folk art these beautiful little baskets with the characteristic conical covers may be seen. Their design differed from one district to another, but few people know what purpose they originally served.

Everywhere in Yemen, with only few exceptions, the Jews lived in separate villages or quarters. In San'a, the capital, and in other cities, they were confined to a suburb outside the main city. This separation has a long history and should not be compared at all with the Ghetto of the European Jews. When the Arabs founded their cities, each tribe was settled in a quarter by itself; the other sections of the population were also accommodated according to their religious or ethnic attachments, as had been the case in the cities of the East which the Arabs occupied at the time of their conquest. The fact of the existence of special Jewish or Christian quarters all over the Arab Muslim world had nothing humiliating in it. In Yemen, however, the situation was somewhat different. Some of the Jewish villages were very old; we have the ancient Hebrew manuscripts written in them many hundreds of years ago to prove it. However, the separate Jewish suburbs outside Muslim towns, such as San'a, have their origin in religious persecution. Earlier, the Jews lived inside the towns, but in 1679, the Jews of San'a and in central Yemen in general were expelled from the country in which they had been living for centuries—an occurrence very common in Christian Europe but absolutely unheard of in Arab Islam. To be sure, after a year or so they were recalled, obviously because they were indispensable as artisans and craftsmen. However, they were not allowed to return to their former homes but were forced to settle outside the cities. The site of the ancient Jewish quarters inside San'a is still known, both by word of mouth and because the architecture of the Jewish town house in Yemen was different from that of the Muslim house. The synagogue of the quarter inhabited by the Jews immediately before 1679 was converted into a mosque, which is still in existence under the name of *Masjid al-Jala* ("the Mosque of the Expulsion").

Despite its hateful origin, the Yemenite Jew was content to live in his special suburb. It provided him with autonomy, especially on Saturday, when Muslims normally refrained from visiting the Jewish quarter. This made it easier for him to fulfill his religious duties, which were to him the very essence of his existence.

Many visitors to Yemen have praised the cleanliness and loveliness of the interiors of the Jewish houses in the towns, while emphasizing, at the same time, the extreme modesty of their outward appearance. This modesty was matched by the extreme simplicity of attire. Yemenite Jews, men and women alike, always were clothed like beggars (and some of the older generation cling to this habit even in Israel). According to a verse repeated twice in the Koran (2:58; 3:108) or at least according to its interpretation, God has ordained that the Jews be poor. In Yemen and other Muslim countries, this is taken literally. The Jews avoid any appearance of affluence. In times of anarchy or in regions beyond the reach of the central government, Jewish property, even houses, were taken away from them under the pretext that they presented a picture of wealth incompatible with the state assigned to the Jews by God.

In general—as far as I am able to judge, and as far as it is allowed to generalize in these matters—the Yemenite Jews did not feel themselves degraded by the forced modesty of their homes and clothes. They regarded themselves as being in Exile both in the literal and the metaphysical meaning. They believed—like other Jews, but perhaps more intensely—that God's presence (*Shekhina*) itself had fled or, in other words, that there was no reason to bother much about a world which was so thoroughly degenerate and God-forsaken. Real life began only after the return to the Land of Israel, in the days of the Messiah. Of that "Perfect World" a foretaste was possible on the Sabbath, when the Jewish men did not leave their quarters. They dressed themselves in white and girded themselves with broad belts of different colors; this they were not allowed to do on workdays or outside their living quarters. Their women would bedeck themselves with their exquisite jewelry, enjoying complete rest and freedom and gay companionship as they gathered in the courtyards of the synagogue.

I have also the impression, although it may be erroneous, that the insults and abuses to which the Yemenite Jews were constantly exposed—for was it not the intention of the law that the unbelievers should be disgraced?—were borne by them with a certain degree of stoicism. In former times—and in remote places even today—it was common for Muslim schoolboys to stone Jews. When the Turks conquered Yemen in 1872, an envoy was sent from the Chief Rabbi of Istanbul to inquire what grievance the Yemenite Jews had against their neighbors. It is indicative that the first thing of which they complained was this molestation by the schoolboys. But when the Turkish Governor asked an assembly of notables to stop this nuisance, there arose an old doctor of Muslim law and explained that this stone-throwing at Jews was an age-old custom (in Arabic 'Ada) and therefore it was unlawful to forbid it. (I am glad to say that this story, which appears also in print, aroused a broad smile on the faces of the Yemenites in whose presence it was told to me.)

There were, however, Muslim laws enforced in Yemen which were felt to be as particularly oppressive although their legal background was fully appreciated. Those who live in a country which discriminates against them most blatantly want to have, at least, one right: to leave that country. But it was precisely this right which was denied the Jews, and those who succeeded in leaving the country forfeited their entire property.

It has been alleged that this prohibition was made in order to fight Zionism. This is not true. The law is much older and was put into effect many years before the Balfour Declaration. Nor is it true that it was purely economic that the Muslim rulers wished to retain Jewish artisans and craftsmen by force. Both explanations are typically modern attitudes toward a measure which has in fact

a strictly inner Islamic legal basis. Christians and Jews are protected by Muslim law, as long as they are under the sway of Muslim rule. As soon as they leave Muslim soil, their life and property
are forfeited if they are not safeguarded by special arrangements.
The Shi'ites of Yemen were sectarians, who regarded their political
foes, the Turks—although these were Muslims too—as heretics
and their country as "out of bounds." Naturally they had the same
attitude toward regions ruled at that time by Great Britain,
such as Egypt or India. Therefore a Jew, a "protected" subject,
was not allowed to proced to such "enemy territory" or, if he did
so, had to leave everything behind. In practice, the former ruler
of Yemen often granted to individuals the right to emigrate, but
for the great masses who strove to leave the country the old prohibition was a source of great suffering.

In order to put this question of emigration from Yemen in its
right historical context, I would like to remark that the wish to
leave Yemen was by no means confined to the Jews. In 1949
an underground Yemenite newspaper (printed in Cardiff, Wales,
and circulated in Aden) estimated that the Muslim emigration
from Yemen during the preceding years was 3,000,000. I suppose
that even with one zero less, the number was still exaggerated, but
the allegation as such is significant. Why and how the present
ruler of Yemen suddenly gave his consent to the wholesale exodus
of the Jews from his country is a topic which lies outside the scope
of this chapter.

A scourge even more terrible than the prohibition against
emigration was the forced conversion of orphans practiced by the
Shi'ites of Yemen. Since 1929, when I first began to study the
language and life—it would be more correct to say the languages and the lives—of the Jewish communities of Yemen, I
have been collecting material on this sad chapter in Arab-Jewish
symbiosis. Its worst aspect perhaps was not so much its coercion
in matters of conscience, terrible as that was, but the fact that
children were torn away from their mothers and brothers from
their sisters. To my mind, this law, which was enforced with new
vigor about thirty years ago, more than anything else impelled

the Yemenite Jews to quit this country to which they were very much attached.

Again the strictly legal aspect of the question has to be understood. The law, which I assume to be in force in Yemen today, says that "protected" persons (i.e., Jews, as there were no local Christians in Arabia), male or female, who had not attained puberty before their fathers died are to become Muslims even if they have meanwhile grown up and married. This law, as I concluded from information given to me as far back as 1929, relates to a saying attributed to Muhammad, which expresses acutely a basic tenet of Islam: "Everyone is born in a natural state of religion (namely, Islam). It is only his parents who have made a Jew or a Christian out of him." The logical consequence of this saying is that in absence of the parents, and in particular of the father, a man must grow up in his natural state, that is, Islam.

In addition to the religious aspect of this law, it has a practical side. Everyone familiar with even the rudiments of the history of the great Ottoman Turkish Empire knows that its brilliant military successes were due largely to its infantry troops, the so-called Janissaries. These Janissaries consisted exclusively of Christian converts who were taken as boys from their parents, converted to Islam and educated for their future profession in special institutes. To the Turks, who were orthodox Muslims, it was perfectly clear that this human tribute from their Christian subjects was not in conformity with Muslim law which guaranteed to the non-Muslims protected by it life, property and the free exercise of their religion. The Shi'ites of Yemen, however, are sectarians, who have their own interpretation of the law. Since both the old Imam, who was murdered in 1948, and his son and successor, Ahmad, the present king of Yemen, are described by their former Jewish subjects as just rulers and completely sincere Muslims, there can be no doubt that by enforcing the law of the orphans they primarily intended to fulfill a religious obligation. But it cannot be denied that vacancies in the "orphanages" of the Imams, which were in effect institutions for the training of professional soldiers, could be filled from time to time by forced Jewish converts.

To be sure, most of the forced converts remained in the homes of those through whom they had received Islam. This applied particularly to female converts. In Yemen, as elsewhere in Arab countries, a bride price must be paid to the relatives of the betrothed girl. If the future bride was of good family, pretty and well-versed in the art of housekeeping, the price would be very high and a young man had to work many years before he could afford to marry. However, a female convert has no legal relatives to whom a bride price is due, for conversion cuts off all family relationships. Therefore such a female convert is a very good bargain, especially if she is attractive and good-natured, as indeed the Jewish Yemenite girls often are. Thus we see that with women too the law of the orphans had practical as well as religious benefits.

Naturally when a Jewish father died, leaving young children —which was extremely common because of the high mortality rate—the family or the community tried to avert disaster; the children were quickly transported to another town where they passed as the children of relatives or of anyone who could take care of them. I have heard of a particularly wealthy and pious man in Lower Yemen who always had eighteen children, and not always the same children, their only common feature being that none was his own child. But very often the efforts of the family or of friends to conceal the identity of the orphans were not successful. It was not exceptional that they were denounced by their own people. The result was that many families arrived in Israel with one or more of their children lost to them, and I have heard of some widows who have been bereaved in this way of all their offspring.

Orphans have not been the sole subject of forced conversion in Islam. To be sure, there exists a principle laid down expressly in the Koran that no coercion may be exercised in religious matters. In practice, however, the wish to make proselytes often proved stronger than the provisions of the law. Non-Muslims in extreme difficulties, particularly because of false accusations entailing capital punishment, were offered and accepted the alternative of embracing Islam. Cases like this have been cited in literature, and I could add a number of examples from personal reports by emigrants from Yemen, including those where a whole village was concerned. Sometimes criminals tried to escape punishment by confessing Islam. I must mention, however, that according to the unanimous testimony of Yemenite Jews questioned by the present writer, both the present and the former ruler of Yemen refrained from accepting such converts.

Again it was sectarian Islam, which deviated from the practice followed by the majority of Muslims and was responsible for forced mass conversion of adults. The most notorious example of this was the Almohad movement, a tremendous political and religious force, which during the twelfth century conquered North Africa and Spain, countries which at that time harbored some of the most flourishing Jewish communities. Those congregations which refused to accept Islam, the town of Fez, for instance, were put to the sword. Those who accepted Islam had no easy life either. The fanatical Almohads understood well that the forced confession of the Muslim faith had little value and therefore put the converts under strict supervision. They had to wear a special garment—described in detail in the sources—and were treated more or less as outlaws. Even those who endeavored to show their zeal for the new religion were brought to court on the slightest pretext, and in many cases the converts were executed, their property confiscated and their wives turned over to Muslims. All the horrors of the Spanish Inquisition were anticipated under Almohad rule. There we may find even discriminatory economic legislation of a most oppressive type, such as was common in Medieval Europe, but normally not in Islam. The neo-Muslims and those who had remained Jews—after the first wave of persecution had passed, it was discovered that many Jews still existed—were prohibited from engaging in commerce, and since commerce was the main Jewish occupation in those countries, the law meant for them economic annihilation.

Our knowledge about the situation of the non-Muslims under the Almohads has been considerably enlarged owing to a recent publication by Abraham S. Halkin of New York, which appeared in the *Joshua Starr Memorial Volume,* New York 1953. In this study, Professor Halkin quotes relevant extracts from a contemporary source, an important but still unpublished Judaeo-Arabic book called *Medicine for the Soul,* written by Joseph Ibn Aqnin, the most prominent disciple of the famous Maimonides. It seems that Ibn Aqnin had been temporarily forced to adopt Islam and, like his master, left the fanatical Muslim West for the more tolerant East. It is interesting to learn from this book that the Almohads, like the Yemenite Shi'ites of our own days, took away the Jewish orphans from their families and delivered them to Muslim guardians. Incidentally, the same saying of the Muslim Prophet which—as we have seen above—was used in Yemen as the legal base for that procedure is quoted by Ibn Aqnin as serving the same purpose eight hundred years ago.

It should be noted that the Almohads were not only non-orthodox Muslims, but in the main also non-Arabs. The movement originated among the Berbers, the indigenous population of North Africa, and bore largely the character of a Berber national upheaval. Indeed the Berber language, instead of Arabic, was attempted for the exposition of the tenets of the new sect. Thus the terrible Almohad persecutions, although carried out in the name of a reformed Islam and ostensibly modeled after the Prophet, cannot be regarded as typical either for Islam or for the Arabs.

Another famous example of mass conversion appears in the opposite, the Eastern, end of the Muslim world. In 1839 the Jewish community of Meshhed, a great city in northeastern Persia, professed to embrace Islam in order to escape annihilation by a fanatical mob. However the community remained intact, preserving under the cover of Islam its allegiance to its old faith. They led an interesting double life, ably described in various publications by Walter J. Fischel of the University of California who visited them on one of his early travels to Persia. The converts bore Hebrew as well as Muslim names, and while making the pilgrimage to Mecca often headed for Jerusalem on their return and remained there. Finally the community emigrated to Palestine where it returned openly to the Jewish faith. As we mentioned before in passing,

Persian Islam is also sectarian, forming a subsection of the Shi'ite branch. Thus the Meshhed case of forced mass conversion also lies outside the orbit of orthodox Islam and of course the Arabic-speaking world.

Any generalizations should be avoided in discussing sectarian Islam. In various places in this book reference is made to the Fatimids, who ruled over Egypt and Palestine for about two hundred years (969-1171). Their reign, despite many disasters, was one of the magnificent periods in the long history of that country. It was indeed the time during which Egypt attained that ascendancy over the Arabic-speaking world, which it has retained to the present time. The Fatimids were sectarians and Shi'ites also but of a very different type from those prevailing in Yemen and in Persia-Iran. In addition, their military strength during the first and decisive years of their rule over Egypt rested largely on Berber troops from North Africa, i.e., the same elements which we found were responsible for the bloody outrages of the Almohads. Nevertheless, the Fatimids were the most liberal rulers of the Middle Ages.

This is apparent from the writings which emanate from their entourage and more emphatically from their deeds. Many Christians and Jews atttained the highest government posts, while retaining their religion. If they adopted Islam, as did Jacob Ibn Killis, the Fatimid Vizier mentioned above, they were able to maintain the best relations with their former co-religionists. The many details available to us concerning the dress worn by the Jews of that time demonstrate that the degrading regulations concerning attire for non-Muslims were either not applied at all or applied most leniently.

Ancient discriminatory laws against Christian and Jewish merchants, as far as we are able to conclude from the evidence at hand, were not enforced. The Fatimid caliphs even contributed to the upkeep of the Academy of Jewish religious learning in Jerusalem. A letter from one of the heads of that Academy to a Fatimid caliph, published in the *Jewish Quarterly Review*, New Series, vol. 45, Philadelphia 1954, reveals that this practice was carried on for many generations. Thus we see that it was not the deviation from orthodox Islam itself or particular racial elements which decided the attitude toward non-Muslims, but the actual tenets and beliefs held by the sect concerned.

Strangely enough, the Fatimid period produced a sudden, unprecedented and violent persecution of non-Muslims. It occurred during the rule of the third Fatimid caliph of Egypt, al-Hakim (996–1021). The first fifteen years of his reign he had adhered to the established principles of his predecessors and was honored by the Jews as a Messiah-like prince of justice and wisdom. The very year the persecution broke out, 1012, a *Megilla*, a poetical "Scroll" written in Hebrew, appeared, praising the caliph in the highest terms. Suddenly everything changed. Muslim historians ascribed the change to the caliph's sudden madness. (One historian, who obviously had great confidence in the medical arts of his time, expressed the opinion that the disaster could have been avoided, if a sufficient quantity of rose oil had been poured into the caliph's nose to moisten his dried-up brain.) But the *Megilla* also reveals that in the very first days of January 1012, the caliph personally had saved two hundred Jews from the hands of fanatics who were about to annihilate them. Obviously the liberal policy of the Fatimids had aroused in the masses a deep reaction. Thus the persecutions unleashed by the sudden madness of the caliph—which seems to be a historical fact—were a response to popular demand.

Although the accounts of that persecution are confused and partly contradictory, the general picture emerging from them is clear enough; it is indeed one of the blackest pages in medieval history. The old laws concerning special garments and other distinguishing marks for non-Muslims were reenforced, accompanied with the most humiliating and ridiculous regulations. All the churches in the Fatimid Empire were ordered destroyed—including that of the Holy Sepulcher in Jerusalem—and their lands and property confiscated. Christians were advised to emigrate to such countries as the Byzantine Empire in the north or Christian Abyssinia in the south. Many Christians, however, embraced Islam. The office where the declarations of conversions were received was so besieged by applicants that some of them were trampled to death in the tumult.

From Jewish and other sources we know that the Jewish community did not fare better. Not only in Old Cairo and Alexandria but in all parts of the kingdom, in Palestine and Syria as far as Tripoli, the Mediterranean port on the north Syrian coast, the synagogues, new and old, were destroyed. In the newly founded town of Cairo itself, on Passover night the caliph ordered the Jewish quarter burned to the ground with its inhabitants. Many Jews emigrated to Yemen and to other distant countries. Suddenly, about seven years later everything changed again: Christians and Jews who had adopted Islam were allowed to return to their respective religions, a step which in normal times was punishable by death. The destroyed churches and synagogues were ordered rebuilt. However, many years passed before the harm done could be repaired. Houses of non-Muslim worship had meanwhile been converted into mosques, non-Muslim property had been seized and occupied by Muslims, and the impoverished communities, both Christian and Jewish, had not the means to bear the expenses of reconstruction.

The al-Hakim episode shows how utterly precarious was the situation of second-class citizens under Muslim law even in the times of an otherwise most liberal regime. Nevertheless, when the known facts are weighed, I believe it is correct to say that as a whole the position of the non-Muslims under Arab Islam was far better than that of the Jews in Medieval Christian Europe.

The reason for this difference between Medieval Europe and the Muslim East is to be sought first in the different legal attitudes of the Church, which did not recognize the right of the existence of other beliefs, and of Islam, which did. Not less important is, of course, the fact that the non-Muslim communities in Arab countries were far stronger and of far greater influence than the small Jewish settlements of unprotected foreigners in Medieval Europe. Consequently, we find that the actual position of Christians and Jews in Muslim lands depended on the varying extent of their power and influence in various periods.

We have already seen how their situation deteriorated as they declined from a majority status during the first century of the Muhammadan era to that of a minority in the third. Their lot became almost unbearable in the later Middle Ages—during the fourteenth and fifteenth centuries of the Christian era. By that time their numbers had so declined that they formed only a small percentage of the population—about the same percentage as in modern times.

There was, however, another reason for the marked worsening of the status of the non-Muslims in the later Middle Ages. At that time foreign barbarian military castes had come into power which exploited the local population mercilessly. This state of affairs was not entirely new; it began as early as the third century of the Muslim era—precisely the period in which, as we have already seen, the discriminatory legislation for the first time became really severe.

The rule of the barbarian soldiery became particularly oppressive from about 1300 A.D., with the effect that the more the Moslem population was humiliated, the more fanatical it became in its treatment of religious minorities. The hysterical intolerance of those times is reflected in the bulky collections of legal opinions given by the Muslim scholars of the fourteenth, fifteenth and sixteenth centuries. Dr. Eli Strauss (now Ashtor), curator of Arabic books and manuscripts of the Hebrew University Library, Jerusalem, has worked through these profuse books, which are still largely in manuscript form, and has summarized the material which relates to the treatment of non-Muslims. His findings, together with other material, is included in his article, "The Social Isolation of Ahl adh-Dhimma," in the *P. Hirschler Memorial Volume*, Budapest 1949. Quite a number of Muslim religious officials have devoted special treatises to this subject, for example, the *Kadi* previously mentioned as responsible for the destruction of the Synagogue of Jerusalem in 1474. The contents of his book, also still in manuscript, have been discussed by me in detail in the quarterly *Zion*, vol. 13, 1949. These scholars of the late Middle Ages were far more intolerant than their colleagues of the early Islamic times and recommended, for example, such measures as expulsion and forced concentration in ghettos for the "unbeliev-ers." One has to remember of course that at that time Muslims were being expelled from Spain and other Christian countries.

The situation changed again in the fifteenth and sixteenth cen-turies when the spectacular victories of the Ottoman Turks brought, as in the first century of the Muslim era, a large non-Muslim population under Muslim rule. Again, reasons of expedien-cy played a large part in the revival of Muslim tolerance for which the Turkish Sultans of the sixteenth century were famed. They, for example, admitted to their country large numbers of Jewish refugees who had been expelled from Spain in 1492. There may have been other reasons for their tolerance having connection with particular Turkish national tradition; discussion of those reasons lies, however, outside the scope of this book.

The gradual deterioration of the position of the non-Muslims in the Ottoman Empire, which then included all the Arabic-speak-ing countries, in the following centuries was mainly due to the general decline of the State with its corollary of oppression of the local population, a state of affairs similar to that of the late Middle Ages, as described above. In short, the actual and the legal posi-tion of the Jews in the Muslim countries, and in Arab countries in particular, depended to a considerable extent on the general situa-tion of the Muslim society of the period as well as on the strength and the influence of the non-Muslim communities. However, the basic principle of Muslim law, which recognized the right of exist-ence of the other monotheistic religions, was, as a rule, adhered to.

The discrepancy between the actual position and the legal status of the non-Muslims, in particular the Jews, in Arab Islam has been studied here in some detail because the question of the rule of Muslim law is of more than historical importance. In these days in which there appears to be a revival of religion, or at least an interest in religion, Islam has come into the foreground again both in the estimate of Western observers and in the Muslim countries themselves. However, religion is one thing and a religious law, created under conditions completely different from those prevail-ing today, is another.

In Saudi Arabia and in Yemen, Muslim law is still in full force. Even a few years ago when the thousands of Americans stationed in Dhahran, the great airfield in Eastern Saudi Arabia, wanted to build a church for their own use, they were unable to do so for, as we know, no new churches can be erected on Muslim soil. This and similar problems are of course minor issues. However, a far more serious affair is the professed aim of the Muslim Brotherhood, which boasts the allegiance of the majority of the Egyptian people: to reinstate Islam as the law of the state. If the Muslim Brotherhood and their counterpart in other countries have their way, it would mean inexorably that Egypt and the other countries involved would relapse into the position of medieval states with local Christians and Jews reduced to the status of second-class citizens. The leaders of the "Military Revolution" in Egypt understood this issue only too well and fought the Brotherhood, although they themselves were eager to reaffirm their devotion to the religion of Islam.

For a religious law, i.e., a law professedly made by God himself, can never be changed in such essentials as the position of the "unbelievers"; therefore, the only way to honor it under entirely changed conditions is not to use it. The fact that canonical law—the law of the Roman Catholic church—is nowhere in force where the masses professing Catholicism are concentrated has not impaired the Catholic faith, but rather strengthened its hold on its believers. The history of the Muslim peoples shows that since ancient times there co-existed with religious jurisdiction civil authorities who in varying degrees preferred to forego the use of the religious law altogether. The introduction of modern civil codes in Egypt and Turkey could rely to a certain degree on precedent. In any case, it has done no harm to Islam, but rather saved it from becoming the target of justified criticism. The very idea that Egypt could give up attainments made eighty years ago (when a modern civil code was first introduced) sounds really preposterous.

This lapse into contemporary issues lends color to the exposition of Jewish-Arab relations under Islam, given above. As we have seen, the position of the Jews inside the Arab Muslim society was relatively better than that enjoyed by them in Medieval Europe. But only relatively. In principle, they and the other non-Muslims were second-class citizens and consequently their position was always precarious, often actually dangerous. The moving plaints of the great Hebrew poet Yehuda Halevi (died 1141), who had lived both in Muslim and in Christian Spain, that the one was as bad as the other is an eloquent testimony to this state of affairs. No discrimination on any grounds, religious or otherwise, can be the basis of a completely satisfactory symbiosis.

6

THE ECONOMIC TRANSFORMATION AND COMMUNAL REORGANIZATION OF THE JEWISH PEOPLE IN ISLAMIC TIMES

In the previous chapter, the position of the Jewish people within the structure of Arab Muslim society has been described from the Muslim point of view—the rights granted by Islamic law to the Jews and the treatment experienced by them at the hands of the Muslims. In the following chapters an even more important aspect of Jewish-Arab symbiosis will be discussed: how the Jews responded to the challenge of the new civilization and how they adapted themselves to the changed conditions.

Let us say it at once: the general picture emerging from the sources at our disposal is one of complete transformation in all fields of economic, communal, and spiritual life. This change did not come immediately in the wake of the Arab conquest. On the contrary, the first two hundred and fifty years following that event are the most obscure in Jewish history. Not until the end of the third century of the Muslim era are we able to discern the results of the transformation, which had affected the main body of the Jewish people concentrated at that time in Arabic-speaking countries. A similar curve of development may be observed in the cultural history of the Persian people who appeared paralyzed and silenced as a consequence of the Arab conquest, but who experienced a revival at the end of the third Muslim century. The reason for the temporary eclipse of Persia was political—it was liquidated as an independent nation through the onslaught of the Arabs. But the Jews obviously suffered economically in the early days of Islam. In any case, at the beginning of the fourth century, the re-emergence of both the Persian and the Jewish cultures was well under way.

The fourth, fifth, and sixth centuries of the Muslim era—corresponding roughly to the Christian tenth, eleventh, and twelfth centuries—must be regarded as the apogee of Jewish-Arab symbiosis, while from the thirteenth Christian century on a decline set in slowly, rapidly increasing with time. The partial revival of the Oriental Jewish communities in the sixteenth and seventeenth centuries, to which various temporarily conditioned outside factors and inner forces contributed, does not come within the compass of the present discussion.

For three reasons we know incomparably more about Jewish life in the Muslim world than we do with regard to the centuries immediately preceding Islam:

1) The Arabs were far more historically minded and left us many more records than the Persians, in whose empire lived the majority of Jews before Islam. The historians and lawyers of Byzantium, where another section of the Jewish people was concentrated, had little to record other than tales of persecution or discriminatory laws.

2) The introduction of paper into the Muslim world in the eighth century increased the production of books and writing to a degree unprecedented in the history of the countries settled by Jews.

3) The fragments of books and documents stored during the Middle Ages in the so-called Cairo Geniza were discovered and brought to European and American libraries at the end of the nineteenth century, thus providing an almost inexhaustible source for the study of Jewish life and literature during the most important centuries of Jewish-Arab symbiosis.

Islam, unlike Christianity, did not incorporate the Hebrew Bible into its canon of religious writings, but adopted, together with the religious and ethical ideas of the Bible, its notion and actual framework of a world history, which began with the Creation, continued with the successive revelations of God to mankind, and concluded with the final Day of Judgment. The eminently historical outlook of the Muslim religion enhanced the natural predilection of the Arabs for recording the more dramatic events of their tribal life. The two elements of a religiously oriented historiography and a national tradition of story-telling, combined with the tremendous widening of the general and geographical horizon experienced during the hundred years' wars of conquest, led to the creation of an enormous historical literature in Arabic. This literature, naturally, was concerned with the fates of the Arab Muslim community. Therefore Jews and Jewish culture are mentioned in it only so far as they were regarded as relevant to Islam. Nevertheless, many important details of Jewish history are known only from that literature: for example, as we mentioned in chapter I, the whole history of the North Arabian Jewish communities in the times of Muhammad and his successors.

In addition, the Arabs were soon acquainted with the science of geography, as developed by the Greeks and their successors on the one hand, and the Persians on the other, as well as with comparative religion, as cultivated by the Harranians, a pagan sect, who had succeeded in surviving into Islamic times. Both these sciences of geography and comparative religion were highly developed by the Arabic scholars and both contribute much to our knowledge of Jews and Judaism in Islamic times. If one compares the well-informed expositions of Muslim scholars about Jewish sects with the ridiculous and completely unfounded fables of Greek ethnologists or Roman historians, one sees how far the Arabs surpassed the ancients in the description of the beliefs of foreign peoples.

Arabic historiography and science could not have created such a gigantic literature had its inception not coincided with the introduction and mass production of paper. Previously writing had been done on either papyrus, a product of a plant cultivated and processed in Egypt, or parchment and vellum, which were made from the skins of animals. All these materials were expensive. However, in 751 the Arabs clashed with the Chinese in Central Asia. They took Chinese prisoners who were familiar with the production of paper and put them immediately to work; and before the end of the eighth century there was a paper mill in Bagdad. Soon the industry spread over the whole Muslim Empire, became extremely ramified, and many types of paper came on the market. For this reason we find Jewish merchants importing paper from Syria to Egypt, although the latter country was a great producer of that commodity too. The existence of a comparatively cheap writing material gave rise to a tremendous output of, and trade in, Hebrew books—both in Hebrew and in Arabic with Hebrew characters—and many of these have survived, at least in fragments. The catalogues of private Jewish libraries in Egypt and other Arabic-speaking countries, which have come down to us by the dozens from the eleventh and twelfth centuries, and which incidentally contain details about the qualities of paper and binding, show that even private persons were able to amass great quantities of books. In addition, letter-writing spread to all sections of the population, the poorest not excluded, and of this activity too many remnants have been preserved. Thus the introduction of paper in the eighth century had an effect on Jewish culture and our knowledge of it, possibly greater than the beginning of printing in the fifteenth century.

This brings us to the third factor which has contributed so much to our knowledge of the Jewish-Arab symbiosis during its most creative period: the fact that the Jews were accustomed to burying their ancient books and letters, and that the most central of those burial places, that of Old Cairo, has been preserved and made accessible to modern research. This is the famous Cairo "Geniza," about which a few words must be said here, for without its treasures our ideas about Jewish life in Arab countries at that time would have been incomparably poorer.

The belief that no writing which may contain the name of God should be destroyed by fire or otherwise is not confined to the Jews; it has its parallels in Christian and Muslim usage. It seems, however, that in this, like many other ritual matters, the Jews have been more consistent, and therefore everywhere in the world pious Jews have laid aside papers bearing Hebrew characters. Many synagogues contained a chamber for the disposal of such papers called *Beth Geniza* or, shortened, Geniza, literally "The House of Concealment" from the Hebrew *ganoz*, to put aside. Such a chamber—a large one—was found in an ancient synagogue of Old Cairo, which, by the way, had been originally a Coptic church. That Geniza was in use for over a thousand years and papers in many languages, including Latin in Hebrew script, have been found there. The language most in use, however, after Hebrew, was Arabic; tens of thousands of leaves covered with Hebrew script expressing Arabic sounds have been stored away there, so that the Geniza has become a most important source for the history of the development of the Arabic language as well as a storehouse of information on the Jews.

Most of the deposits consist of fragments of books, many of which had been known before only by title or quotation, or totally unknown. Our knowledge of Hebrew literature in Arab times (approximately between 700 and 1100) has been completely revolutionized by the Geniza findings, and work on them is still going on most vigorously.

I do not believe that all of the early Arabic *Muslim* books which have made their appearance in the Geniza in Hebrew have been found elsewhere.

For the historian naturally the most interesting part of the Geniza are the letters and documents. The Geniza has given us autographic letters and fragments of books, often of considerable length, of the most famous personalities in the orbit of Judaeo-Arab culture, such as Maimonides, his son Abraham, Saʿadya, and many others. No less than seventy letters of the Palestinian *Gaon* (the Head of the Academy and spiritual leader) Solomon ben Yehuda, an eminently interesting personality (died 1051), have been preserved, mostly in Hebrew but partly also in Arabic. And the letters of persons of humbler position are also available to us and are of great historical significance. The Geniza has preserved letters in considerable numbers from almost every country of the

Muslim Jewish world, from Spain and Morocco in the West to Aden and India in the East, from the Byzantine Empire and naturally many from the smaller Egyptian towns and villages. Of particular interest are the many letters from Palestine. As to the language of the letters, most of those dealing with public affairs were written in Hebrew; most, but by no means all, private letters were written in Arabic since business was normally conducted in Arabic.

The documents preserved reflect practically every aspect of public and private life. Every Monday and Thursday, sessions of the Rabbinical Court were held in the Geniza synagogue and many of its proceedings have come down to us. As we know from instructions to the clerk of the court, he was bound to write down the depositions of the parties and witnesses verbatim and, since people spoke Arabic, it became the normal practice—from the second part of the eleventh century—to compose the main, non-technical parts of the proceedings in Arabic. The court kept a book in which every case coming before it was recorded in chronological order, and many pages of such books from the eleventh and twelfth centuries have come down to us, providing a most vivid picture of the daily life of the community. The same can be said of the many deeds and contracts preserved. A collection of hundreds of modern Jewish marriage contracts would make dull reading, for they are more or less nothing but formularies. To be sure, those of the tenth, eleventh, and twelfth centuries also followed fixed forms, but, in addition, were real contracts, which differed widely from case to case. Often a list of dresses, ornaments, and furniture brought in by the bride has been preserved, which gives us a deep insight into the material culture of the Jewish community concerned. Many an Arab word, which appears in no dictionary, and perhaps also in no literary text, does occur in those lists. All in all, the Geniza papers can be regarded as a very important source for the history of Eastern civilization in general.

The main stock of the Geniza then available—over a hundred thousand leaves—were brought in 1897 to the University Library, Cambridge, England, as a result of the enthusiastic efforts of Dr. Solomon Schechter—later President of the Jewish Theological

Seminary of America, New York. However, many other libraries possess greater or smaller collections of Geniza material with the result that page 1 of a book or letter may be found in Cambridge, page 2 in New York, and page 3 in Leningrad. For this and many other reasons—in particular the fragmentary state of many of the papers—Geniza studies require a high degree of workmanship. During the first part of this century a galaxy of distinguished scholars were engaged in identifying, publishing, and discussing the treasures of the Geniza. Of the many names, there should be mentioned in particular Samuel Poznanski of Warsaw and Jacob Mann of Cincinnati, who worked mainly in the field of History; Simha Asaf of Jerusalem (Cultural History); Solomon Schechter himself, Louis Ginzberg, and Israel Davidson, all of New York City (Hebrew Literature); and of those who are still alive, Paul Kahle, formerly of Bonn, who revolutionized our ideas about the text of the Bible largely through the aid of Geniza fragments, and his former pupil, Menahem Zulai of the Schocken Research Institute, Jerusalem, who has reclaimed whole provinces of previously lost medieval Hebrew poetry.

There is, however, one section of the Geniza—precisely that which is most important for our purposes—which has not yet been adequately investigated. These are the letters, contracts, and documents written in the Arabic language. Scholars of the School of Oriental Studies of the Hebrew University, Jerusalem, are preparing at present to publish that material. Owing to the vastness and the difficulty of the material, considerable time will pass before it will be available in print in its entirety. From the specimens quoted later on, the reader may grasp its significance.

Because the period of full Jewish-Arab symbiosis is comparatively well-known, while the centuries both preceding and following the rise of Islam are the most obscure in Jewish history, it is very difficult to gauge the impact of the creation of the Muslim State on the Jewish people. What happened to the Jews during the first two hundred and fifty years of Arab rule has been dealt with far too sweepingly on the basis of information from later generations. Furthermore, political and religious changes have been the paramount concern of the historian, where it is my opinion that the far-reaching economic and social transformation of the Middle East during the eighth and ninth centuries contributed more than anything else to the "New Look" of tenth-century Jews.

We will make an attempt to show how the advent of the Arab Empire and the subsequent developments in the Middle East affected the destinies of the Jewish people. As new material is expected about these questions from various quarters, some of the findings outlined here may have to be qualified in the light of further research.

Even prior to the hundred years' wars of Arab conquest, which united the whole region between central Asia and northern Spain in one single empire—at least for a few decades—there extended an unbroken chain of Jewish settlements from northeastern Persia through Mesopotamia (Iraq) to Syria, Palestine and Egypt, and on the shores of the Mediterranean Sea, including Spain, France and Italy. Before Islam, most of this area was divided between two rival Empires, the Roman or Byzantine West and the Persian East who were engaged in continuous warfare, interrupted by shorter or longer periods of armistice. Nevertheless, talmudic literature demonstrates that up to 500 A.D. there was continuous coming and going between Mesopotamia, then a great Jewish center and part of the Persian Empire, and Palestine, which was under Byzantine rule. There is little information about the period immediately preceding Islam—approximately the years 500–650 A.D.—but it is exactly this lack of information which may indicate that the conflicts between the two empires made communication among various Jewish centers precarious.

It has been unanimously assumed by Jewish historiography that the unification of the area under Arab rule resulted also in uniting the widely dispersed Jewish communities. There is, however, little evidence for this in the source material, as far as the first two centuries of Islam are concerned. The silence of the sources conforms with what is known about the character of the early Muslim state and the position of the non-Muslims in it. Political unity is, after all, of very little advantage for a population which has neither the right nor the means to move freely, and there was little freedom of movement in early Islam. The Arabs themselves were regarded normally as soldiers stationed in a certain district, which they were not allowed to leave except by special permit. The subject population was even more restricted due to the exigencies of taxation. Each adult non-Muslim had to pay a poll tax, called *Jizya*, which was graded according to income, consisting of one, two, or four gold pieces in the western, formerly the Byzantine part of the Muslim Empire, and their equivalents in silver in the eastern, formerly the Persian, section. Women, children, and old or disabled men were solely exempt. It has often been stressed that this poll tax was the means by which to emphasize the second-class status of non-Muslims rather than an economic discrimination. Because of its humiliating character, high-standing non-Muslims often tried to exempt themselves from payment. The Jews originating from Khaibar in North Arabia produced a document—certainly fake—that Muhammad himself had granted them exemption. On the other hand, it is repeatedly stated in Jewish and Muslim sources that payment of the poll tax was sometimes a benefit because it designated the payer as a "protected" person, whose life and property were safeguarded. There are stories about caliphs who wished to protect their Jewish friends from the obligation, but were asked by them not to do so as it would bring them more harm than good.

Whatever the attitude towards the *Jizya* poll tax was, large sections of the population were so poor that it constituted for them an unbearable burden. Naturally, they had to pay other taxes also for the products of their soil and of their flocks. Certainly the sum of one gold piece a year seems to be very modest. This is, however, as the Arabic proverb says: "A camel for a penny! How nice!—but I have not got the penny." As we know from an Arab papyrus of the ninth century (when money had less value than in the earlier days of Islam), an agricultural laborer received as his yearly wage six gold pieces. We can gather from various Geniza papers that he could barely sustain himself, let alone his family, on such a salary. In these circumstances, payment of one gold piece as a poll tax was a very heavy imposition. It is not surprising to find in contemporary sources that flogging, imprisonment, exposure to the burning sun, and other punishments had to be used in order to collect the tax. As people possessed so little, the most common way to evade taxation was to flee to another village or town. For this reason, movement from one place to another was not permitted. Only in very special cases were permits given (some such permits have been preserved). From Geniza letters coming from rural Egypt it may be gathered that even in later, more liberal times, nobody could leave his village without his tax receipt in his pocket. In Iraq, the receipt was attached to the neck of the non-Muslim. Anyone found not bearing that seal was liable to be put to death. So common was this procedure that for some time it was even administered to peasants who had embraced Islam.

The second reason for the restriction of the freedom of movement was a corollary of the first: the fear that the agricultural population might flee the country. It is indeed a very sad picture which Abu Yusuf, the Chief Justice of the famous *Harun ar-Rashid* of the *Arabian Nights*, paints of the position of the peasants in the caliphs' Empire at the end of the eighth century. It took the Arab conquerors some time before they learned discretion. As the Arabic saying goes—"one cannot slaughter a cow and milk it at the same time." We do not know exactly in what circumstances the Arabs found the Middle East when they conquered it. However, there can be no doubt that in comparison with later Roman times, the state of the agricultural population as a whole deteriorated in the Muslim period and that this deterioration set in very early. In any case, we find the Arab rulers in the first centuries of Islam trying hard to keep the agricultural population on the soil by restricting the free movement of their subjects.

In view of all this we cannot assume that the unification by conquest of areas belonging previously to the Byzantine and the Persian Empires had an immediately salutary effect on the Jewish communities scattered throughout them. On the contrary, it seems that the blackout prevailing in Jewish history during the first two centuries of Islam reflects the dire situation of a people who belonged in the main to the much-oppressed lower classes. This was the time, apparently, when the Jews were thrown out of agriculture. While the Talmud assumes that a Jew, even in Iraq, normally possessed farm land, Jewish legal literature emerging from the third Muslim century onwards presents an opposite view. The Jewish law, which up to 500 A.D. had been essentially that of a peasants' population, had to be completely reshuffled. However, the lawyers succeeded in this transformation only partially. As many transactions could legally be made only "in connection with soil," they adopted the legal fiction that every Jew ideally had a part of the soil of the Holy Land. Hundreds of documents have been found in the Geniza in which one party confers upon another four square cubits of its share in the Holy Land "together" with this or that right, which forms the real content of the contract. In some catalogues of Geniza papers such documents are listed as "transfer of land," but wherever I had the opportunity to check, they contained only the legal fiction. It is true, the Geniza reveals that as late as the twelfth century some Jews were engaged in agricultural activities, but those were the exceptions which confirm the rule.

In the towns the situation of the Jews was not enviable either. According to the scanty information at our disposal, the Jews in early Islamic times took no considerable part either in commerce or in the professions, although we know of some great Jewish merchants and one or two notable doctors. There were some crafts, dyeing, for example, which seem to have been monopolized by the Jews all over the Muslim and partly over the Byzantine Empires. Supposedly they preserved that monopoly by keeping certain technical details of their manufacture a secret. However, these crafts, although indispensable, did not rank high in social esteem.

The low position of the Jewish people in the first Muslim centuries is reflected also in the spiritual field. To be sure, certain branches of Hebrew literature flourished in those times: the type of religious poetry known under the name *Piyyut*, which presupposed a deep knowledge of the Hebrew language and Jewish lore; the *Midrash*, which in its form is a kind of homiletic exposition of the Bible, but in its content a treasure-house of popular thought, belief, and wit; and mystical speculation and legal discussion.

However, all these branches of literature had developed in Roman and Byzantine times (the very word *Piyyut* is of Greek origin), and often it is only some more or less veiled allusion to Arab rule which reveals that a particular piece is from the time of Islam.

The contributions of the Jews to science seem to have been entirely sporadic. The historians usually quote, as an indication of the early participation of the Jews in the new Muslim civilization, the example of Masarjawaih, a Jew from Basra in southern Iraq who bore a Persian name and who is reputed to have written on medicine and translated treatises on that subject from Syriac into Arabic. Another famous example is Masha'alla (the word means "whatever God will" and was used in later times as a protection against the evil eye), an astronomer and writer on general subjects, whose treatise, *On High and Low Prices*, is still extant. His name, curiously enough, became a byword in Muslim religious literature as the representative of science, as opposed to religion. As far as we are able to judge at present, however, those were special cases. The bulk of the Jewish people indulged, in early Islamic times, in a popular religion divorced from the abstract thinking required by theology, philosophy, or science. It is curious that the famous Muslim scholar al-Jahiz (died 869), who was himself of Negro extraction, thought that the Jews were physically unfit for abstract thinking because of their continuous inbreeding ("you have never heard of a Jew marrying anyone but a Jewess"), while the bulk of the Muslim population was a mixture of all the peoples of the world. Things changed when, through the complete transformation of the Middle East, which was described in Chapter I as the "bourgeois revolution" of the eighth and ninth centuries, an entirely new Jewish society emerged, not similar at all to that of Medieval Europe, but resembling rather the nineteenth century when Jews became prominent in commerce, banking, industry, and the free professions, while maintaining a large substratum in the more humble walks of life, particularly in Eastern Europe. Since this "bourgeois revolution" of the eighth and ninth centuries was of decisive importance for Jewish history and has not yet been described to any extent elsewhere, some of its main aspects will be discussed here. A special study on this subject is in preparation by the writer.

1) In the upheaval caused by the Arab conquests a general "move of capital" set in in all the countries between Spain and India. Treasures guarded for so long by kings and churches, and by noblemen, were seized by the conquerors and thrown on the market. An instance of this is the fate of the golden Madonnas of Sicily which were made into money after the Muslim conquest, by being shipped to India and sold there to idolaters; the famous bronze Colossus of the Isle of Rhodes was bought from the Muslims by a Jewish scrap dealer who converted the Colossus into nine hundred camel loads of bronze. Many of the conquered were dispossessed; large fortunes were accumulated. To be sure, often these newly won riches were not administered by the conquerors themselves but by their "clients," the so-called *Mawali,* members of the subject population who embraced Islam, adopted Arab names and became affiliated with the Arab tribes to which their masters belonged. It seems also that capital often passed into the hands of these Mawali or into the possession of the Christians and Jews who followed the conquering armies and aided them in disposing of the spoils. A first indication of the rise of a new class of capitalists was the overthrow of the Umayyad Arab regime in 750, an event largely engineered by capitalist-financiers who directed the anti-Umayyad propaganda.

2) The accumulation of fluent capital was paralleled by the creation of a large reserve of cheap labor. Many factors contributed to this: the impoverishment of large sections of the conquered population; the flight from the country into the towns; and the large-scale application of forced labor (corvée), about which much is known both from literary and archaeological sources. If in the ruins of an Umayyad palace north of Jericho, Palestine, a tablet is found on which a mason had scribbled Hebrew and Arabic letters (obviously a Jewish master who wanted to learn Arabic), we may safely assume that the man was brought there as one of many artisans whose forced enlistment in the Umayyad labor armies we read of in Arab historians. Labor was cheap,

because it was free. Slaves bought with money normally were used for personal service and not for industrial purposes. Only in the third century were large contingents of Negro slaves employed as a labor force—in southern Iraq, where a formidable slave revolt unparalleled in Muslim history took place.

3) The new Arab towns were an immense economic factor, not only because of the enormous building activities involved but more, because these towns were essentially large garrisons and sumptuous courts for rulers or provincial governors. Thus a permanent, economically powerful consumer population of necessary commodities and of luxury goods came into existence. Indeed many an influential Jew is known to have made his fortune by supplying either to the rulers or the army.

4) The new towns could easily sustain large populations because the wretched conditions of farm life made agricultural products generally cheap. The frequent failure of local crops and other calamities caused much fluctuation in the prices of basic commodities—recorded by the historians. This last, however, was a great stimulus to the trade in cereals and other food articles.

5) The great war expeditions to distant countries were in themselves large capitalistic undertakings, accompanied by great economic booms. Before such an expedition started, each commander and each soldier received a specified sum with which to equip himself for the long journey and for the fighting. The effect on the local market can be easily gauged and is sometimes described expressly by the historians.

6) The enormous mixing of the population and the great enrichment of certain groups produced many new habits in food, clothing and housing. These vogues must have had great importance in the minds of the people, because we read so much about them in our literary sources. Naturally they were a great spur to international trade. While writing these lines I have before me a letter sent by a Jewish merchant from Aden in South Arabia to Cairo about 850 years ago. In this letter he asks his business correspondent in Cairo to buy for him all kinds of goods for the needs of his household. Among the forty-odd items are wares manufac-

tured in Jurjan, far north in Persia, in Amid in Kurdistan, in Bagdad, Beirut, Cairo itself, and various other places in Egypt, as well as in Spain. It seems that the more remote a piece of merchandise was the more fashionable it was believed to be.

7) Many other, more secondary reasons contributed to the spread of commerce and the rise of capitalism in the period following the heroic age of Islam: the construction and reconstruction of roads, originally made for military and administrative purposes; the existence of exact route books (travel-guides) originally made for imperial needs; improvements in travel facilities, especially by sea; and the rise in the purchasing power of the Christian West, about which more will be said in connection with Jewish trade; etc.

8) In addition to the economic and technical reasons, it was certainly of importance that at the head of the Arab State stood the mercantile aristocracy. Originating from the birthplace of the Prophet of Islam, they certainly had deeper sensitivity to the exigencies of business than the knights and noblemen of the Persian Empire, who believed that an aristocrat should pass one half of his life in war and the other half at banquets. All in all, it would seem that despite its limits the Arab Muslim rule, at least at its beginning, was more efficient and more just than preceding regimes. In addition, Muslim law was largely based on Arab custom which we have already noted was flexible and well adapted to the needs of a nation of merchants.

9) Another most important social factor in the rise of Middle-Eastern capitalism was the destruction by the Arab conquerors of the former ruling or privileged classes who were superseded by the new aristocracy of money. What actually happened was that money became the path by which the gifted or the lucky ascended the social ladder.

10) In addition to the economic, technical, and social changes contributing to the creation of Middle-Eastern capitalism, a very strong religious element was active in its rise.

The occupational ideal of the first Muslim century had been that of the warrior-saint. Naturally something of this ideal remained in force in subsequent centuries, and pious men of pugnacious inclination could always find self-expression in the incessant border warfare with the infidels. However, by the end of the second century of Islam, the military profession, which was at that time already composed mainly of non-Arabs, soon became the exclusive province of barbarian slave corps and definitely lost its former glamor. The other great field of state service, bureaucratic administration, attracted many good brains, again mainly non-Arabs, and that bureaucracy, "the people of the pen," as they were called, was largely responsible for the development of the peculiarly syncretistic Arabic literature of the third and fourth Muslim centuries. But religious people shunned government service and regarded government in general as the very substance of the forces which opposed God's rule on earth. A pious man would not accept an invitation to dine from a government official. The food offered there could not be regarded as *halal*, (religiously permissible), in the moral sense of the word since most of government's revenue was thought to emanate from extortions, law-breakings, and oppression of the weak.

But the religious attitude toward commerce was completely different. The income of the honest merchant is regarded in Muslim religious literature as a typical example of *halal*, as earnings free of religious objections. In addition, the merchant was particularly able to fulfill all the duties incumbent on a Muslim; he could pray at the five daily times prescribed, for according to the slow pace of oriental bargaining such an interruption was conducive to a propitious conclusion of business. A merchant could also find time for the study of religious books. In a really Arab Muslim town such as San'a, the capital of Yemen, it was quite common to find a merchant reading a manuscript on religious law, while sitting in his shop. When traveling, a businessman could more easily fulfill his duty as a pilgrim to Mecca; he could visit famous religious scholars or saints. He was in a position to comply with the commandments of almsgiving. He would find it easier to keep the fasts than his co-religionists with lower incomes who did physical labor. Finally, had not the Prophet himself and most of his prominent companions been engaged in business?

In short, just as the rise of modern capitalism in Europe was accompanied by a new religious attitude toward making money, so the "bourgeois revolution" of the Muslim Empire of the eighth and ninth centuries had a strong religious foundation. This fact certainly expedited the process by which the Jews were transformed from a people engaged mainly in manual trades into one whose most characteristic occupation was commerce.

This transformation by no means went on unopposed. An early Jewish writer of the Karaite sect—about which more will be said later—stigmatized the devotion to the business profession as un-Jewish and as an aping of the Gentiles—meaning the Arabs or the Muslims in general. His tirades show that although commerce had become quite common among Jews, it was still regarded as somewhat novel. Indeed three times in their ancient and medieval history, the Jews, an essentially agricultural people, took to business as a means of survival. After the destruction of the First Temple (587 B.C.) and the deportation to Babylon (modern Iraq), they learned business from the Babylonians, an old nation of traders. During the Hellenistic period, the Greeks served them as masters. In Muslim times, they again found themselves confronted by a highly mercantile civilization but responded to the challenge so completely that they became themselves a nation of businessmen.

Certainly the Jews were not complete novices in Islamic times to business and the trades connected with it. That Jew who made the Colossus of Rhodes into scrap metal at the time of the first Muslim conquests was charged with that task because he had been in the metal business before (later on, a business in which many Jews were engaged, as we may learn from the Geniza papers), and because he had the capital to finance the transaction. I would like to provide other instances of Jewish trade in early Muslim times, one often quoted and one hitherto unpublished, which show us that known Jewish economic activities from that period obviously were the continuation of those in which they had been engaged even before Islam.

The first example is of course the famous story of the Radanites, to whom Dr. L. Rabinowitz, Chief Rabbi of the United Hebrew

Congregation, Johannesburg, South Africa, has devoted a whole book, called *Jewish Merchant Adventurers*, London 1948. Their story is contained in one of the Muslim travel-guides. The particular guide, which contains the details about the Radanites, was composed around 870 A.D. by Ibn Khordadbeh, a high official of the imperial postal service. What he has to tell about those Jewish merchants—whose name still defies explanation—is indeed very remarkable:

> These merchants speak Arabic, Persian, Roman (i.e., Greek, which was spoken in the Eastern Roman Empire), the language of the Franks (the inhabitants of present-day France), of the Andalusians (the Christian inhabitants of Spain), and of the Slavs. They journey from west to east and from east to west, partly on land, partly by sea. They take ship in the land of the Franks, on the Western Sea and steer for Farama (an ancient port in Egypt, which was situated not far from the northern end of the present Suez Canal). There they load their goods on the backs of camels and travel by land to Kolzum (a port on the southern end of the Suez Canal). There they embark into the Eastern Sea and go to India and China. On their return they carry . . . the products of the Eastern countries to Kolzum and bring them to Farama, where they again embark on the Western Sea. Some make sail for Constantinople to sell their goods to the Byzantines; others go to the palace of the King of the Franks to place their goods.

The author describes further three other routes taken by the Radanites: the first by sea from France to Syria, and from there via Iraq and the Persian Gulf to India and China; the second, overland through Spain, and, after crossing the Straits of Gibraltar, along the coast of North Africa to Egypt, Palestine, Syria and Iraq to Persia and India; the third, through the center of Europe to the land of the Khazars, a Turkish people living around the shores of the Caspian Sea, whose leading classes professed at that time the Jewish faith; from the land of the Khazars the Radanites crossed the mainland of Asia until they reached China.

The exploits of this company of merchants were extraordinary, perhaps unparalleled in the history of early medieval trade. We are now in a position to judge their achievements in the light of subsequent developments. In the Cairo Geniza, many documents relating to the Jewish trade to India during the eleventh and twelfth centuries have been found, but in none of them is China or any other country east of India and Ceylon mentioned. Those later India merchants, on their return, regularly visited Spain, which then was Muslim, and North Africa, but did no business with Christian Western Europe.

Therefore I would conclude that the great international trade connected with the history of the Radanites has no connection with the socio-economic transformation of the Jewish people in Islamic times. Rather it was a continuation of pre-Islamic Jewish trade, which gained an unprecedented importance when the advent of Islam erected a temporary barrier between East and West. The Jews who combined political neutrality with long-standing international connections could, in the first centuries of Islam, cross the frontiers more easily than either Christians or Muslims. The headquarters of the Radanites obviously were in Christian Europe although, as the polyglot character of their business shows, they had partners in the whole area of the Muslim world, in which Hebrew, perhaps, served as a common language. In any case, Radanite activities appear to have ended in the tenth century. The rising merchant republics of Italy literally killed off the Jewish trade. Simultaneously, in the Muslim world the economic transformation of the Jewish population into a predominantly commercial class was in the process of being completed.

A similar phenomenon can be observed in another field of Jewish activity. We learn from the Geniza papers that Jews owned ships and traveled or sent cargoes in ships owned by them in the Arabian and Indian Seas. But I have never come across a single reference to Jewish *sailors* in that part of the world. But in the

Mediterranean, occasional mention is made in the Geniza of Jewish sailors (*navati,* a word derived from Greek, found both in Hebrew and Arabic and echoed in the English *navy*). This difference no doubt goes back to the fact that the sporadic mention of Jewish sailing in the Mediterranean in later Islamic times indicates merely the lingering traces of a Jewish activity, which, we know from Christian sources, had been much more flourishing in preceding periods.

From these I wish to offer one example which is interesting both in itself and because it involved a Jew and an Arab two hundred years before Muhammad. I am referring to the really charming account of Synesius, a Greek savant, about his voyage, in the year 404, from Alexandria to a small port on the North African coast. The boat in which he happened to travel belonged to a Jewish skipper; the crew also was predominantly Jewish. The writer humorously explains that the rather eccentric skipper had separated the women passengers, who were mostly young and fair, from the men by a screen. A terrible storm arose, but the skipper suddenly let the rudder go, lay down and began to read from a scroll. All the eloquent remonstrations of the passengers were to no avail, for it was Friday night, and, as Synesius explains, Friday night belongs to the following day of Sabbath, on which no Jew is supposed to work. However, on the boat were many Arabs serving in the Roman cavalry. One of them drew his sword and threatened to behead the skipper if he did not resume immediate control of the vessel. But the Jew remained obdurate. Only at midnight, when things looked really bad, did he resume his duties with the following announcement: "Now we are clearly in danger of death in which case it is permitted to work on the Sabbath." Naturally that reassuring announcement caused a great tumult, but the ship landed safely—although not at the port of destination. (The account may be read in full in the very useful source book, *The Jew in the Medieval World,* by Jacob R. Marcus, Cincinnati 1938.) Although the Geniza has preserved hundreds of documents referring to the Mediterranean trade in later Islamic times, nothing about a Jewish sailor's life comparable to Synesius' account can be found in them. The impression is that by the twelfth century the Jews had been thrown out of the profession altogether.

The way is now cleared for a balanced appreciation of the great socio-economic transformation of the Jewish people during the second and third centuries of Islam. Our sources do not allow us to describe that process itself, but they contain sufficient information for showing clearly its results.

First, with the sole exception of a small part of North Arabia, from which they were driven in the early days of Islam, we find, at the beginning of the tenth century, Jews well entrenched in all parts of the Arab Muslim realm. We have no statistics to prove that their numbers had increased there since the inception of Islam, but this is indeed the over-all impression, as flourishing Jewish communities were encountered everywhere, even in places such as Yemen and North Africa where the important former Christian populations had disappeared. From the Muslim sources it is evident that, in early Islam, only sporadic conversions of Jews occurred, while in Egypt, for instance, a Christian writer states that at the time of the Muslim conquest, the Jews, unlike many Christians, did not succumb to the pressure of the victorious religion.

All this shows that (a) there were no forced conversions to Islam during its early, really Arabic, period; (b) the economic and social advantages to be gained by acceptance of the ruling creed were not strong enough to induce the Jews to forsake their faith. Obviously, it was the very fact that Judaism and Islam were so closely related that obviated the inner urge which might have led a Jew to embrace Islam. Only in the later Middle Ages, it seems, did the ecstatic mysticism of Islam offer a definite attraction to the decaying Oriental Jewries and then only until the tremendous upsurge of Jewish mysticism in the sixteenth century led to a temporary revival of those communities.

The second great fact which impresses any student of the sources available to us from the tenth century on is the enormous mobility of the Jewish communities in the Muslim world, as well as the close and lively connection between all of them. That period was indeed one of a strong, inner migratory movement.

As we have seen, it was not the very temporary political unification of the Middle East under Arab rule which created this state of affairs. During the obscure first century of Islam we hear about forced transfer of segments of the Jewish population, e.g., from Palestine to the Mediterranean coast of Northern Syria, which were exposed to the naval attacks of the Byzantines. Here the caliphs tried to replace the Christian population with Jews on whom naturally they might rely more readily. Another example of migration involves the foundation of Kairuwan, the capital of the country known today as Tunis. The caliph ordered the governor of Egypt to send there a thousand "Jewish or Copt" (Egyptian Christians) families, which shows, by the way, that the non-Muslims were essential to administration. As Kairuwan soon became a notable seat of Jewish learning, it may well be that it was inhabited by Jews from its very inception. The repopulation of Jerusalem by Jews after its conquest by the Arabs also falls into the first century of Islam. The story, repeated in many history books, that the Christians, before surrendering Jerusalem, stipulated that no Jew be allowed to live in it, and that the Arabs accepted that condition, is completely untrue, as this writer has pointed out in a special study. The information, contained in a Geniza paper that seventy families from Tiberias—then the main Jewish center in Palestine—moved to Jerusalem shortly after its fall, is plausible for more than one reason; it is also probable that Yemenite Jews settled there together with Yemenite Arabs, who, as we know, formed the first Muslim garrison of the Holy City.

To be sure, all these are sporadic cases. From Jewish sources we know next to nothing about Jewish population movements during the first two centuries of Islam. For the third century we have a little more information. However, in the fourth (the tenth Christian century), precisely at the time when the Muslim Empire had become completely dismembered and had fallen into its natural geographical units, the relations among the various Jewish centers and the movement among them were at their height. In this, as it may be stated at once, the state of the Jewish community only reflected that of the Muslim world. Precisely at the moment when there had arisen so many political frontiers inside Islam, Muslim writers began to talk about *Mamlakat al-Islam*, "the Realm of Islam," as a single unit. It was the Muslim merchant, the real bearer of Muslim civilization, who was stronger than all political frontiers and who moved incessantly in the whole area between Spain and Morocco in the West, and Central Asia and India in the East.

In this, the Muslims were emulated and possibly surpassed by the Jews. The Geniza documents, which often enable us to follow the movements and connections of a single man during periods of years, reveal how amazingly agile the Jews had become. We would find a man one year in India, the next in Aden (Yemen) and Egypt, and from there he would embark on two successive trips to Spain and Morocco; in between, he would apologize to his business friend in Aden that, for special reasons, he was unable "this year" to travel again to Yemen and India. It was apparently quite common for a man to make the long journey from Morocco or Spain to India more than once in his lifetime.

It should not be implied that the Jews had no commercial traditions of their own prior to the rise of the Islamic mercantile civilization. Ample reference has been made before to the Radanites, and we will examine later the pre-Islamic activities of the Persian Jews. It remains without doubt, however, that never before in Jewish history have commerce and international traffic affected so large a section of the Jewish population, as it did from the tenth, and particularly from the eleventh, century on. What impresses one most, while studying the Geniza papers relating to the Jewish trade between the Mediterranean and India, is the fact that so many small fry took part in it. It is evident that by the twelfth century international trade affected the whole community.

The participation of the rank and file in international business was possible because it was conducted largely on the basis of partnership. At a time when travel was exposed to so many dangers, people preferred to spread the risk and invest in a number of undertakings rather than putting all they had into one venture. A merchant setting out to another country normally would travel in the company of a friend and would not do business for himself alone, but would always take with him a large number of orders, often limited in scope. Therefore, people with small resources were able to take part in business, between Egypt and India, for instance, or between the same country and Spain. Partnerships between capitalists and merchants or between traveling merchants of various, sometimes rather distant, countries were indeed rather common occurrences. In a letter found in the Geniza, a Jewish merchant from Tunis writes to his business friend in Egypt that he hopes that their sons will continue to entertain the close relationships that had prevailed between the two houses for generations. In general, business relationships in those days were regarded as bonds of personal friendship. Possibly it could not have been otherwise. The element of trust was most important in view of the distance and general insecurity. Most of the business letters have an attractive personal touch and often close with a list of presents sent by the writer as a token of friendship. Those lists, by the way, allow us an intimate picture of the daily life of the recipients, e.g., of the Jews from Arabian countries living in India. An item which looms large in the letters to India is *halal* cheese which was *kosher* (religiously permissible) and which traveled the long way from Egypt to where, in some cases, it had been imported from Sicily.

Business connections very often also furthered the creation of family relationships. Here again the Geniza gives us many details. For a man from North Africa to marry a woman from Aden (Yemen), or a Spanish Jew to take home from his travels to the East a wife from Cairo was quite a common occurrence. As we know from one literary and one legal document—paralleled, by the way, by similar statements in Muslim literature—the attractiveness of the young women of Yemen gave a special lure to the adventurous journey to the East. Reference has been made earlier to the possible adverse results of endogamy among the Jews in the earlier days of Islam. Perhaps the fresh "circulation of blood," which coincided with the revival of business, may have had a wholesome effect from the point of view of eugenics!

In addition to commerce, migration contributed enormously to the unification of the Jewish people inside Islam. From the third to the fifth centuries of Islam, the movement was from East to West, from Persia and Iraq to Palestine, Egypt, North Africa and Spain. In this field, too, the Jewish movement was paralleled, and possibly preceded, by the Muslim. Africa and Spain were colonial areas for the more developed and more enterprising Muslims of Asia, the Arabs, and the Persians. Palestine, of course, was a special case. Large parts of its Christian population, especially that of the Greek towns, emigrated after the Muslim conquest to the Greek Christian empire of Byzantium. Owing to the attraction of the holy places, the gap left by the Christians was soon filled by Muslims and Jews. Possibly more than any other country, Egypt demonstrates the great changes brought about through the migration movements. In the early days of Islam, it was an agricultural province, used largely for providing food for the Muslim armies which were stationed in Syria (to fight the Byzantines) or elsewhere. By the end of the tenth century it had become the commercial pivot of the Muslim world, second to none, not even to Iraq and its capital Bagdad. There were two main causes for this change: a negative cause, the deterioration of the political situation in Iraq and Persia; and a positive cause, the fact that the colonial areas of Africa and Spain had developed so immensely in the preceding centuries. We have definite accounts in Arabic sources of the emigration of whole groups of Muslim merchants from Iraq to Egypt, and abundant evidence for similar movements among Jewish merchants.

The two main synagogues of Old Cairo were called "that of the Iraqians" and "that of the Palestinians," showing the foreign origin of most of its Jewish population. In various towns in Palestine, there were Iraqian synagogues. In fact, so numerous was the Iraqian element in Palestine that some of their religious rituals were adopted by the ancient inhabitants of the country. If a large section of the Muslim population of Jerusalem during the tenth century was Persian, exactly the same was true with regard to the Jews. Thus Persian, in addition to Arabic and Hebrew, was continuously heard when the Jews assembled for prayer in the neighborhood of the ancient Temple. So strong was the Persian influence in Jerusalem at that time that the great Hebrew lexicographer David ben Abraham al-Fasi, who lived there, used Persian words, although, as his name indicates, he hailed from Fez in Morocco.

These facts about the great Jewish migration from Iraq and Persia to Palestine and the countries of Africa and Spain have long been known, although perhaps they have not yet been put into their proper historical context. Once, however, the documentary Arabic Geniza is published in full, a far more accurate and detailed picture of that migration will emerge. The mere names of the persons mentioned in them are most telling. Many Jews in Africa bore names of towns in Asia, such as Samarkand and Nisabur (Central Asia and North Eastern Persia), Hamadhan and Tustar (Western Persia), Bagdad and Basra (Iraq), Aleppo, Hama and Damascus (Syria), Jerusalem, Acre, Ascalon, and Ramle (Palestine), and even of countries of the Arab peninsula, such as Hijaz and Yemen. In addition, the Geniza contains actual dates of migrations from Asia to Africa.

By the beginning of the twelfth century, the tide had turned; a movement began in the opposite direction—from the Muslim "West" (Spain and North Africa, west of Egypt) to the East, which included Egypt as well as Asia. The most famous example in Jewish history of this migration movement is Moses Maimonides, who was born in 1135 in Cordova, Spain, lived some time in Morocco and emigrated, when in his thirties, via Palestine to Egypt, where he died in 1204. He was followed by his disciple, Joseph Ibn Aknin, and preceded by many others. The immediate cause of Maimonides' emigration was the Almohad persecution, to which reference has been made in the preceding chapter. However, he followed much-trodden paths. For the Muslim West, although originally a colonial territory, had accumulated in the centuries subsequent to its colonization sufficient wealth to seek expansion itself.

This was particularly true of the Jewish population, which was largely descended from merchants coming from the East and far more exclusively engaged in commerce than the long-established Jewish communities of Egypt and Asia. There is abundant evidence in the Geniza papers that the majority of the Jewish merchants engaged in the Far Eastern trade came from the Muslim West. Many of them settled temporarily or permanently in Egypt, Yemen or India itself. (One document tells of two North African Jewish silversmiths, who emigrated to Ceylon in approximately 1140.) Some of the most prominent Jewish merchants in Aden in the first part of the twelfth century hailed from the Muslim West, while for religious reasons—which were sometimes combined with commercial considerations—Jews from Spain and North Africa had made Palestine their home even earlier. All in all, we see that the great Jewish migration movements in Islamic times were largely connected with the entrance of the mass of the Jewish population into commerce.

It would be interesting to know how far Jewish migration and commerce stretched beyond the confines of the Arab Muslim world at the time of the acme of Jewish Arab symbiosis. At the borders of Islam and Western Europe, that is, Spain, southern France and Sicily, the biographies of many Jewish celebrities indicate a continuous coming and going. The complicated situation in the center of the Islamic world, especially Egypt, about which we know a good deal, may be summarized as follows:

Jewish merchants from Byzantium and France frequently visited the Egyptian ports, acquiring there not only Eastern merchandise but also books, and seeking answers to religious questions. If they were in trouble of any sort, captured by pirates or molested by greedy officials, they could rely on the brotherly help of the Egyptian Jews, just as any co-religionist from an oriental country. However, if one judges from the thousands of documents preserved in the Geniza, the business connections of the Jews of Egypt with those living outside the area of Islam were limited in scope. Names indicating European origin are almost absent from the Geniza; even the name Rumi (coming from Byzantium. Constantinople and its dependencies) is not frequent. A notorious example of a French Jewish scholar, who became prominent in the Arab East, was Anatoli, Chief Justice to the Jewish community of Alexandria in Maimonides' time. Once he was insulted by a high Jewish dignitary because of his inferior, European origin. But generally he was held in high esteem, and there were other scholars from Christian countries in Maimonides' entourage.

An even more significant question is that of the role played by the Jews in the development of medieval Middle-Eastern capitalism, and their relative importance in the economic life of the Muslim world. According to the present state of research, both Muslim and Jewish, no definite answer is as yet possible. It is certainly correct to say that the Jewish contribution was important, but exactly how important we cannot yet make out.

As far as banking is concerned, the list of Jewish bankers in Iraq who were able to grant substantial loans to the government during the tenth and eleventh centuries is very impressive, as Walter J. Fischel emphasizes in his book, *Jews in the Economic and Political Life of Medieval Islam,* London 1937. Dr. Fischel rightly points out that a tenth-century caliph might change his prime ministers fifteen times, but he retained his Jewish court banker almost from the beginning of his reign to its very end. (This reminds one of the early twenties of this century, when Hezkiel Sassoon, the Minister of Finance in modern Iraq, held office in various successive cabinets.) One Muslim geographer states that in the second half of the tenth century most bankers and money-changers in Syria and Egypt were Jews. I have the definite impression, however, that Christian bankers are mentioned in Muslim sources more frequently and far earlier than Jewish bankers; certainly the Jew does not appear in Muslim classical literature as the typical banker and money-lender, as he does in medieval Christian writings.

The wealth of material about the Jewish trade in Arab countries preserved in the Geniza enables us to specify the branches of commerce in which Jews were engaged; however, we are not able to appraise their relative importance, as relevant Muslim sources have not yet been made available. The Jews were prominent in the great Indian trade of spices, aromatic, dyeing and medical herbs;

in the textile and clothing business; in the metal trade, both in raw metals and ingredients for the metal industry and in finished metal vessels of all descriptions. They exported iron and steel from India and brought there copper and lead; in addition, it seems that the Jews were active not only as gold- and silversmiths (i.e., makers of ornaments)—as they were in all Muslim countries from pre-Islamic times down to the present day—but also as manufacturers of brass-, and possibly also of silver and gold vessels. (As late as 1924, I found the Jews in Damascus specializing in metal vessels; the Christians, working in the same factory, processed mother-of-pearl, and the Armenians made woodwork.) Pearls, imported from the East, corals, found in the Mediterranean and shipped to India, chemicals, drugs, and paper were other commodities handled by Jews. I have not found much about Jewish trade in agricultural products—the many details about food shipped refer almost exclusively to presents made to business friends, not to trade in food articles—and I have not come across a single case of a Jew trading in timber, although the importing of this material to the Arab Muslim countries was of great significance, and the business itself became in the nineteenth century a typically Jewish occupation in eastern Europe.

Any future appraisal of the Jewish contribution toward the great mercantile civilization of the Middle East in medieval times will have to take into consideration the fact that our main source of knowledge on Jewish economic activities, the thousands of documents preserved in the Geniza, is one-sided; it centers around Egypt and the eleventh and twelfth centuries. However, we already know that Egypt originally was a colonial area, which attracted the Jewish merchants from Persia and Iraq, and that the process of the mercantilization of the Middle East was in the main completed by the tenth century. The ancient Jewish merchants' company of the Radanites, as we have seen, by-passed Egypt, using for transit only the Isthmus which is cut through at present by the Suez Canal. So unimportant commercially was Egypt in their time that when we compare the sums which were handled by Jews in southern Persia and Iraq—recorded by the Muslim historians—with those appearing in the Geniza papers, we come to the conclusion that the really great Jewish wealth had its seat in the countries around the Persian gulf. Nor is the source of that wealth unknown. A Christian writer mentions that as early as pre-Islamic times the Persian Jews had amassed fortunes through their trade by sea to India; Saʿadya Gaon, the spiritual leader of Babylonian Jewry in the second quarter of the tenth century, alludes to the same source. However, the moist and often flooded soil of Iraq and southern Persia cannot preserve paper documents as does the dry soil of Egypt. Therefore we can never expect to secure from the more ancient and possibly more important commercial activities of the Babylonian Jews the same wealth of information that we possess about the Jews who lived on the great route between Spain, Egypt and India during the late Middle Ages. Nonetheless, re-examination of the extant literary sources—both Jewish and Muslim—by a competent scholar may provide us with a new picture of Babylonian Jewry in Islamic times and therewith offer a balanced view of the role of the Jews in Muslim civilization in general.

Obviously a most vital reason for the self-organization of the Jewish merchants was the need for the protection of their interests and even their very lives. On the long route from Spain and North Africa to India, there existed many petty rulers, sometimes not distinguishable from pirates or brigand chiefs. Even in the well-established kingdoms, it was almost impossible to obtain access to the local governor should a merchant be robbed, cheated or otherwise damaged. In addition, in many countries it was customary or legal to confiscate the property of a foreign merchant who died en route. To protect themselves against these dangers, the Jewish merchants had in every important commercial town a "Representative," who brought their cases before the rulers of the country, who had special agreements with "all the lords of the seas and the deserts" in the interest of his clients, and who took care of a client's assets in case he was shipwrecked or died in some other fashion.

In addition to "foreign relations," the Representative of the merchants (in Hebrew, *Peqid ha-Soharim*; in Arabic, *Wakil*) had many functions directly concerned with business. To his warehouse the foreign merchants sent or brought their merchandise. There the prices were fixed, and often the Representative was charged with the distribution of goods among different partners or with the selling itself. He served as a banker. Money was deposited with him and through him payments were made. He acted also as a postoffice; letters were delivered to him and he passed them on to the foreign merchants on their arrival. There can be little doubt that other communities besides the Jewish had similar representatives and it is probable that the *Consuls* of the Italian merchants' colonies in the Middle East, which were the forerunners of the modern consuls or representatives of foreign states, were modeled after the ancient institute of the *Peqid ha-Soharim* or *Wakil*.

As far as we know, there were no formal elections to the office of the Representative. A successful and respectable businessman gradually assumed such a position and transmitted it to his son if the latter was able and so inclined. Thus we find in Cairo at the end of the eleventh century a Representative called Yequtiel, the son of a doctor; he was followed in this function by his son, but his grandson returned to the profession of his great-grandfather and became a physician. Instead, Joseph ben Yehuda Cohen, whose forefathers had occupied the highest religious dignities, first in Babylonia and then in Palestine and Egypt for about two hundred years, assumed the office. Access to him obviously was not easy. We find a group of merchants, who were robbed by Byzantines off the coast of Sicily, asking a business friend to bring their case before him, as they themselves were not eloquent enough to do so. We are particularly well informed about the family of the Representatives of the Merchants in Aden, whose fate we are able to follow through three centuries. The same office was found in Ramle, then the capital of Palestine, in Tyre, then the main port of the Lebanon coast, and even in a small town in Lower Egypt. In Iraq, the court banker seems to have filled partly similar functions.

We have discussed the office of the Representative of the Merchants in some detail because it is the most novel venture in Jewish communal organization in Islamic times of which we know. All other Jewish communal institutions, although considerably developed under Arab rule, had been in existence in pre-Islamic times. Even the most central Jewish institution, the office of the *Resh Galutha*, the Head of the Jewish community in exile, or "Exilarch," as he is referred to by historians, must be so considered. He had his seat in Iraq and was regarded as a descendant of the royal house of David, and probably was so. In pre-Islamic times he bore the title "King," just as the provincial governors of the Persian Empire did. (Thus the official title of the Persian Emperor was "King of Kings.") At that time, when large tracts of land were still inhabited by Jewish peasants, the Resh Galutha was part of the administration of the Empire and was charged with the collection of taxes, supervision of the markets, and even had jurisdiction over criminal cases. He was one of the high dignitaries of the state. Of one of these Jewish "kings" it is known that his daughter, Shushan-Dukht, was married to the Persian King, Yezdegerd I. (399–420). It was she who founded the Jewish colonies in Isfahan and Hamadan, which became so prominent in Islamic times.

The position of the Resh Galutha changed considerably under Islam. The Arab armies took Iraq by force, thus its whole soil was regarded as Muslim property. The Jews, possibly more than other members of the rural population, forsook agriculture and concentrated in the towns in order to preserve their religion. Furthermore, the Muslim State was far more tightly organized than the loose-knit Persian Empire. All this contributed to the fact that in Islamic times the Resh Galutha occupied a very honored position as the general representative of the Jewish community. According to a Christian source, he had precedence over the Christian dignitaries at the caliph's court, but as a rule he had no administrative functions within the Muslim State. He was addressed by the Muslims as "Our Lord, the son of David," and as David is described in the Koran as one of the greatest prophets, naturally his office was surrounded by the halo of sanctity. He was installed in his office by the caliph (one such document of installation has been preserved by a Muslim writer), and it was a sign of the times when, in the year 918, one of two rivaling Exilarchs succeeded in being appointed by reciting an appropriate piece of Arabic poetry in the presence of the caliph. In his turn, the Exilarch confirmed the appointment of the Jewish religious dignitaries in those countries which had previously belonged to the Persian Empire, even in Yemen, although that country formed since the tenth century a part of the Fatimid Caliphate, which was a permanent foe of the rulers of Iraq. The Spanish Jewish traveler, Benjamin of Tudela who visited Bagdad about the year 1168 was deeply impressed by the splendor of the Exilarch's court and describes in detail his weekly reception by the caliph. (This example of Jewish-Arab symbiosis may be read in M. N. Adler, *The Itinerary of Tudela*, London 1907, pp. 39–41, or in Jacob R. Marcus, *The Jew in the Medieval World*, Cincinnati 1938, pp. 186–187.)

But all the splendor of the Exilarch's office could not conceal the fact that he had very little executive power. He had no jurisdiction in criminal cases, and his income was confined to the proceeds from his own lands and to more or less voluntary contributions. It is most indicative that al-Biruni, a great Muslim scholar, who lived around the year 1000 when the caliph had become a mere figurehead of the Muslim world, explained that in his time the caliph occupied a position similar to that of the Jewish Resh Galutha.

Of far greater importance for the Jews in Islamic countries than the office of the Resh Galutha was another ecumenical dignity, that of the *Gaon*, which became indeed so prominent in Jewish life during the first five centuries of Islam that these are labelled in Jewish history as "The Gaonic Period." Gaon was the title borne by the heads of the two great Jewish academies of Babylonia-Iraq (originally only one of the two) who were regarded by Jews all over the world as the highest authority in all religious matters, which, to be sure, also included at that time civil law. The so-called *responsa* of the *Gaons*, i.e., their written answers to legal and ritualistic questions—thousands of which have been preserved —are indeed the most characteristic literary product of Judaism in that time. The responsa sometimes covered whole books and were collected under various titles. Thus the Jewish scholars of Sijilmasa, a town in far-away Morocco, would collect and publish all the responsa they had received from the hands of the academies in Iraq, a procedure which has its parallel in Muslim religious literature. In addition, the Gaons would send out apostles (called *Peqidim*, representatives) to decide matters on the spot, settle disputes, and collect funds.

It has been maintained by such authorities as the late Professor Louis Ginzberg of the Jewish Theological Seminary of New York that the Gaonate developed under the influence of Islamic rule. This statement, however, needs closer definition. The institutions of the Jewish academies, their heads, apostles, and responsa are, of course, very old and go back to pre-Christian times. The title Gaon itself appears half a century before the Arab conquest of Iraq. Furthermore, Muslim scholarship was organized differently from the Jewish academies; it was of a very loose texture. Between its informality and the strict hierarchy of Christian clergy, the Jewish religious authority occupied a middle position, as the faculties of the academies consisted of scholars of different grades who were promoted according to rather fixed rules, whereas scholars outside the academies and even laymen were admitted to the meetings of the academies twice a year, during the month preceding the holidays of the spring and fall respectively, the off-season in agriculture. No similar arrangements are known to have operated in contemporary Islam; consequently, no Islamic influence can be assumed to have modeled the life of the ancient Jewish academies of Iraq.

Indirectly, however, Arab civilization influenced the Gaonate in many ways. Without the migrations and the commercial travel all over the Muslim world, the institute of the responsa could never have reached the importance it had during the ninth, tenth, and eleventh centuries. Journeys whose aim was a visit to famous scholars and schools were an old Jewish custom, most conspicuous in talmudic literature, and this tradition received new impetus under Arab rule, where travel for study's sake became a characteristic aspect of Muslim civilization. Even in Byzantine times Jews used to visit the ruins of Jerusalem for prayer and mourning, but it is easy to understand that under Islam this custom gained new momentum, for the Muslim pilgrimage to its holy places is one of the main religious duties. Thus a Jewish scholar from Spain or North Africa would try to visit Jerusalem—or, as the saying goes, "behold Jerusalem"—at least once in his lifetime and, while in the Muslim East, perhaps try to visit the seats of Jewish scholarship, particularly Iraq. Many of the letters of the heads of the Jewish academies to Egypt or to the countries of the Muslim West show that their addressees were known to them personally.

From the end of the ninth century on, the political and economic life of Iraq deteriorated steadily. The Jewish population, as we have seen, suffered from this decline. Certainly the academies and the Exilarchs were not immune, although the latter preserved its ancient luster for some centuries to come. Just as the Muslim world became dismembered politically so did the Jewish communities of the various states begin to have heads of their own, the *Nagid* (prince). Such Nagids are known from Spain, North Africa, Egypt, Palestine and even Yemen, where they were identical with the Representatives of the Merchants mentioned above. The most conspicuous example of such Nagids were the descendants of Moses Maimonides, who occupied this office in Egypt for about two centuries. Like the Resh Galutha, these Nagids were installed or confirmed by the governments of the respective countries, and like their ecumenical model they had little executive power.

The most active units of Jewish life in Muslim countries were the local congregations. Although Arabic terms were used concurrently with the Hebrew, e.g., for the head of the congregation (*Muqaddam*), or for the congregation itself (*Jama'a*), the Geniza papers, as well as the responsa of the Gaons, reveal that no particular Arabic influence can be discovered in their inner make-up. The reason for this is the simple fact that the Muslims had nothing that corresponded to the local Jewish organization which held religious and social, to some extent even political, functions. As an analysis of the modern Yemenite congregation seems to indicate, the Jewish congregation in Islamic countries obviously had preserved some of the characteristics it had in later Roman times.

Local needs were attended to first, in accordance with the talmudic maxim that "The poor of your town have priority over others." But even the smallest congregation contributed toward Jewish ecumenical and regional needs. Jerusalem and Palestine in general with their seats of learning, scholars and mourners, ranked first, but the academies of Iraq and, of course, those of the capitals of the various countries, were also supported. Ransom for Byzantine Jews brought to Egypt by Arab pirates were collected throughout the little congregations of the Egyptian countryside, and similarly the refugees from Palestine and Syria in the times of the Crusaders were cared for by methods reminiscent of the modern American United Jewish Appeal. A Jewish merchant in India would send donations at one and the same time to the main synagogues in Old Cairo, to Jewish holy places in Iraq and in Egypt, and to the needy of different congregations. Muslim charity had exactly the same, interterritorial character. To each of the instances given above, parallels could be adduced from Arab sources.

Our survey of the economic conditions and social institutions of the Jews during the first, creative, five centuries of Islam, has shown that there were many agents which worked toward a revival and a gradual unification of the Jewish people inside the Muslim world: the economic rise and entrance of the Jews into the class of business and professional people; commercial and family relations connecting Jews from many Muslim countries; the new institution of the "Representative of the Merchants"; the allegiance to ecumenical and regional central authorities; travel for "the seeking of wisdom" and for pilgrimage to holy places; the application of the same law to all Jews wherever they lived; and, finally, Jewish charity which, like its Muslim counterpart, was not limited by political boundaries. The new economic and social conditions did not fail to exercise a marked influence also on the cultural life of the Jews inside Islam.

7

THE CULTURAL DEVELOPMENT OF THE

JEWISH PEOPLE INSIDE ARAB ISLAM

1. *Jewish Participation in the Medieval Civilization of the Middle East.*

The medieval civilization of the Middle East—approximately up to 1300—was far more modern than that of contemporary Europe in many respects—economic, social and spiritual. It was a basically intermediate civilization linking up Hellenistic-Roman antiquity with modern times.

Its dominant religion was Islam. Christians and Jews were therefore relegated to an inferior legal status, which made their position always degrading and often precarious. On the other hand, this civilization was largely secular, so that non-Muslims could feel themselves to be equal heirs to a great cultural tradition.

The language of this civilization was Arabic. In the beginning this meant social predominance for Arabic-speaking Muslims—so much so that the restrictions imposed on non-Muslims (according to some sources) included a prohibition against teaching their children Arabic. However, the Arabs were soon absorbed into the old sedentary population of the Middle East, imposing their language on it even while they themselves lost their national identity.

From the tenth century A.D. onward, there was no longer any question of a contrast between Arabs and non-Arabs, but rather between the civilized, Arabic-speaking citizens of the Middle East and the foreign barbarian soldiers who ruled over them. Arabic, like Latin in Europe, had ceased to be a national language and became the language of a civilization. But, owing to the far more secular character of Eastern civilization in that age, it was far less closely connected with the ruling religion than Latin was with the Catholic church. Therefore, Christians and Jews unhesitatingly used Arabic even while expounding sacred topics to their co-religionists, just as a modern Muslim or Jew might make use of English, when preaching or working on religious subjects.

I hope that all that has been said so far will explain the position of a Jew inside that medieval civilization of the Middle East and how far it is correct to speak at all of "Jews in an Arab environment" at that time. Owing to the prevailingly unnational and secular character of that civilization, Jewish participation in it must be regarded rather as contribution to human progress in general than to a specifically national culture.

Recently the Cultural Committee of the Arab League held a congress in Bagdad in honor of the millenary of Ibn Sina, Avicenna, the famous medieval doctor and philosopher. A most spectacular millenary congress was also held by the Government of Persia. The Turks in their turn celebrated Avicenna as one of their own. All three were right: for Avicenna, according to some authors, was of Turkish descent. He passed most of his life in Iran and wrote his scientific works in Arabic.

The Greeks would have had even greater right to celebrate him as a national hero because Hellenic ideas and ways of thought occupied him all his life long. I mention this fact in order to point out that the work of medieval Jewish doctors, philosophers, mathematicians, astronomers, etc., should not be described as Jewish contributions to Arab civilization, since they wrote neither for the glorification of the Arabic language nor to prove the vitality of the Jewish race; but, while engaged in scientific work, they rightly regarded themselves as the disciples of the ancient Greek masters.

Nor can the writer attach much importance to the fact that some poets of Jewish descent wrote fine Arabic verses like Ibrahim ibn Sahl al-Israili (the Israelite) of Seville (died in 1260; his *Diwan* or collection of poems was printed about ten times!), or that Jewish converts were first-class experts on Arabic philology and antiquities. Abu Ubaida, a Persian Jew, was so great an authority on Arabic language, genealogy and tribal wars that he could boast: "Two horses (—in a battle—) never met before or after Muhammad without my knowing it."

These and similar cases were cited in the twenties of this century by well-meaning Arabs in order to show how great a *khidma*, a service, was done by Jews to Arab culture. However, it would be difficult to find in the work of these men a specific Jewish contribution to Arab letters: at least I would not see anything Jewish in the facts that ibn Sahl of Seville devoted many of his poems to a Jewish boy whom he loved, or that Abu Ubaida was so hated for his caustic criticism that nobody followed his coffin. . . . These men were, so to say, Jews in the flesh, but not in the spirit. They were simply members of the vast subject population of the Middle East which was assimilated to Arab ways of thinking and expression.

Originally, the present writer had intended to include in this book a chapter on the oft-treated subject of the contributions made by Arab-speaking Jewish scholars to the progress of science in the Middle Ages. However, he felt that those contributions had little bearing on the relations between Jews and Arabs or Islam and Judaism. The subject has been exhaustively treated in the first three volumes of George Sarton's monumental *Introduction to the History of Science*. And there exist good popular expositions, e.g., *Jewish Contributions to Civilization*, Philadelphia 1919, from the graceful pen of Joseph Jacobs; *The Legacy of Israel*, edited by E. R. Bevan and Charles Singer (who wrote the relevant chapter); and Cecil Roth's *The Jewish Contribution to Civilization*, London 1938, which contains important corrections and additions to the other two books.

It is, however, correct to speak of a great Jewish-Arab symbiosis if one confines oneself to the vital contributions made by the cultural elements inherent in one civilization to the autonomous spiritual life of the other. Such was the influence of Judaism on the creation of Muhammad and on the subsequent development of

Islam, touched upon in chapter IV, and such diverse ways in which Arab Muslim civilization affected Judaism and even Hebrew literature.

If we disregard the social and cultural creations of the Jewish groups living in the United States of America and other English-speaking countries and which have come into prominence in comparatively recent times, there are three great civilizations with which the Jewish people have come into close contact after developing a most unique culture of its own: first, the Greek civilization, which the Jews encountered in many countries where Greek was spoken, and particularly in Palestine, which was included successively in Hellenized states for almost a thousand years; secondly, the Arab Muslim civilization, with which we are concerned in this book; finally, that of the Romanic and Germanic peoples of western and central Europe—a connection which began over a thousand years ago, reached its climax in the nineteenth and the first quarter of the twentieth centuries, and at present is rapidly approaching its termination.

The most eloquent testimony to the Greek-Jewish symbiosis is the Greek New Testament, large parts of which must be regarded as a product of the Jewish genius and intrinsically Jewish in every respect. There exist important writings in Greek by professing Jews—the philosophical writings of Philo of Alexandria. which are regarded by some experts as the very basis of medieval thinking, or the books on Jewish history by Flavius Josephus, once a priest officiating in the Temple of Jerusalem. However, none of these creations have ever been translated into Hebrew (except in modern times) and only a very faint echo of them reached the bulk of the Jewish peoples during the Middle Ages. With the New Testament, however, owing to a tragic, but inevitable, political and spiritual constellation, Judaism had to part altogether. Thus the contact with Greek civilization, stimulating as it certainly was in many respects, did not result in a fully satisfactory cultural symbiosis. We shall have to return to this question in another connection later on.

The Romanic and Germanic peoples of western and central

Europe have influenced the Jewish groups living among them in many ways. The most conspicuous result of that connection was the rise of two specific Jewish languages: one of Romanic origin, Ladino; and one Germanic, Yiddish—which were most vigorously developed by the Jews after most of them had left the countries of western and central Europe and moved eastward to the Turkish Empire where most of the Jews spoke Ladino, and to the Slavic countries where Yiddish thrived both in quality and in quantity. At the beginning of the nineteenth century the majority of the Jewish people spoke Yiddish, which explains why the kindred German language became the means of literary expression for the Science of Judaism and other Jewish cultural and social activities throughout that century and up to the end of World War I. Until that time, even Zionist Congresses were conducted in German and their protocols published in that language.

The Science of Judaism, i.e., the creation of a full and coherent picture of the history and spiritual life of the Jews as a whole, came into being through the efforts of scholars like Zunz, Graetz and countless others, who wrote in German, and certainly contributed much to the rise of the self-respect of the Jewish people and to a better understanding of its fate among non-Jews. It paved the way for world-embracing Jewish philanthropy and even for the nationalist movement which led to the erection of the State of Israel. The modern philosophy of Judaism, as it was developed by men like Nachman Krochmal (who wrote in Hebrew, but was deeply indebted to German philosophy), Hermann Cohen, or Franz Rosenzweig helped especially the thinking Jew to find his place in an impermanent world. Finally, gifted Jewish writers of fiction in the German language gave expression to the strains of mood prevailing among the Jews in modern times.

No wonder that Moritz Steinschneider, himself an outstanding German-Jewish scholar, in his *Introduction to the Arabic Literature of the Jews*—which he wrote at the age of ninety—compared the German-Jewish with the Arab-Jewish symbiosis, regarding the two as of equal importance.

Here, however, I venture to disagree with the great master. Despite their great relative importance, none of the creations of the Jewish authors writing in German or conceived under the impact of modern Western civilization has reached all parts of the Jewish people or have influenced the personal inner life of every Jew to the profound degree as did the great Jewish writers who belonged to the medieval civilization of Arab Islam.

The reason for this difference is self-evident. Modern Western civilization, like the ancient civilization of the Greeks, is essentially at variance with the religious culture of the Jewish people. Islam, however, is from the very flesh and bone of Judaism. It is, so to say, a recast, an enlargement of the latter, just as Arabic is closely related to Hebrew. Therefore, Judaism could draw freely and copiously from Muslim civilization and, at the same time, preserve its independence and integrity far more completely than it was able to do in the modern world or in the Hellenistic society of Alexandria. It is very instructive to compare the utterances of Jewish authors of the Middle Ages about Islam and the Arabs with those of the nineteenth and twentieth centuries which deal with a surrounding culture, for instance, *Germanism and Judaism* (*Deutschtum und Judentum*) by Hermann Cohen. In Cohen's book Judaism is "justified," because it is regarded (rightly or wrongly) as essentially identical with the highest attainments of German thinking. However, most of the Jewish authors of the Middle Ages who wrote in Arabic never had the slightest doubt about the absolute superiority of Judaism. I emphasize this fact not because I believe that such an attitude should be adopted in our times, but simply as an indication that Judaism inside Islam was an autonomous culture sure of itself despite, and possibly because of, its intimate connection with its environment. Never has Judaism encountered such a close and fructuous symbiosis as that with the medieval civilization of Arab Islam. Some of its particularly significant aspects will be discussed in the following sections.

2. The Linguistic Aspects of Jewish-Arab Symbiosis.

The first and most basic aspect of Jewish-Arab symbiosis is the simple fact that the great majority of the Jews, like the rest of the populations of the Caliph's Empire, adopted the Arabic language. It is by no means easy to account for the comparatively rapid and almost complete diffusion of the Arabic language in the countries of Southwest Asia and North Africa. One most important factor has been explained in chapter III, namely, the fervent attachment of the Arabs to their beloved language, an enthusiasm which simply infected the populations which came under their sway, and we must take into account the merits inherent in that highly developed language itself. However, what occurred in the seventh and ninth centuries A.D. with Arabic had its counterpart, for over twelve hundred years, in the adoption of Aramaic as the common language of the whole Fertile Crescent in the sixth to the fourth centuries B.C.

Aramaic, unlike Arabic, had not the advantages of being the language of a state, a ruling religion and society; it was not a "national" language at all; nor could it compete with the clearly cut and highly refined Arabic grammar. Still, it achieved, almost surreptitiously, what Arabic accomplished in the wake of the spectacular victories of the Muslim armies. This shows that, in addition to the obvious factors, other agents must have been at work in the process of the diffusion of these international languages.

However, as the Jews were only one of the peoples affected by it, there is no need to dwell on this problem here in detail. Nor is it necessary, or even possible, to state when exactly Arabic became the language of the majority of the Jewish people. In the main, the process was completed around 1000 A.D., about 350 years after the great Muslim conquests, at the time when the Arabs themselves had been replaced throughout the Caliph's Empire by Turkish and other foreign rulers.

Only in the rugged mountains of Kurdistan and Armenia have the Jews retained their old Aramaic dialect, while Hebrew, as we shall see, not only retained its position as a second and literary language, but experienced an unprecedented revival.

By adopting the Arabic language the Jews did not become Arabs. They only exchanged one international language, Arabic, for another, Aramaic. However, there was a great difference between the two processes. As far as we know, there did not exist a non-Jewish Aramaic literary language and literature, which influenced to any extent the thought and the writing of the bulk of the Jewish people. Various Aramaic dialects were spoken by Jews in countries such as Palestine and Babylonia, and developed by them into literary languages. In addition, as far as we can see, the patterns and contents of the talmudic and midrashic literatures were to all intents and purposes a purely Jewish creation.

The situation was quite different with regard to Arabic. It was adopted by the Jews at a time when the Arabs had already developed a national literature and a religious terminology (a development, to be sure, in which many Jewish converts had taken part). Therefore, the acquisition of the Arab language by the Jews meant also their adoption of Arab ways of thinking and forms of literature, as well as of Muslim religious notions.

Arabic was used by Jews for all kinds of literary activities, not only for scientific and other secular purposes, but for expounding and translating the Bible or the *Mishna,* for theological and philosophical treatises, for discussing Jewish law and ritual, and even for the study of Hebrew grammar and lexicography.

For all these literary purposes Arabic, as developed in the post-classical period, was used. It was recognized long ago that the deviations from the ancient models of Arabic style found in Judaeo-Arabic literature are not due to a specific Jewish idiom, but to the stage of development reached by Arabic in the latter Middle Ages, a change, however, more conspicuous in Jewish literature, because the Jewish writers, who used Hebrew characters, felt themselves less bound by the classical models than the Muslims.

On the other hand, for letter-writing and other non-literary purposes a more colloquial form of Arabic, interspersed with Hebrew words and phrases, was used. These documents, thousands of which have been preserved, are extremely interesting, not only for their content but also for linguistic reasons. Many peculiarities of present-day colloquial Arabic, which is a language quite apart from classical, can first be traced in these non-literary medieval Jewish documents.

The Judaeo-Arabic vernaculars of our own days, such as those of Morocco, Tunis or Yemen, cannot be compared with Yiddish or Ladino, for these, as explained in the previous section, are languages preserved by the Jewish people in an environment foreign to them (Yiddish, which is Germanic, on Slavic soil; Ladino, which is Spanish, in Turkey, Greece, etc.). Still they differ markedly from the language of the Muslim population, first in pronunciation, secondly, with regard to details in grammar and vocabulary, and, thirdly, by the use of Hebrew words and phrases.

However, the Arabic-speaking Jews introduce far less Hebrew elements into their speech than is common in Yiddish; precisely because their knowledge of living Hebrew was far more developed than was the case in eastern Europe, they refrained from mixing up the two languages. In any case, the contemporary Judaeo-Arabic dialects and their literatures constitute a storehouse of Jewish tradition, folklore and wit, and bear a living testimony to the creative power of Jewish-Arab symbiosis.

Not only that, but just as the medieval Judaeo-Arabic texts constitute a most valuable contribution to our knowledge of the development of spoken Arabic, thus, in more recent times, Judaeo-Arabic writing is able to contribute to the solution of a most serious problem facing the Arab world today, the discrepancy between literary and spoken Arabic.

In western Europe the surrender of Latin to national languages and the rise of the local vernaculars marked the transition from medieval to modern times. The Arab countries are in a similar situation today. The difference between the literary language and the colloquial—even that spoken by the most educated persons—is immense, with all the negative effects of such a dualism on literature, the spiritual development in general and even on morals.

Twenty years ago it seemed that Egypt would actually do something about this grave problem, and I venture to surmise that if at that time Egypt had been a really independent state with some outstanding creations—not only some pleasant collections of short stories—available in the local vernacular, we would have had today a national Egyptian language, which would have done away with that linguistic dualism that is so detrimental to the Arab mind.

Why then is it true to say that Judaeo-Arabic writing is able to contribute to the solution of this problem? Because Jews, while using Arabic for literary purposes, have created what could be called "a literary vernacular," a language based on the living local talk, while avoiding its vulgarities. This idiom can be studied in Judaeo-Arabic newspapers, weeklies and monthlies (some, in the Iraqian and Tunisian dialect, were among the earliest periodicals to appear in Arabic) and books written for entertainment or religious and other purposes.

A characteristic example of this style might be found in the book *Travels in Yemen*, written by a shrewd coppersmith from San'a, who accompanied the famous French-Jewish scholar Joseph Halévy during his journey through Yemen in 1870. Despite some indelicacies, the book is written in a pleasant, vivid language, which betrays its roots in the living local vernacular, but is "common Arabic," easily understood by any educated Arab all over the world with the aid of the small vocabulary and the short linguistic notes provided in the Introduction to the printed edition (Hebrew University Press, Jerusalem 1941). For the various local dialects are more closely related to one another than they are to classical Arabic.

This shows, by the way, that the development of national languages, a process which would contribute much to the mental health of the Arab world, would not impede its unity.

The various stages of the development of Judaeo-Arabic are most conspicuous in the checkered and extremely interesting history of the translations of the Jewish Bible into Arabic. Originally, the reason for this activity was not so much that Hebrew was no longer understood, but an endeavor to provide by these translations (which had the character of explanatory free renderings) an authoritative interpretation of the text, in particular in theological matters, (e.g., the inculcation of a spiritual-abstract conception of the human-like qualities attributed to God in the Bible).

That is why the most famous of the classical translations, which superseded all the others in popular usage, that of Saʿadya (died 942), was called by him *Tafsir*, commentary. (In order to avoid misunderstanding: Saʿadya wrote also an Arabic commentary on the Bible.) Saʿadya, although of Egyptian origin, was so great a scholar that he succeeded in becoming Gaon, that is, the spiritual head of the Jewish community, who had his seat in Bagdad. In addition to his substantial greatness as a doctor of the Jewish law, Saʿadya excelled as a philosopher and theologian, as a linguist of great originality and even as a composer of religious poetry.

All these qualities made him an ideal interpreter of the Bible. His translation became a sacred text, which was copied, and later printed, beside the Hebrew original and the old Aramaic version. This procedure was followed even in the latest standard edition of the Pentateuch for Yemenite Jews printed in Tel Aviv in 1940.

As with other sacred texts, Saʿadya's version was often memorized, but soon became largely unintelligible to the majority of the Arabic-speaking Jews, because of the discrepancy between literary and spoken Arabic, which has been in existence for many centuries. Therefore, it became necessary to translate the Bible anew, and this time into the various local dialects. A fine collection of such vernacular Bible translations, called *Sharh*, which also means "explanation," is found in the unique fund of Oriental Jewish books and manuscripts brought together by the late Mr. David Sassoon and preserved by his learned son, Solomon Sassoon, in Letchworth, Hertfordshire, England.

In his introduction to his translation of the Bible into the vernacular of Morocco, Rabbi Susani, a very scholarly-minded man living in the sixteenth century, most lucidly explains the problems of turning the Bible into Arabic. The book, which he had written in his own hand in Safad, Palestine, where he had emigrated as a young man, was read in Damascus, Syria, and Basra, Iraq, which shows that despite its local flavor the version was "common

Arabic" (colloquial) enough to be understood by Jewish readers all over the Arab world.

However, the history of the Jewish translations of the Bible into Arabic did not stop at this stage. The popular *Sharhs*, although not committed to writing, but memorized by the elementary-school teachers, became themselves semi-sacred and traditional, and, with the further development of the colloquials, partly unintelligible. They were still memorized in schools, but complemented by explanations in the contemporary vernacular. This is the position in our own times, when the Jewish-Arabic symbiosis in the old sense of the word is rapidly coming to an end. It is highly desirable that we preserve some of these orally transmitted Bible versions in print (and even by recording), not only because of their linguistic interest, but because they are a living testimony to the popular traditional conception of the Bible in the Arab East.

Together with the study of the Bible, there came into being the study of its language and of language in general. Writing in Arabic and using Arabic methods and terminology, the Jewish scholars assiduously explored and described the Hebrew of the Bible and soon also that of the *Mishna* or post-biblical Hebrew. For the first time, the pronunciation, the grammar and the vocabulary of Hebrew were scientifically treated and, so to speak, brought under control; thus Hebrew became a disciplined and well-organized means of expression under the influence of Arabic.

The vast literature on the subject has come down to us only in part and not everything of what has been preserved is available in printed editions. Thus only recently the huge Bible dictionary of David ben Abraham al-Fasi, a tenth-century scholar originating from Fez, in Morocco but living in Jerusalem, was made known to the public by Professor S. L. Skoss of Philadelphia in an excellent edition, while the dictionary of post-biblical Hebrew by Tanhum Yerushalmi (thirteenth century)—as his surname shows, also a man from Jerusalem—has not yet been published in full up to the present day, although its edition was described as a major "desideratum" by most competent Gentile and Jewish scholars.

Al-Fasi's dictionary—the first of its size and age yet published in full—was written, before the great grammarians of the West (Morocco and Spain), Yehuda Hayyuj and Jona ibn Janah, discovered and developed the principle that all Hebrew words, just as Arabic, went back to "roots" consisting of three letters, a principle which has become basic to all Semitic philology.

However, subsequent discoveries did not make obsolete the independent collections of the older generations. As a whole, the Hebrew philology of the Arabic-writing Jewish scholars of the tenth through thirteenth centuries is an imposing body of research and knowledge.

These philologists did not confine themselves to the study of Hebrew. It was a commonplace among both Jewish and Muslim scholars that Arabic, Hebrew and Aramaic were basically one and the same language. However, it was left to the former, who alone were fluent in all three languages, to do the actual work of comparison and mutual explanation, thus laying the foundations for the field of comparative linguistics, a science which to the present day seems to have had particular appeal for Jews.

Considering the fine work done by medieval Jewish philologists and the fact that so many men of Jewish faith or descent have excelled in linguistics during the last hundred years, one is tempted to ask: why did the Jews wait for the Arabs to give them the impetus to study their own language and why had they not developed a system of Hebrew grammar and lexicography of their own during, say, the time of the *Mishna*, when the nucleus of the Jewish people was still firmly rooted in its native soil?

This deficiency is the more astonishing, as in the first centuries of the Christian era there prevailed in Palestine almost ideal conditions for such a creation:

(1) The Rabbis were versed in two or even three languages, classical (i.e., biblical) and colloquial (*mishnaic*) Hebrew, as well as Aramaic—it is precisely the discrepancy between the classical language of old Arabic poetry and the argot spoken in the newly-founded towns which served as one of the most important incentives to the rise of Arab philology;

(2) In *mishnaic* times the canon of biblical literature was finally

fixed—in Alexandria it was the similar work on the "edition" of
Homer and Plato which laid the foundation of the Greek science
of language;

(3) The powerful faculty of abstract and syllogistic thinking
displayed in the Talmud, if applied to the study of language,
would have made the rabbis excellent linguists;

(4) The work of the *Masoretes*, the scholars who lay down the
correct pronunciation of the text of the Bible, shows that its
creators had a very fine "ear" and an excellent faculty of observation of linguistic facts.

If despite all these favorable conditions no genuine Hebrew
philology was created by the Jews, while on their own soil, some
special reason must be sought, such as that innate disregard of the
importance of a national language and that concentration on ideas,
which in chapter III was defined as characteristic for old Israel in
contrast to the Arabs.

Thus it was the contact with the Arabs—"the worshippers of
language," as they have been called—that directed the Jewish mind
to a field of activity, for which, as it was proved subsequently, it
was particularly gifted, and which bore its mature first fruits to the
benefit of the national language of the Jewish people itself.

A particularly telling trait of Jewish-Arab symbiosis are the
Arabic names borne by Jews from pre-Islamic times up to the present day. In his *Introduction to the Arabic Literature of the Jews*,
Moritz Steinschneider devoted no less than 236 pages to this subject. Today, however, with the new research resulting from access to
the letters and documents of the Cairo Geniza, on the one hand,
and the life of the still-existing oriental communities on the other,
the material brought together by Steinschneider could be doubled.
Particularly has our knowledge of the Arabic names borne by Jewish *women* increased enormously. Those names often have a very
tenacious life. Some of the Karaite Jewish ladies of Cairo, mentioned in the Arabic weekly of their community, still bear in 1954
the same awkward Arabic names as did their grandmothers nine
hundred years ago.

A great piece of cultural history is preserved in these names.

Thus I doubt, for example, whether any Jewish girl bore the name Sitt attujjar, "The Princess of the Merchants," found in a twelfth-century marriage certificate prior to the social transformation of the Jewish people described in chapter VI of this book. Neither would Jewish girls ever have been called Siniya, Tuerkiye, or Rumiye, i.e., the Chinese, Turkish, or Greek (or, rather, European) girl, if Jews had not emigrated to Yemen or other near-tropical areas. The climate of that country, which is both near to the equator and yet Alpine, has a darkening effect on the human complexion. The result is that the mothers in Yemen would wish their daughters to be as fair-skinned as their sisters in more northern countries.

Space does not permit us to enlarge on this fascinating subject. There is, however, one point which deserves special attention. Arabic names have been used by Jews for religious purposes far more extensively than is the case with non-Hebrew names in Europe and America. Normally, in the West, a person is called up or mentioned in a synagogue by his Hebrew name and so addressed in such documents as marriage contracts. In the East, however, Arabic names are used for the same purposes without scruple, and the custom of bearing double names, one in the language of the country and one in Hebrew, is by no means common. Thus in certain times and certain countries a man called Hasan ("the handsome") in Arabic would bear also its Hebrew equivalent, Japheth; or, conversely, a Moshe (Moses) would be known also as Musa (the Arabic form of the name)—as was the famous Maimonides. However, in other places, e.g., in Yemen, people are called either by Arabic or by Hebrew names and these are used for all purposes. Thus, a Hasan or a Musa, even if he were a rabbi, would be always addressed by his Arabic name even during the synagogue service or in documents, while a Moshe would be addressed in this Hebrew form by his Arab acquaintances. (They might distort the name and pronounce it Moesai but it is the Hebrew form which they have in mind.) All this is natural where Jews had spoken in the vernacular of their neighbors for hundreds of years and yet are segregated from them by a special attire. If a man is discernible from a distance as a member of a separate community, he does not need to conceal his identity by giving up his Hebrew name. On the other hand, a non-Jewish name was not regarded as "profane," because the whole life of the community was confined to the narrow circle in which religion was paramount. We must remember, however, that the alliance between Hebrew and Arabic contributed to the fact that Jews in Arab countries bore mainly Arabic names.

3. *The Rise of Jewish Philosophy under Muslim Impact.*

In the first part of this chapter, the linguistic aspects of Jewish-Arabic symbiosis have been discussed in some detail, for these, although most tangible in everyday life, are usually overlooked. Fortunately, and most characteristically, the same cannot be said about the study of the impact of Muhammadan spiritual life on the Jewish mind.

Many Jewish scholars engaged in Islamic studies directed a part of their activities to this subject. They were led in this by I. Goldziher, the Nestor of modern Islamics (1850–1921), who regarded his own work on Jewish-Arab philosophy as so essential, that in private letters he complained that it did not find the same attention as his widely read books on Islam.

A tremendous amount of scholarly work, some of first-rate quality, has been devoted, during the last hundred years, to the rise and development of Jewish philosophy and theology under the influence of the Islamic culture. Beginning with Solomon Munk's *Mélanges de philosophie juive et arabe,* and his classical edition and translation into French of Maimonides' *Guide of the Perplexed,* down to the masters of our own times, H. A. Wolfson of Harvard, or the lamented Julius Guttmann of Jerusalem (whose *Philosophy of Judaism,* Jerusalem 1951, certainly deserves an English translation), many experts on Jewish philosophy or on philosophy at large have devoted their lives to the study of the relations between Muslim and Jewish thought. This work is being vigorously continued by a younger generation of scholars in the United States, France and England—as well as in Israel.

It is due to the activities of scholars of this type that some of the Jewish-Arabic authors, to whom comparatively little attention has been paid before, have come into the foreground in our own times, e.g., the enigmatic Ibn Kammuna, a thirteenth century author of a comparative study on Islam, Christianity and Judaism, or the original thinker, Abu'l-Barakat ibn Malka (twelfth century), whose philosophy has been lucidly explained by Solomon Pines, Guttmann's successor to the chair of Jewish philosophy at the Hebrew University, Jerusalem.

Abu'l-Barakat's main philosophical work has been recently edited by Muslim scholars in India, while Pines is preparing an edition of his philosophical commentary on Kohelet (Ecclesiastes). In his criticism of Aristotle's *Physics*, Abu'l-Barakat, like the Hebrew-writing Hasdai Crescas of the fourteenth century, (who, however, worked independently of him), anticipated that destruction of Aristotle's authority, which marked the beginning of modern science.

The basic fact about Jewish-Arabic thought is that Greek science and Greek methods of thinking made their entrance into Jewish life mainly through the gates of Arab-Muslim literature. With the Arabic-writing Jewish doctors, mathematicians, astronomers and philosophers of the ninth and tenth centuries, science, in the Greek sense of the word, for the first time became known and practiced among the bulk of the Jewish community. All genuine Jewish reasoning before that time consisted either of simple, practical observations and conclusions, or of mythological conceptions, no matter how profound.

Systematic, scientific thinking, such as that developed by the Greeks, was practiced by the Jewish people only under "Muslim" influence. There were, at the turn of the ninth and tenth centuries, close connections between the Jews of western Upper Mesopotamia, in particular of Raqqa, which, for a short time served as the capital of the Muslim Empire, and the Harranians, a non-Muslim community, which was especially devoted to Greek science and philosophy. However, these partial and sporadic contacts—which, by the way, used Arabic as the means of understanding—were of no great historical importance and cannot change the basic fact that it was Arab Muslim civilization through which the Jewish people were introduced to Greek science.

Here, of course, we are confronted with a question similar to that set to us while studying the history of the creation of Hebrew grammar and lexicography: How was it possible that the Jews, who for a full thousand years, from Alexander the Great down to Muhammad, had lived inside the Hellenistic civilization, did not make themselves acquainted with its highest product, the scientific method, until they became surrounded by another civilization, which only imperfectly preserved that heritage of Greece?

This is the more astonishing, as great numbers of Jews, living in the Diaspora, spoke Greek and, as the example of Philo of Alexandria shows, were deeply involved in Greek philosophy. Philo, according to H. A. Wolfson the main originator of the philosophical thinking of the whole Middle Ages, remained completely unknown to the bulk of the Jewish people living in Palestine and Babylonia, while those innumerable traits from Hellenistic life found in talmudic literature—many of which have been explained so admirably by Professor Saul Lieberman of New York in his *Hellenism in Jewish Palestine* and other publications—betray a knowledge of only the surface, not the essence, of Greek civilization.

This strange fact can be explained only by the very unique role, which the message of the Jewish people—ethical monotheism—imposed on it in an almost totally hostile, heathen world. When the mad Roman emperor, Caligula demanded godlike adoration for himself, the whole civilized world, including the Greek philosophers and scientists, bowed their knees to him. It was only a small barbarian people of peasants, living on the hills of Judaea, and their co-religionists in the Diaspora, who refused to do so and who would have died rather than profess what they regarded as a lie and an abomination. It is evident that the Jewish people could not carry out its unique mission without spiritual sacrifices. It had to keep aloof in order to keep intact. It had to forgo the participation in Greek civilization, if it did not want to become absorbed by it.

Only many centuries later, when the monotheistic aim of Judaism had conquered most of the known world in the form of Christianity and Islam, did a more conciliatory attitude toward "Greek Wisdom" become possible, although some of the best men of medieval Judaism refused to accept it (even the Spanish Hebrew poet and thinker, Yehuda Halevi—despite the fact that he was a doctor and trained in Greek science).

Islam itself was able to digest Greek philosophy only after it had been previously adapted by Christian theology to suit the use of believers in a revealed religion. Even so the Muslim world soon split into two main camps, one orthodox Islam, which, though using some Hellenistic material for the formulation of its creed, firmly condemned any philosophical approach to religion as unbelief, and one, the more esoteric circles of doctors, men of letters and government officials, who adopted a conciliatory attitude or were so imbued with Greek thinking that they denied Islam in all but public profession.

Needless to say that in so vast and complex a civilization as the Islamic, there were innumerable shades of attitudes, from the mere mythological conception of religion, which was not touched even by the slightest contact with Greek thought, to the atheist, who relied on philosophy alone. As a whole, however, in this respect, as in economic and social matters—referred to in chapters I and IV, Muslim culture lay between the ancient East and modern civilization, insofar as Greek thought and science, however reduced, formed a basic ingredient in its spiritual and material life.

This process of absorption of the legacy of Greece was in the main completed in the fourth Muhammadan and tenth Christian centuries, precisely at the time when the Jewish people began to take its full share—and soon possibly even a little more than the share appropriate to its number—in the new civilization.

The change in attitude toward philosophy and science was no

doubt connected with the "bourgeois revolution" of the eighth to ninth centuries, the rise of a considerable part of the Jewish people to leading positions in business, industry, banking and the free professions.

Having shown that the majority of the Jews living in Palestine and Babylonia did not take to Greek thinking in pre-Islamic times —we may add the following: even in its Christian form, despite the close relations between the Fathers of the Church, such as Eusebius and Jerome, and the Rabbis—the reason, additional to the one offered before, was no doubt social: at that time most of those Jews were farmers and artisans, who, as a rule, have not much use for abstract thinking.

Things became quite different after the social changes. At a time when the new learning had taken firm root in the well-to-do families, it became a question of survival for Judaism, whether it could stand the test of being interpreted in progressive, contemporary terms or not.

Judaism stood the test successfully. While adopting many of the most advanced results of the new science, it developed an independent, particularly Jewish attitude to the basic questions of religion and life. Thus the works of the Jewish theologians and philosophers of the tenth to twelfth centuries became classics of Judaism, which have not lost their significance even in our own day.

There exists, of course, the greatest possible variety between the many attempts at reconciliation of the Jewish tradition with Greek-Muslim thought. Unfortunately some of the books concerned have come down to us only incompletely or are not yet available in printed editions.

There is a great difference between the scholastic mind of Saʿadya Gaon, the pietist mood of Bahya, the synthetic thinking of the poet Yehuda Halevi, and the systematic original reasoning of the "rationalist" Maimonides—to name just some of the most prominent authors.

While evaluating them, one must be extremely careful to locate each in his proper historical setting. Thus, to my mind, Mai-

monides (born 1135 in Cordova, Spain, died 1204 in Cairo), although active during the major part of his adult life in Egypt, is to
be understood historically against the background of the Almohad
upheaval in the Muslim West (Morocco and Spain). There, extreme orthodoxy made a temporary truce with philosophy, the
notable meetings, at Marrakesh in Morocco, between the fanatic
Almohad ruler Abu Ya'qub and the famous philosophers Ibn
Tufail and Ibn Roshd (known to the West as Averroes) marking
the apogee of this strange alliance.

In Egypt, too, strict orthodoxy seized the upper hand shortly
after Maimonides' arrival there, when the famous Saladin and
his family, the Ayyubids, replaced the more tolerant Fatimids.
These, as we have seen in chapter V, were the figureheads of a
Muslim sect, which, for both religious and practical reasons, had
adopted a more liberal attitude toward other religions.

This change from tolerance to strict orthodoxy is reflected also
in the Jewish thought of the time. Maimonides, as befitting a
great man, was tolerant by nature; this can be proved convincingly
from many of his letters. Theoretically, however, he was an un-
compromisingly orthodox Jew who regarded Judaism alone as a
real religion. On the other hand, Nethan'el Fayyumi of Yemen, a
man of far smaller stature than Maimonides, who had undergone
the influence of Fatimid religious literature, takes quite another
stand on this question. To him, the different religions are like
various medicines, each fitting the people to whom it is applied.
Religions must be different in order to suit the different tempers of
men; in essence, however, they are all alike.

No such simile would have been acceptable to Maimonides. To
him, Israel's religion was to be compared to a human being; all
other religions are only images of a human being, beautiful images
perhaps but imitations nevertheless. Maimonides' attitude, which
was shared by most of the other Jewish thinkers who wrote in
Arabic, certainly was in conformity with the Bible—which, of
course, was composed at a time when Israel's faith was the only
existent monotheistic religion. Even Maimonides must be seen in
the light of the general spiritual trends of his time.

Maimonides' main philosophical work, the *Guide of the Perplexed*, however, was studied and used copiously by non-Jewish scholars, both Muslims and Christians, and even taught by Muslim lecturers to Jewish audiences who were less familiar with the scientific thinking of the time. All this was possible because the great theological problems which occupied the medieval mind were essentially the same in the three religions. Just as in our own time the same scientific problems are handled by the scholars of the Western democracies and those of the countries behind the Iron Curtain, in the Middle Ages religious philosophy was a meeting ground for the thinkers of the three rival religions.

Naturally many of the problems which occupied the medieval Jewish philosophers have become obsolete for us, especially as far as they were concerned with the explanation of the physical world. They were embarked on an exploration of the nature of God rather than the needs of man. Their very aim is foreign to modern thinking which centers most intensely around the human mind. Precisely because of this difference, however, it is most challenging to become acquainted with those grand edifices erected by creative minds under circumstances so distant from ours.

I can never read the last chapter of the *Guide of the Perplexed* without the deepest emotion. Here Maimonides tries to prove— and his arguments sound so perfectly convincing!—that the only ultimate goal for which it is worthwhile to live is pure, abstract thinking. Even ethics which, after all, deal essentially with the imperfections of human nature, must be regarded only as a preparatory stage. This ideal of pure thinking, which has its roots in Greek philosophy and its Muslim interpretation, is illustrated by Maimonides through a series of such brilliantly chosen quotations from the Bible and other Hebrew literature that one leaves the book with the impression of the perfect harmony which prevailed among the three worlds united as they were in the mind of the great thinker. Thus, the *Guide of the Perplexed* is a great monument of Jewish-Arab symbiosis, not merely because it is written in Arabic by an original Jewish thinker and was studied by Arabs, but because it developed and conveyed to large sections of the ʃewish people ideas which had so long occupied the Arab mind.

Although Jewish-Arab philosophy cannot be regarded as uniform, it constitutes notwithstanding a definite body of thinking, which is characteristically distinct from its Muslim counterpart. It is, of course, impossible to describe the difference in a few words; questions about which so many generations have thought so intensively have produced subtle and elaborate answers that make any short definition outrageously crude.

One might gain an insight into these matters by comparing the 13 Articles of Faith, printed in every Jewish prayer book, with the various Muslim creeds, translated and lucidly explained by the Dutch scholar A. J. Wensinck in his book, *The Muslim Creed* (Cambridge University Press 1943, particularly p. 191).

However, after all the necessary reservations have been stated, it is truly said that the unanimous belief of the Jewish thinkers, most emphatically expressed by men so different as Saʿadya, Bahya and Maimonides, was that man is free and lord of his destiny, and, therefore, inexorably responsible for all he does, while the prevailing mood in Muslim theology was that man is determined, subjected to predestination and consequently forced to rely on mercy rather than on his own good deeds.

In a recent painstaking study on the nature and origin of Muslim fatalism (W. Montgomery Watt, *Free Will and Predestination in Early Islam*, London 1948) the author assumes (pp. 168–9) that "the sense of being determined, of being passive in the hands of some other, was a thought deep in the . . . unconscious of the peoples of the Middle East" before Islam, obviously as the outcome of many centuries of foreign domination.

It would appear that it is not actual experience—for who could have had a more crushing lesson of life than the Jewish people? —which makes man fatalistic or free-minded, but an inherent, fundamental, religious attitude. That of Israel is expressed in the teachings of the Book of Deuteronomy (30:19): "I have set before you life and death . . . therefore, choose life"; that of Islam is found in the extensive utterings of Muhammad on the subject during the latter part of his prophetic career. The innumerable shades of doctrine expounded by Muslim and Jewish theologians were only variations of the one fundamental belief of each religion.

There were other differences, e.g., the insistence of orthodox Jewish theologians on a purely spiritual conception of God—although in early Islamic times, in the pre-philosophical period, it was precisely the Jews who were rightly blamed for their gross anthropomorphisms—while official Islam was less opposed to popular ideas about God's appearance. The attitude of the Jewish theologians in this matter goes back also to the beginnings of Israel's religion, which was born out of the fight against "any graven image and any likeness."

However, nothing is perhaps more telling than the fact that the most authoritative doctor of Jewish law and theology, Maimonides, was a physician—i.e., a man of secular erudition—and a philosopher, while in Islam this combination was the exception rather than the rule. The most representative Muslim theologian was of another type; he combined the study of law and theology with the "Way" of Mysticism. This leads us to another profound difference between the two communities, one which will be discussed presently.

4. *Islamic and Jewish Mysticism.*

Besides its exquisite art and handicraft, possibly the finest contribution of Islam to general human culture is *Sufism*, its pietist and mystic movement, which, during many centuries, meant highest exaltation for the select few and an elixir of life for the masses. To renounce the world, to wipe out one's own small personality and to find oneself again in the all-embracing unity of God—this is the ultimate goal of *Sufism*, which man can reach only in the rapture of ecstasy, after passing through many "stations" on a "way" to ever-higher perfection.

Like Muslim theology and philosophy, *Sufism* was not a homogeneous, uniform body of tenets and practices, but an extremely ramified movement with distinct stages of development. A succinct, but most substantial account of the mystics of Islam is found in Professor A. J. Arberry's *Sufism* (London 1950), while in another small but equally informative volume by the same author, somewhat misleadingly called *The History of Sufism* (London 1952) the history and problems of the research into this unique movement are discussed. These short books may serve also as an authoritative guide to the literature on the subject.

In its higher form, the main inspiration for *Sufism* seems to lie in Greek sources. Plato's theory of knowledge, which teaches that in order to be able to know a certain object, the student must have in himself something of the nature of the object studied, logically leads to the assumption that man cannot know God fully except by sharing God's nature, by—being God.

In its earlier stages, however, as has become evident recently, *Sufism* is the direct outcome of the ascetic trend of religiosity, prevailing in original Islam itself which, later, was supplemented and enriched by foreign sources, in particular Christianity and Buddhism. To these often-discussed borrowings, we have to add those taken from Judaism.

The literary evidence for these connections is to be found in a monograph, published in the quarterly *Tarbiz* (vol. 6), on Malik ibn Dinar, the head of the second generation of the Iraqian mystics, who quotes copiously from Jewish sources. No such habit was ever indulged in by his master, the famous Hasan Basri. However, it is not so much these express quotations as the great similarity between the early Muslim pietists and the *Hasidim* known to us from talmudic literature, which suggests some connection between the two.

These *Hasidim* excelled in observing most minutely the commandments of the law and doing more than is prescribed in the law in their dealings with their fellowmen. Indeed, loving kindness and overscrupulousness in their dealings with other people marked the early *Hasidim*. They criticized all luxury, even in the building of synagogues; they were particularly careful in avoiding any contact with government or even Jewish authorities, as these were regarded as unfair to the common people; in dress and behavior the *Hasidim* appeared as mourners; their favorite biblical book was the Psalms and their saint, so to speak, was David, the pious king, who spent his nights in prayer; they used to formulate their tenets in short, enigmatic utterings of a mystical flavor and purposely addressed people in paradoxically styled admonitions, and cared not at all whether they were regarded as fools. Anyone familiar with the literature on the ancient Muslim mystics will agree that each detail mentioned here with regard to the *Hasidim* of the Talmud applies also to them.

Many of the early *Hasidim* were famed for being holy men, whom the Prophet Elijah visited as a matter of daily occurrence, or whose prayer for rain was believed to be absolutely effective. This *Hasidism* was a way of life rather than an organized movement, although the Talmud speaks of a special burial-place for *Hasidim*, just as there were in use special graveyards for priests, judges, and other distinguished groups.

It was related to, but not identical with, the early Jewish mysticism or gnosticism of the *Hekhalot* (The Heavenly Palaces), which reached its peak in the centuries immediately preceding Islam (most authoritatively described in the second chapter of Gershom Scholem's *Major Trends in Jewish Mysticism*, Jerusalem 1941, New York 1946). Both *Hasidism* and *Hekhalot* mysticism, both of which found expression also in a highly developed religious poetry (the *Piyyut*), were careful to remain inside rabbinical Judaism, and in particular the more famous *Hasidim* were at the same time notable bearers of the Oral Law—just as the pious ascetics of early Islam.

It was necessary to give some details about the seldom treated *Hasidism* of talmudic times, in order to bring out in full relief the peculiar relation between Judaism and *Sufism*, the great pietistic movement of Islam. As we have seen, there existed some contacts between the early ascetics of Basra and the Jewish *Hasidim*, and in Sufic writings in general the "pious men of the Children of Israel" were a favorite object of edifying stories, some actually found in Jewish literature and some spurious. However, the influence of

Islam on Judaism in this respect was of far greater moment, although, as we shall presently see, at a certain stage, there was a point beyond which Judaism firmly refused to go along.

Islam had two advantages over Judaism. First, it could draw on a huge reservoir of human resources. The hundred years' war of Muhammadan conquests were a great catastrophe for the countries affected. Millions of people were reduced to slavery and dragged from one part of the world to another. However, this great mixing of classes and races had also the beneficial effect that fresh minds were prepared for the new Arabic-speaking civilization of the Middle East. Thus, of the two leading figures of early Iraqian asceticism mentioned above, the first, Hasan Basri, was the son of a captive, who followed his master to Medina from Maisan in southern Babylonia, while Malik ibn Dinar's father was made a slave in Kabul in far-away Afghanistan.

The Jews, however, were famous for their strict endogamy (a fact to which, as we have seen, an early Muslim writer attributed their incapacity for philosophical reasoning) and were necessarily limited in number.

Secondly, the Muslims had a superior tool in the rich and well-organized Arabic language. Where the Jewish gnostics of the fifth and sixth centuries stammered, the Muslim mystics of the ninth and tenth centuries were able to speak out eloquently. Thus, despite the largely common background, Muslim pietism became a far more complete and impressive system of thought and morals than early *Hasidism* was, and was able, in its turn, to exercise a tremendous influence on Jewish minds, who were well prepared to accept it.

About direct contacts with a Muslim *Hasid* we hear, most significantly from the Palestinian Gaon (spiritual head of the Jewish community) Solomon ben Yehuda, who died at a very ripe age in 1051 and whose letters, of which about seventy, mostly written in beautiful Hebrew, have been preserved, betray the atmosphere of the Muslim pietist mood.

Definite traces of Sufic influence are to be found in the poems of the Gaon's Spanish contemporary Ibn Gabirol, while Bahya's

The Duties of the Heart, written in Arabic about 1075, denotes the first full reception of Muslim "ascetic theology" into Judaism.

In its Hebrew translation, *The Duties of the Heart* became the most popular Jewish book of devotion, so much so that even the great Goldziher confessed that he could not escape its spell; it was translated into the various Jewish vernaculars, including spoken Arabic. (Such a retranslation in the vernacular of the isle of Djerba, Tunisia, appeared in print as late as 1919). There are renditions into all the main modern languages used by Jews.

Although Bahya, as D. H. Baneth has shown, has made use of sources other than Muslim (Greek doctrines, transmitted probably by an Arabic-writing Christian), he is, in spirit as well as in matter, a direct offspring of Muslim pietism. Goldziher and A. S. Yahuda, the editor of the Arabic original of Bahya, and a number of other scholars have collected much material to prove this, and recently George Vajda of Paris has defined Bahya's relation to his Muslim models more exactly.

Bahya's teachings, which designate the Love of God as the center and goal of human life and postulate permanent examination of one's conscience and the practice of world-denial, echo the great pietists of the Muslim East. So greatly was Bahya—by profession a doctor of the Jewish Law—impressed by them, that he uses their writings profusely even when he might as easily have quoted a passage from the Talmud for the same purpose.

Of Bahya's various successors only one must be mentioned here: Abraham Maimuni, the worthy son of the great Maimonides. As Professor Abraham J. Heschel of New York and others have emphasized of late, even the "rationalist" Maimonides was not devoid of mystical elements in his thinking. With his son Abraham, however, Pietism in the Sufi sense of the word became the rallying cry of the day.

In his great Compendium called *The Complete (Guide) for the Servants of God,* two volumes of which have been edited and translated into English by Professor Samuel Rosenblatt under the title *Highways of Perfection* (Baltimore 1927 and 1938), Abraham Maimuni states expressly that, to his mind, in some respects the

Sufi masters have more faithfully preserved the ways of the prophets than the Jews themselves.

Unlike Bahya, however, he finds the whole material for his teachings in Jewish sources. On the other hand, he did not confine himself to preaching and writing but, in collaboration with other *Hasidim*, tried to introduce a number of Muslim religious practices, congenial to him, into the Jewish rite—a detail to which we will return later.

Despite the great dependence of medieval Jewish piety on Sufism, there was one point on which it parted company. Judaism never consented to blur the distinction between the Creator and the created. Love of God, emulation of God, nearness to Him, longing for Him—yes; but union or identification with Him, this idea meant to Jews—at least to Jews living inside the Muslim civilization—nothing but blasphemy and self-deification.

The joyous cry of a Muslim mystic: "Glory to Me! How great is My Majesty" would have been an abomination for Orthodox Jews and Pietists alike. Some daring verses by al-Hajjaj, the mystic of Bagdad famous for his saying, "I am the Truth (i.e., God)," who was "crucified" in 922, certainly were used by Jews, as they have been found in Hebrew transcriptions, but, as a whole, Muslim impact on Jews has not led them to ecstatic mysticism.

The reason for this absence of ecstatic mysticism of the Sufic type in Jewish piety may be accounted for by the greater inner unity of Judaism, while Islam, as Professor Levi Della Vida explained in a searching analysis, published in the *Crozer Journal* 1944, never reached that integration. However, there may be other reasons for this difference.

Ecstatic *Sufism* made extensive use of the social phenomenon of the exclusively male society of Islam. "The unbearded young man" was taken as an image of the divine beauty. Gazing upon him could convey an idea of the beauty of the original. Conceptions like these might have given rise to the loftiest relations between Master and Disciple; they became, however, too ready an excuse for a vice, which Judaism has always regarded with par-

ticular abhorrence (although, naturally, it also sometimes penetrated into Oriental Jewish circles).

Whatever the reasons may have been, it is remarkable that one
of the most exquisite aspects of Muslim civilization, ecstatic mysticism, is missing from the Jewish religion of that time. Jewish
mysticism, the *Kabbala*, developed along quite different lines, and,
in the main, on Christian soil. It seems, however, that individual
Jews—like other non-Muslims—have sometimes been attracted by
Sufism and through it by Islam in general—a fact which possibly
contributed to the decline in the number of Jewish intelligentsia
in Muslim countries in the latter Middle Ages.

The revival of Oriental Judaism in the sixteenth and seventeenth
centuries is no doubt due largely to the Kabbalistic reform movement of Isaac Lurya and his successors, which directed the craving
for mystical exaltation into new, original, Jewish channels. The
spell of Sufism did not cease, however, to exercise its influence on
Jews in later times. The missionary Joseph Wolff describes in 1831
"a sort of Judaized Sufism," practiced by the Jews of Meshed
(quoted by W. J. Fischel in his *Israel in Iran*), while as late as 1941
a professing Jew presided over a circle of non-Jewish *Sufis* in
Teheran. How far the close connection between present-day Jews
and Muslim mystics of Damascus, described in a well-known
novel of the prominent Hebrew writer Yehuda Burla, are fiction
or based on reality—escapes my knowledge.

For various reasons, Sufism, in particular in its organized form
of *Dervish* orders, has sunk into deep disrepute among modernish
Muslims. Not only in Turkey, but even in Egypt, the *Sufi* con-
vents have been converted into schools or other buildings of public
utility. There are, however, already significant beginnings of an
intellectual Neo-*Sufism*, which forms an interesting parallel to the
Jewish Neo-*Hasidism*, associated by many with the name of Martin Buber.

5. *The Acme of Jewish-Arab Symbiosis: The Hebrew Poetry of the Middle Ages.*

The most perfect expression of Jewish-Arab symbiosis is not found in the *Arabic* literature of the Jews, but in the *Hebrew* poetry created in Muslim countries, particularly in Spain.

A poem by, perhaps, Yehuda Halevi—graceful in form, unfailing in wording, forceful in feeling and thought, overwhelms the reader with that complete harmony which is the surest indication of true culture. This applies especially to religious poetry which is our most precious heritage from Hebrew-Arab Spain. Although one can respond to Halevi without knowing anything about the Arabic language, literature or prosody, it is, precisely, because the Arabic influence is subtle in him that it is the more significant and vital.

Religious poetry had been a very important branch of Hebrew literature before Islam. It had a permanent place in life, for the synagogue service consisted partly of fixed prayers and partly of improvisations which were recited by their authors—as a kind of offering to God—during the intervals between the prayers or after their conclusion. Successful poems themselves became part of the official service which thus grew longer and longer in the course of time.

By contrast, the Muslim service is short and consists of a few impressive prayers and formulas, repeated as often as fourteen to twenty times a day. The common service on Friday or on Festivals varies little. Even the collections of prayers for the assemblies of pietists or mystics consist mainly of passages from the Koran or other religious books, or in litanies of little poetical value. The Muslims do not possess a prayer book composed of religious poems, such as that used by the Protestant or Jewish communities. I cannot recall an Arabic word which corresponds to *Siddur*, the Hebrew "mass-book," which contains the official rites of the service, or the *Mahzor*, the "collection," which includes the additions for the Festivals and other special occasions. (The Yemenite Jews have an Arabic name for the latter; they call it *Tiklal*, that which

contains everything; the official prayers—although very extensive
—are known by heart and are therefore not contained in a separate
book.)

In any case, nothing in Islam can be compared to the rich development of the Jewish prayer book. Each country, and often
various towns in the same country, possessed a body of religious
poetry of their own. A number of these books have been printed.
And yet, all of them taken together contain only a fraction of the
poems actually created, as we may conclude from the *diwans*, collections of poems, of various authors, or, as we may judge, from the
many poems which have been retrieved from the Cairo Geniza.

Nevertheless, the influence of Arabic on Hebrew medieval poetry
was enormous. A secular Hebrew poetry came into being, or, more
correctly—as we will explain later—its production became fashionable and was practiced by the most prominent authors. As is natural, and verifiable in talmudical literature, there also existed in
the centuries preceding Islam a popular secular poetry among the
Jews. But it has not been preserved. Only religious subjects were
deemed worthy of transmission to posterity. To be sure, even the
greatest Hebrew poets of Arabic times, whose output of secular
poetry was considerable, had scruples. They wondered whether the
holy language of the Bible should be applied to such subjects as
love, such forms as panegyrics or satire. But, as very devout Muslims so occupied themselves all their lives, Jewish poets felt that
they could do the same. They even came to believe that by so
doing they strengthened Jewish self-respect by proving that the
holy Hebrew language was able to achieve the same feats as its
younger sister, Arabic.

Thus, it was the influence of Arabic on Hebrew which made the
rise of medieval Hebrew poetry possible. The language of the
Piyyut, the Jewish religious poetry which arose in pre-Islamic
times, was rich and imaginative, but it was undisciplined, erratic,
and sometimes even bizarre. It was from Arabic that the Jews received the idea of a "pure," classical language. As a model, there
served the text of the Bible, whose pronunciation, spelling, grammar, and vocabulary were eagerly studied by the Jews in all Islamic

countries. The Hebrew poets, however, did not confine themselves to biblical Hebrew. Detailed modern research from Leopold Zunz to our own time proves that they used many words and forms not contained in the Bible. But the biblical text—just as the text of the Koran and the classical poetry served for Arabic—was always offered as "proof," as "testimony," as the criterion of good form. Like any purism, such classicist rigor had its drawbacks. As a whole, however, it contributed much to the revival of the Hebrew language; it perfected it as a working tool which could be handled with ease and precision.

Apart from the general impact of Arabic on Hebrew, the very forms and motifs of Hebrew poetry, like Persian, were largely indebted to the Arabic model. Pre-Islamic Hebrew poetry employed rhyme, and, as J. Schirmann's searching study, "Hebrew Liturgical Poetry and Christian Hymnology" (*Jewish Quarterly Review*, Philadelphia, October 1953) has shown, it may even be that it was there adopted for the first time systematically. But many other formal elements, such as the use of different meters, and the subtle and most effective arrangement of the stanzas were directly borrowed from the Arabic.

Fortunately, in the eleventh century, when Hebrew poetry had fully perfected its new style, Arabic poetry had already given up much of its old rigidity and had absorbed many of the elastic and graceful forms of the popular song. It may be that even Spanish songs have found their echo in Arabic and, ultimately, in Hebrew poetry. At least we find in both, and even in a poet of the rank of Yehuda Halevi, the strange practice of concluding love-songs with a verse in Spanish. As M. Stern has convincingly demonstrated (in his *Les chansons Mozarabes*, Palermo 1953), these Spanish verses had come to the Jews through Arabic. The Hebrew poets, like their Arab colleagues, sometimes concluded with a verse in vernacular, local (not classical) Arabic, which may also show the influence of popular poetry on their themes, and, in particular, on their prosody. In the latter Middle Ages it was common—and had its counterpart, for example, in Persian or in Italian—to write alternately one stanza in Hebrew and one in Arabic, and even in a third or fourth language. Such "play on language" did not, generally, produce real poetry. In Yemen, however, where the Jewish-Arabic symbiosis had been most prolonged and intensive, the situation was unique. There the Hebrew poets of the sixteenth and seventeenth centuries and, in particular, the greatest of them, Shalom Shabazi (or Abbo Sholoem, as he is called in his native district) wrote many poems alternately in Hebrew and Arabic stanzas, and these appeal to the reader as sincere creations. They are sung even today, and may be heard at many a wedding or circumcision feast, or other social gatherings. More and more, however, the singers skip over the Arabic stanzas, as their semi-classical language is no longer fully understood.

The Arabic influence on Hebrew rhetoric was also great. Striking metaphors and similes, audacious comparisons and contrasts, "surprising" openings and endings and many other devices of artful speech were borrowed by the Jews from the Arabs. To be sure, many prophetic speeches preserved in the Bible betray powerful eloquence and talmudical sayings are often formulated in pointed and effective language reminiscent of Greek oratory. But these sporadic outbursts of a natural gift for speech are a far cry from the refined, systematic and self-conscious art of rhetoric displayed by the Hebrew poets of the Middle Ages under Arabic influence.

For our taste, the Hebrew poets, like their Arabic masters, indulged a little too much in their newly acquired art. Nevertheless, to the traditional (and not only the Oriental) listener, the mere intellectual delight in the rhetorical refinement of a piece is apt to arouse feelings which the contents of the text itself would not warrant. I remember attending a Yemenite funeral at which a professional mourner, using (as I knew) hand-written specimens of dirges, praised the dead; he had hardly begun his artistic performance when the whole audience burst into tears. It was not the force or novelty of feeling but the striking and subtle formulation which produced that effect.

But it was in dealing with religious themes, which stirred the hearts of the medieval Hebrew poets more deeply than anything else, for which their training in rhetoric prepared them to make the most glorious performances. Their claim that the holy Hebrew language surpassed in beauty even the Arabic seemed to be justified in this field. While reading their works, one, so to speak, takes part in the creative mastery of the language. The old Hebrew peasants' speech became pliable, almost elegant under their trained hands. The particular charm of their style lies in the exquisite refinement and artistry of Arabic rhetoric, moderated by the innate simplicity and straightforwardness of Hebrew.

Naturally, much depended on the personal talent of each poet. However, of the three great masters of Spanish Hebrew poetry, Solomon Ibn Gabirol, Moses Ibn Ezra, and Yehuda Halevi—above all the latter—it can be said that they reached the highest degree of both forceful and sincere poetical expression in their religious creations—religious in the widest sense of the word. Many others, such as Samuel the *Nagid* (or head of Spanish Jewry), Abraham Ibn Ezra, and Yehuda al-Harizi, also attained in many of their poems a highly dignified and imaginative style.

It is interesting to note that the very themes which ran through the Arabic models were taken over by the Hebrew poets; more precisely, it was their aim to express in Hebrew the ideas which were regarded by existing temporary society as proper for poetical formulation. Every detail, even in the most moving elegy on such apparently subjective themes as lack of recognition, the faithlessness of friends, the stupidity of one's compatriots, must be scrutinized to determine whether or not it contains a traditional motif rather than a personal experience. (Of course, then, as always, people usually experienced only what they had read first in books, or, in our time, seen in movies.)

One example may suffice. Since the times of *The Song of Songs*, the hair of the beloved has been described as being as black as a raven, as dark as the night. The latter simile is artistically expanded in one of Yehuda Halevi's poems (see *Selected Poems*, translated into English by Nina Salaman, Philadelphia 1946, p. 48). Normally, however, his lady has golden hair (*sahov* in Hebrew, which may be red or auburn). Therefore, while admiring her glowing cheeks, which, so to speak, lent their color to her hair, he says (*ibid*, p. 55):

> She was like the sun, making red, in her rising,
> The clouds of dawn with the flame of her light.

Similarly, in another poem, not included in the selection just quoted, Halevi sees the perfection of beauty in that golden hair. Now *Sefaradi* girls, i.e., girls from the Jewish community which originated in Spain, often are endowed with particularly lustrous, auburn hair. In addition, even in pre-Islamic poetry Jews were described as having hair of such color (*suhb*, which is the same word as the Hebrew, mentioned above). Thus it is perfectly feasible that Yehuda Halevi's mistress—if he had one at all—had indeed such coloring. We know, however, that some of his Arab compatriots also used to attribute to their mistresses that particular charm. Thus it is more than likely that it was the simile of the sun and the golden clouds rather than a lady with golden hair herself that enchanted the poet—as well as his audience.

This brings us to a most important point: the social function of Hebrew poetry in Arab countries. This subject, which has been particularly emphasized by the late Benjamin Klar and by J. G. Weiss, needs further study. In the light of the Geniza findings—and other manuscript sources from the eastern countries of Islam, which have been somehow neglected, this aspect of medieval Hebrew poetry demands further treatment.

As we saw in chapter VI, a new Jewish society of business and professional men emerged during the ninth and tenth centuries, a society with time and money at its disposal, a society of wider spiritual needs and a more refined taste. The fashionable pastime of Arabic-speaking society, whether Muslim, Christian or Jewish, was poetry. Between that pastime and the traditional education of the Jews, which consisted in the study of the Bible, the Talmud, the contemporary religious literature, and the synagogical poetry, there lay a gap which threatened to destroy the very unity of the Jewish people. Here, the new secular Hebrew poetry fulfilled a great social function inasmuch as it employed all the traditional elements of Jewish education for producing those aesthetic objects which were regarded as indispensable to social life.

Thus, a love-song, although addressed to a girl in the most personal terms, certainly was composed for recitation to a large crowd, presumably at a wedding or a similar occasion. A genuine Jewish or Muslim wedding was a very extended affair, lasting sometimes two weeks, with several days and all the evenings devoted to social gatherings. The poets and the musicians had to provide entertainment. As can be observed today, perhaps at a Yemenite wedding, three types of poetry were recited on such occasions: one had direct bearing on the event and even on the personalities of the young couple, the families and their guests (countless poems of this type exist in Hebrew); secondly, religious poems, those which praised Israel as God's bride, or others which had no relation to the subject of the wedding at all; and, finally, "songs for pastime"—those which are connected with the subject of love, but which would not appear at all to modern taste to be appropriate for the occasion of a wedding. Among these one would hear the most vehement complaints of a wife against the husband who neglected her, or listen to tales of the misery of married life in general, or hear of love scenes, quite incompatible with the social standing of the young couple. We can safely infer that the many medieval Hebrew poems about "the separation from the beloved" or "the chiding of the cruel girl" or similar subjects actually were recited or sung at weddings and other social gatherings.

But poetry to the Arabs was more than a pastime. It was their most powerful means of publicity. Just as a well-to-do and influential man of our own day wants to have appropriate coverage by a respectable newspaper of the engagement or marriage of his daughter, the promotion of his son to a professorship, the birth of an heir, or the death of his father, exactly in the same way did an Arab or Jewish notable of the Middle Ages publicize and possibly perpetuate such events through one or several poems, written by a distinguished poet especially for the occasion.

A passage in a letter by a prominent Hebrew writer of the tenth century to Hasdai Ibn Shaprut, the leading Jewish statesman of that time, is illustrative. He describes how the latter came to him at midnight by foot (and not on his mule—the equivalent of the modern car), asking him to write a dirge for his mother who had just passed away. He found the poet already engaged in the task! Such dirges, as we know from another passage by the same writer, were recited at the funeral and repeated by the whole congregation during the seven days of mourning.

Furthermore, men engaged in business or in the service of the state, needed publicity for the very preservation of their respective positions. Business, as we have seen in chapter VI, was largely denominational in organization. Even a Jewish court banker had to have, first of all, the confidence of the Jewish merchants, who would lend their money to the government through him. Therefore, a panegyric by a Hebrew poet served well the purpose of publicity. We find that a *Nagid*, or head of the Jewish community, in Aden durng the thirteenth century, sent ample donations to a well-known Spanish poet whose home-town was on the international highway between Spain and India. The Representative of the Merchants (see chapter VI) in the same town, who died in 1151, was eager to receive formal eulogies from the merchants who passed through his city and who were poets themselves. Indeed, the ability to write Hebrew verses was an accomplishment often found in Jewish gentlemen within Arab Muslim civilization. Just as an Arab historian quotes many a verse written by a Muslim merchant stopping at Aden, the Geniza has preserved not only the business papers of a very successful Jewish India merchant from Tunis who arrived in Aden but also his songs of praise and a dirge which he composed on the death of the Representative there. One of his panegyrics has been found (in Cairo, of course!) in two copies, which indicates that it carried out its publicity purpose well.

As medieval Hebrew poetry served such an important function in the Jewish society inside Muslim civilization, it can serve, to a certain extent, as a true mirror of that society. This applies in particular to the type of poetry which is known in Arabic under the name of *Maqama*, and in Hebrew, *Mahberet*, a mixture of narrative, description, and satire with special emphasis on puns and verbal witticisms. The crown of achievement in this genre is unanimously given to Hariri, a citizen of Basra in southern Iraq, who lived at the beginning of the eleventh century. The rendering of his *Maqamas* into Hebrew by al-Harizi, who lived in Spain about a hundred years later, is the greatest linguistic feat ever performed in that language. However, for the modern reader, al-Harizi's original book of Hebrew *Maqamas*, the *Tahkemoni*, is far more interesting. For the journeys of Hariri's hero were all imaginary, but al-Harizi actually made the long trip from Spain to Bagdad and puts into the mouth of his hero his many experiences with the Jewish communities along the way. But even the purely literary sections of the *Tahkemoni* and even those which are imitations of older sources possess deep significance for the social life of their period and at the same time make excellent reading.

Of these literary sections I wish to mention one, the *Maqama* of the successful businessman, which is in the main a Hebrew replica of an Arabic original of the tenth century. The poet visits a rich merchant, with the intention, of course, of receiving from him remuneration for services done or offered. However, the latter is so busy explaining to him how wonderful, how really first-class is everything he possesses, that the poet never gets an opportunity to utter his request. The merchant takes him through his house and his garden, and shows him—with great pride and many enthusiastic comments—all his furniture, his dishes and vessels, his garments and slaves.

His enthusiasm reaches its summit when he leads his unhappy visitor to his ultra-modern bathroom which shines in its glazed tiles and other modern conveniences. When, during a stay in the United States, a successful businessman concluded the tour of his home with the same detail, I got a vivid feeling for that mercantile civilization of the medieval Middle East to which reference has been made so often in this book!

Considering the origins of medieval Hebrew poetry, one is not surprised to learn that the leading work dealing with the theory of Hebrew poetry, a book by the great master Moses Ibn Ezra, was written in Arabic and not in the language with which it deals.

Moreover, while other Jewish-Arabic books dealing with theoretical subjects (the Hebrew language, philosophy, and even astronomy and mathematics) were eagerly sought after by the Jews living in Christian Europe and were translated into Hebrew for their benefit, often shortly after having been written, no translation of Moses Ibn Ezra's *Ars Poetica* is known from the Middle Ages. (A Hebrew edition by Professor B. Halper of Dropsie College, Philadelphia, appeared in 1924). What is clear from this example is that Hebrew poetry in Spain was a product of Arab Muslim civilization. Nevertheless it found its way to the Jews of Christian Europe, partly—particularly as far as its secular portions are concerned—through the mediation of Hebrew poetry in Italy, and mainly through the synagogue service which admitted the creations of the Spanish Hebrew poets in many places.

It is indeed the religious poetry of the Spanish Jews which is of universal and permanent value. Second to none in sincerity of feeling, richness of ideas, and force of expression, its particular contribution can be described as a passionate romanticism, which, in its turn, had its origin both in the mental make-up of the Jewish people of that time and the philosophical and mystical notions discussed in the previous sections.

According to that religious romanticism, the immortal, purely spiritual soul is full of longing for the "house of her Father." Renouncing the pleasures of this world—hard as that may be—should be no sacrifice to her, for it is the only way to real beatitude. Searching, often painful self-examination is the beginning of that path; complete satisfaction and eternal bliss its end. She—the soul is of the feminine gender in Hebrew and therefore always represented as a female being—constantly dreams of her reunion with God, the fountain of her life, and her dreams often take color from those scenes in which God was, according to the Bible, actually manifest—during the revelation on Mount Sinai or in the Temple of Jerusalem or in Elijah's vision in the desert.

From here, almost inadvertently, the poets shift to the fate of the people of Israel, which is, according to Yehuda Halevi, the heart of the world. Like the soul, which is held in the prison of the body and of this earthly existence, Israel is not where it really belongs; it lives in physical, and even more, in spiritual exile. To be sure, the pleasures of plentiful Spain are certainly more attractive than the dusty ruins of the Holy Land. But Israel—also permanently represented as a female—is prepared, like the soul, to renounce all the good things she enjoys, if her Beloved, the Almighty God, forgives her her short-comings and reunites with her in the country of her spiritual origins. The Hebrew poets of Spain, who lived during the period of the great struggle for that country between Islam and Christendom and afterwards for Palestine, naturally lived in an intense state of expectation of the religious and even the political restoration of Israel. This romantic expectation, however, was irrevocably intertwined with the general notion of the freeing of the soul from its earthly fetters and its return to its real home.

All this appears to the modern reader as very remote and abstract. However, precisely because these things were the real issues for the medieval poet, we find in his religious poems more actual experience than in his love scenes. When in a "vigil," a song to be recited in the nightly services, Yehuda Halevi describes how, while rising from his sleep at midnight, he was overcome by the majestic beauty of the starlit sky, we believe with all our hearts that he has actually had that experience. When in a morning meditation, showing him on the way to the service, he is enraptured by the marvels of the dawn, we share his feelings. No wonder that Spanish Hebrew poetry reached its peak in the cycle of poems composed by Yehuda Halevi when he decided to give up his respectable position as a physician and set out on his long journey to the Holy Land (May 1140 to February 1141), at the end of which he died. "To behold Jerusalem" at least once in one's life was regarded almost as a religious duty by the Jews living in Islamic countries. At a time when Palestine was in the hands of the Crusaders, when continuous warfare was going on in all parts of the Mediterranean, such a journey was dangerous and a great strain, particularly for a man of fifty-five, Halevi's age. However, the physical reunion with the soil of the Holy Land was to him a fore-taste of the final restoration of Israel and of the reunion of the soul with its eternal roots, while the renunciation of the pleasures of life in Spain he regarded as a practical step on the road to spiritual fulfillment. Precisely because these issues were the innermost concern of the pilgrim to Zion, Halevi's poems about his departure from Spain, his travels on the sea, and his sojourn in Egypt turned out to be intensely lively and lovably human.

What, other than the formal elements discussed at the beginning of this section, has the Arab Muslim environment contributed to the contents and development of this religious poetry? No doubt, some Islamic phrases can be discovered even in the religious language of the Spanish Jewish poets. More than one of them emphasizes that "refuge *from* God can be found only *with* God," an idea which echoes a well-known passage in the Koran. However, as J. D. Abramski has shown, the Koran passage itself was preceded by a Midrash on Exodus 14:27, where it is said of the Egyptians, "they fled *toward* Him." "One flees *from*, but not toward," muses the Midrash, and answers, "If God pursues you, it is He alone with whom you may take refuge." Thus one must be careful in ascribing to Muslim origin even those phrases which are rather common in Arabic literature, because these themselves may date back to an ancient Jewish source and which, possibly, was known to the Hebrew poets.

It is also possible that phrases which resound in Arabic literature may be nothing but actual descriptions of Jewish religious life. In one of his wonderful "vigils," Yehuda Halevi admonishes himself to follow in the footsteps of those "whose days are passed in fasting and whose nights in prayer"—a phrase familiar from Muslim pietist literature. Still, we know from medieval Jewish sources that during the forty days preceding the Day of Atonement pious men used to fast in the daytime; "vigils" were, and still are, held in Jewish communities all over the Muslim world during that period. I may remark in passing that the forty days' fast is also still observed by some Oriental Jews of the older generation. Thus Yehuda Halevi, while using the phrase quoted above, no doubt alluded to the realities of Jewish life, while his formulation probably echoed Arabic usage.

However, the most important contribution of Arabic literature toward the development of Hebrew religious poetry—as far as I can see—does not consist in the provision of actual models, or even in the formal elements, but in the spirit which pervaded Islamic civilization as a whole and which enabled the Jews within it to develop intensive, completely harmonious spiritual life of their own. Muslim philosophy and theology, pietism and mysticism, through their Jewish counterparts, are mirrored in the Hebrew poetry of the Middle Ages. The result was perfect. The Hebrew poet could draw in full measure from a civilization which was closely akin to his own, while at the same time cherishing a strong transcendental belief in the mission of Israel.

6. *Other Spiritual Contacts.*

a. SECTARIANISM AND MESSIANIC MOVEMENTS

The most characteristic but also the most evasive field in which Islam stamped itself upon Judaism is the rise and development of the Jewish sects during the early centuries of the Muslim era. Impressed by the theological and legal terminology of the Arabic-writing sectarians of later times, or misled by seeming similarities, Jewish historiography, with such notable exceptions as S. A. Poznanski or Salo W. Baron, has been inclined to see Muslim influence where indeed far more complicated historical processes were in operation.

Similarly, ancient Muslim historians—out of, of course, completely different motives—attributed to Jews a decisive influence on the rise of the first Muslim sects. While reading Saif Ibn Omar, one of the earliest Muslim writers, one receives the impression that the great schism between the Sunnites, the main branch of the Muslim community, and the Shi'ites, the followers of Ali, the son-in-law of Muhammad, was mainly the outcome of the machinations of a Yemenite Jew, called Abdallah Ibn Saba. This Jew taught the Muslims that Ali was not really dead, but only hidden, and would come back in time to establish the kingdom of God. And there were other heretical notions attributed to Ibn Saba, which formed the theoretical base of the early Shi'ite creed. Now, the idea that the Messiah would be defeated, hide, and eventually reappear, is indeed found in pre-Islamic Jewish literature, and, as we shall see later on, the Jewish sagas about "the End of the Days" were eagerly sought after by the Muslim storytellers. However, there can be no doubt that Jewish influence on the formation of the early Muslim sects was at most of secondary importance.

Naturally, the case was somewhat different with regard to the rise of Jewish sects inside Muslim civilization. Our knowledge of the early sects and of the beginnings of Karaism, which finally united all the dissenting movements, is at present incomplete, for the sectarian writings of the seventh and eighth centuries have not yet been retrieved; even of those of the ninth century only short compositions or small portions of works have come down to us. Extensive and complete books survive only from the tenth century onwards, about 250 years after the first beginnings of the sectarian activities. One can easily imagine how incomplete and biased such late information is. Fortunately, information about the early sects is contained also in Muslim writers, but these too are not older than the tenth century and their descriptions, naturally, are limited in scope.

Sectarians are men who strive to win over their whole community to certain tenets, practices, and actions, and who, on failing, become a minority, more or less loosely connected with their people. Like their Muslim counterparts, all the early Jewish sects in Islam were of a religious-political character. It is significant that they first arose where Jews lived in compact groups—around the Persian towns of Isfahan and Hamadan, the two colonies founded by the Persian Jewish Queen Shushan-Dukht, mentioned in chapter VI.

We are comparatively well informed about the founder of the oldest known Jewish sect in Islamic times, Abu 'Isa al-Isfahani, who was called in Hebrew, Isaac son of Jacob, but who was known under his bynames, "the Servant of God," "Abu 'Isa," which means Father of (a man called) Jesus, or even "Muhammad son of Jesus." According to the tenth-century Karaite writer Kirkisani, our best source, Abu 'Isa was active under the Umayyad caliph Abd el-Malik (685–705), certainly in the years 685 to 692 when the Muslim world was divided betwen two rivaling caliphs and was plagued by the riots of bellicose religious factions. In Iraq, the Shi'ites were led at that time by an Arab who was both a prophet and an astute politician and who acted on behalf of a son of Ali. Similarly, but even more outspoken, Abu 'Isa insisted he was a prophet and a forerunner of the Messiah. He collected an army to redeem the Jews "from their oppressors." It is not impossible that he believed himself invulnerable or, further, that he surrounded himself by an impregnable, magical circle made of myrtle twigs, although such beliefs are more characteristic of the time of the later sources which report those stories (see below). In any case, he was killed in battle and his army dispersed. Other uprisings of this kind were also crushed, and it may well be that the disappearance of the Jewish village population in the Arab East was partly caused by the negative outcome of such Messianic upheavals. Abu 'Isa's movement became a religious sect, the remnants of which were found as late as the tenth century even in Damascus, a town rather remote from Isfahan, its place of origin.

The greatest innovation in Abu 'Isa's teachings was the doctrine that Jesus and Muhammad were true messengers of God and that it was, therefore, recommended, although not obligatory, that Jews study the holy scriptures of Christendom and Islam. At the same time he declared that the rabbis of the Talmud and their contemporary successors were equal to the prophets. This doctrine (which —according to his enemies—he had adopted in order to explain more easily his own gift of prophecy) coincides with the religious conceptions of the Muslim Prophet at the beginning of his career, but is not at all characteristic of the Islam of Abu 'Isa's time. While we may assume that he was inspired to describe himself as a religious-political leader from contemporary examples in nearby Iraq, Abu 'Isa's main spiritual inspiration originated from the same pre-Islamic theory of successive prophetical revelations which had induced Muhammad to assume the role of a prophet.

Abu 'Isa's religious injunctions bear little reference to Islam. He prohibited divorce—like the Christians—and ordered his followers to hold prayers seven times a day; this, although originating in Psalm 119:164 ("Seven times a day I praise Thee") may have something to do with the seven *Horae*, or hours of prayer, of the Christian monks. According to him, the Jews in exile should refrain from consuming meat or wine, for these were permissible only so long as animal sacrifices and wine libations were offered in the Temple of Jerusalem. Here also we find the pre-Islamic trait of Jewish asceticism and mourning for Zion.

Strangely enough, Abu 'Isa's followers were not completely repudiated by the bulk of the Jewish people, and although their writings are lost their influence is discernible in the so-called Apocalypse or Revelation of Simeon bar Yohay, which was composed in the last years of Umayyad rule (around 750). In this Apocalypse, Muhammad is described as a true prophet, sent by God in his mercy to the Arab people. There seems, however, to exist no connection between this liberal attitude of early, simple religious men and the similar approach adopted by later philosophers, such as Nethan'el Fayyumi or Ibn Kammuna (discussed above in section 3).

There were many so-called Messianic movements in Islamic countries, which, although opposed by Jewish leaders, did not result in sectarian segregation. Similarly in Islam, countless usurpers, combining personal ambition with religious and political slogans, arose and were crushed, leaving behind them no trace of sectarian formations. Closer observation reveals that there is often some coincidence in place and time between the Jewish and Muslim movements. Thus Yemen is the classical land of false Messiahs. It has become famous in Jewish literature because of Maimonides' *Epistle to Yemen* which deals with a false Messiah of his time. In the sixties and seventies of the nineteenth century, Yemenite Jewry was shaken by Messianic ardor; stirred first by a genuine saint, who paid for his beliefs with his life, and then by an impostor who took up the latter's role. A third Messiah was reported there as late as the last decade of that century. In Yemen, whose ruler is also the spiritual head of the community, each political upheaval, by force of circumstance, is mingled with religious propaganda. As such turmoils were a constant feature of the history of that country, it is natural that Jews too sometimes tried to present themselves as religious-political leaders of their own community.

From a responsum by Maimonides it is known that the Yemenite Messiah of his time literally lost his head because he firmly believed that no sword could do him harm. We have already seen that a similar belief was attributed to Abu 'Isa of Isfahan, although I doubt the accuracy of that allegation. All this has, however, a striking parallel in the death of the Central Asian Muslim saint, Abu l-Karam, who in 1239 led sixty thousand of his followers completely unarmed against the invading Mongols. The Mongol commander, taken aback by the manifestation of such faith, cautiously left his army behind and encountered Abu l-Karam alone. The Mongol commander easily killed him and then allowed his soldiers to cut down Abu l-Karam's followers.

A contemporary of the Yemenite Messiah, of whom Maimonides wrote, David Alroy, the twelfth-century Messiah of northern Mesopotamia, formed the subject of a novel by Benjamin Disraeli. Owing to new Geniza finds, we know now of four Messianic stirrings in Mesopotamia during that century. The first was originated by a woman visionary (who, by the way, tried—unsuccessfully—to remain unmarried, as befitting a saint) in Bagdad, in the years 1120 and 1121. At the same time, in 1121, a Muslim religious teacher from the same town, having gained followers in Mecca through his preaching of repentance, tried to proclaim himself caliph and usher in the era of justice, which the Muslims, like the Jews, expected at "the End of the Days." In the very same year, a Karaite Jew declared himself Messiah in Palestine, which then was largely in the hands of the Crusaders. This double coincidence is certainly significant.

A few years later, the rich and clever Bagdad Jews became the laughingstock of the whole world when they were induced by a new Messiah to renounce their earthly possessions and gathered on the roofs of their houses, expecting, as promised by their Messiah, to be miraculously flown to Palestine. In 1950, most of the Jews of Bagdad actually *were* brought to Israel by air, but eight hundred years earlier, despite great faith, the operation remained unsuccessful; "the Year of the Flight" became proverbial and a chronological landmark. It is to be noted that during the night in which the Bagdad Jews awaited their miraculous transport to Palestine, they put on green garments—what the Muslims expect to wear in Paradise.

The great schism in the Jewish community which is connected with the name of Karaism also seems to have received in its original stages general impulses from the Islamic environment rather than influence in details. It is characteristic that Anan, the founder of the sect (eighth century) still wrote in Aramaic, the language which the Jews in Iraq, Syria, and Palestine had used for over thirteen hundred years. The Karaite authors of the ninth century, such as Benjamin Nehawendi and Daniel Kumisi, wrote mainly in Hebrew, either because Aramaic was no longer generally understood or because they, who came from Persia, were not as well versed in that language as Anan, who, as a member of the family of the "Head of the Diaspora," lived in Iraq. Contrariwise, the Karaites of the tenth century composed their extensive writings almost exclusively in Arabic, and, by that time, Muslim jurisprudence and theology had indeed made its unmistakable imprint on Karaite thought and terminology.

However, the main issues which originally and chiefly occupied the early Karaites—the denial of a binding oral tradition, with the corollary of a return to the Bible (*Mi-kra*, hence the name Karaites), and the mourning for Zion, which made obligatory residence in Palestine—obviously had their origin in pre-Islamic Judaism. The two issues were interrelated. For, as Daniel Kumisi, who himself had left his homeland and settled in Palestine, pointed out, the Rabbis, the bearers of the "Oral Law," were "the teachers of the Diaspora" (or exile, *Galuth* in Hebrew). Accordingly, their teachings applied to a life in exile. With the return to the Holy Land, the law of the Bible would be reinstated in its purity.

The rise of Muslim religious law was an extremely complicated process (see, e.g., Joseph Schacht, *The Origins of Muslim Jurisprudence*, Oxford 1950). Still, the obligatory character of the *Sunna*, the living tradition traced back to Muhammad—which is different from the Koran, the verbatim word of God—was not contested by any of the contemporary religious factions of Islam, least of all by the Shi'ites, the followers of Ali, as has been assumed by Jewish historians of the nineteenth century and is still repeated in Jewish history books. On the other hand, it well may be that the general spiritual unrest of the early centuries of Islam and the tremendous dissensions among Muslims on interpretation and application of their holy book and their oral tradition, affected the Jewish community on its side by renewing the long-standing controversy on the binding nature of teachings which were not included in the canon of the Bible. It is well known that this controversy formed the main point of difference between Sadducees and Pharisees, the two leading Jewish factions in Jesus' time.

The mourning for Zion and the ideal of asceticism in the Holy Land, although pervading the whole of talmudic literature, may have received new impetus from the interest taken by the Muslim pietists and mystics in Palestine, which was regarded by them as the cradle of revelation and the refuge of the saints. There is literary evidence for the assumption that the model of the Christian hermits, who led a lonely life in the hills of Judea and the Lebanon, inspired the Muslim ascetics to follow suit. It is reported that many of the early Muslim mystics of Persia took up a solitary life in Palestine (in the wider sense of the word including the Lebanon), and it is quite possible that the increase of the Persian Muslim population in Jerusalem, referred to in chapter VI, had something to do with this trend.

In addition, just as Muslim asceticism was largely a reaction against the worldliness which set in as a result of the material prosperity following the Arab conquests, Jewish asceticism was a protest against the transformation of the Jewish people into a nation of businessmen. Iraqian and Persian Jews were the first to become prominent in business; they were also the first to produce a strong ascetic movement. It remained for the Karaites, who were critical of everything in contemporary Judaism, to become the most vociferous in their invectives against the worldliness and the oppressive ways of the rich. "The rich of the Diaspora" and "the merchants of the Diaspora," who amassed wealth abroad instead of coming to Palestine and there living a Jewish life, are a favorite topic of Daniel Kumisi, as noted in Jacob Mann's interesting summary of his Karaite studies in the *Yearbook of the Central Conference of American Rabbis,* vol. 44 (1934), especially pp. 228–9.

There may be still another medium through which the Muslim environment contributed to the rise of the great Karaite schism: by its polemics against the Judaism of the time. We have already alluded to the accusation voiced by the Muslim writer al-Jahiz that the Jews adhered to a gross, anthropomorphic conception of God. This accusation is borne out by the writings of the Jewish theosophists in vogue at that time, some of whose material was even incorporated into the official compilation of the Jewish oral teachings, the Talmud. It was against these trends of Jewish popular religion that Karaism waged war incessantly—with such complete success that all prominent representatives of Judaism in Islamic countries dissociated themselves from those elements until they came to be regarded as incompatible with Jewish religion altogether.

It is evident, however, that both the early Muslim criticism and the Karaite reaction against popular Jewish religion had its pre-Islamic antecedents. The very first Karaite author who deals with these matters at length, al-Jahiz' contemporary, Benjamin of Nehawend, does not confine his fight against anthropomorphism to the later Jewish scriptures. He tackles the problem with regard to the Bible itself, in a manner reminiscent of Philo of Alexandria and some of the prominent early Christian thinkers. According to Benjamin, the God who created the world or talked to Moses on Mount Sinai was not God himself, who is a completely spiritual essence, but an angel, who can take on bodily forms and come into contact with our physical world. There can be little doubt that, with this solution of the problem, the early Karaites followed an ancient tradition. Subsequently, the doubts or the criticism which gave rise to such solutions must also have been far older than the Muslim writers who voiced them.

The Karaite schism took advantage of the political divisions in the Muslim Empire. Anan, the founder of the sect, was heir to the throne of the *Resh Galutha*, or "Head of the Diaspora," and it is said that he started the schism because his younger brother was nominated to that office in his stead. In any case, his descendants emigrated to Palestine, which, from the middle of the ninth century onwards, was largely connected with Egypt and independent of Bagdad. There was, of course, no point in assuming in Palestine the title of *Resh Galutha*. Therefore, Anan's descendants styled themselves *Nasi* or Patriarch, the title held by the head of Palestinian Jewry in Roman times. With the growing importance of Egypt, a Karaite *Nasi* came to be found there as well.

It has rightly been stated that the Karaite schism was a great rejuvenating force in Judaism. In itself it was by no means uniformly rational in its approach to religion; nevertheless, its leading authorities were rationalists, who forced their opponents to fight them with their own weapons. The outcome was that Judaism became a well-defined and logically constructed system of ideas and tenets, freed from the deformities of popular superstition. No less important was the stimulus it gave to Hebrew studies and biblical research. Finally, the ascetic of "Zionism" of the Karaites did not fail to challenge other sections of the Jewish people.

Karaism itself was a failure. It failed because it was inconsistent, because it betrayed its own principles by accepting in practice almost the whole "burden of inheritance"—Karaism's own phrase—of rabbinical Judaism. Theoretically the Karaites repudiated the "Oral Law," but accepting it in practice forced them to look for its new theoretical justification. This they found in the Muslim conception of *Ijma'* or general acceptance by the community. But the Muslim jurisprudents had developed this idea—which corresponds to the Jewish "Custom of Israel which is law"—*in addition* to their *Sunna* or "Tradition of the Prophet." By destroying the traditional theoretical base of Judaism while retaining it in practice, the Karaites created merely confusion. They expounded the Bible according to the same logical principles which had prevailed in the Schools of the Rabbis (and afterwards the Muslim lawyers), but in details their results were often different from those accepted by the majority of the Jewish people. Thus the historically sound principle of "general acceptance by the community" was constantly crisscrossed by audacious analogies drawn from a biblical text or by ingenious logical constructions made by this or that Karaite doctor. Reading in the great compendium of Karaite law of the tenth-century Kirkisani (whose Arabic original has been edited recently by Leon Nemoy), one is impressed by the immense acumen and resourcefulness of the author, but regrets that his brilliant talents were wasted on findings of little permanent value. The general reader may get an idea of the vast, but, as a whole, rather barren Karaite literature from Leon Nemoy's recently published *Karaite Anthology*.

The Karaite eclipse may have been due partly also to special historical circumstances. Palestine was the main center of Karaite activity during the most creative and flourishing period of their existence, the tenth and eleventh centuries. However, Palestine suffered very much during the eleventh century from internal disorders and barbarian invasions, particularly in the second half of the century, and with the conquest of Jerusalem by the Crusaders in 1099 the Karaite settlement there practically came to an end. For reasons which still need further elucidation, the center of Karaite activities moved to Constantinople and other Byzantine towns, where writers fluent in both Arabic and Greek codified their doctrines and practices in *Hebrew* books. From there they proceeded to the Crimea and scattered in Russia. Of the Muslim countries, it is only Egypt, the ancient seat of the Karaite *Nasi*, where a sizeable and active community survived. Of late, most of its members emigrated to Israel, where the antagonism of sects has completely lost its ancient bitterness, just as the Muslim sects today have largely ceased to form mutually hostile camps.

b. Law and Ritual. The Position of Women

It was not only Karaite jurisprudence which was affected by the Muslim environment. The same holds true, although in different ways, for Jewish law and ritual in general. These relations have not yet been investigated sufficiently. Quite a number of innovations make their appearance in Jewish law in Islamic times. It can be safely assumed that some of the innovations, as we discussed in chapter VI, came into being as a response to the new economic and social conditions. With regard to others, however, it is difficult to decide whether they owed their existence to the activities of the great Babylonian academies, to Muslim models, or whether they had been established before Islam, and by chance omitted from literary mention.

The important institution of *Stopping the Prayer*, the right of a person to interrupt public prayer, especially on Saturdays, until redress was given or promised, seems to have had an entirely inner Jewish development, but there are parallel phenomena in Muslim practice.

A similar case is the institution of the *Accredited Witness*, which corresponds roughly to that of a modern public notary. Both in Jewish and in Muslim law the moral, religious, and social virtues required of a witness appearing before a court were so high that it was difficult to find persons fulfilling these requirements. At some time in the history of Bagdad, the greatest city of Islam, only three hundred persons were qualified to give witness. Such a state of affairs was incompatible with the exigencies of economic and social life, particularly since, in both Jewish and Muslim law, legal documents are signed by the witnesses and not by the parties. Therefore, it became customary that each court had some qualified persons at hand who witnessed, signed, and even drew up legal deeds. The beginnings of this development go back to the talmudic period, but, as it was completed only in later Islamic times, it well may be that the Muslim environment was of some influence in this matter.

This brings us to a very characteristic aspect of the relationship between Judaism and Islam, namely, the cases in which Jewish institutions or ideas touched Islam, underwent a period of development there and returned to Judaism in a modified form.

Such a case, according to the late Orientalist, Joseph Horovitz, is the *Chain of Tradition*, the custom of assigning authority to an oral tradition by adding to it a preamble containing the names of the scholars who had handed it down from the first authority—in Islam, normally Muhammad. As this procedure was by no means general in early Islam, and as the name of this branch of Muslim knowledge incorporates some Jewish expressions—as e.g., the very term *Chain of Tradition* itself—Joseph Horovitz may have been right in assuming that in this point Islam was influenced by the highly developed Jewish "Oral Law." However, in Islam, this *Knowledge of the Men*, the study of the biographies and mutual relations of the thousands of scholars mentioned in the preambles to the laws, became a huge science, indeed one of the important branches of Muslim cultural historiography. In Judaism, it had its counterpart in such books as *Seder ha-Dorot* or *Sequence of the Generations*, dealing with the teachers of the Talmud, or in the famous *Letter* of the Gaon Sherira, which is in the form of a responsum, an answer to a query, but actually contains the history of the heads of the Babylonian academies from their inception down to the author's own times. These Jewish books cannot be compared to the Muslim *Knowledge of the Men*, which is indeed a fully developed science, but it stands to reason that this Muslim science did not fail to impress the doctors of Jewish law. When Maimonides, in the introduction to his codification of Jewish law and lore, enumerates an unbroken chain of forty authorities from Moses to Rav Ashi, the editor of the Babylonian Talmud, it is very possible that he was influenced by the Muslims, who, in later times, required strict completeness in these matters.

Another good example of the relationship between Judaism and Islam is the idea of *Kawwana*, in Arabic *Niyya*, the religious intention or devotional frame of mind, which, in the two religions, has to accompany certain acts of worship. As soon as formal, obligatory prayer—as a substitute for Temple offerings—became a fixed Jewish institution, it created a problem: whether a man had really fulfilled his duty of saying the prayer if he did so absent-mindedly and without concentrating on the contents of the prayer. Lengthy discussions about this matter are found in the Talmud; therefore it seems feasible—as the late Dutch scholar A. J. Wensinck has pointed out—that this notion, which is equally important in Islam, first came there from Judaism. However, the Arab scholars, in their formal approach to things, were not content in requiring "intention," but composed formulas in which the devout, before complying with a religious duty, would expressly state that he intended to do so. In Judaism, such formulas appear late and in pietist circles in particular, which, as we have seen, were receptive to foreign ideas. I wonder whether this formal expression of the religious intention has not been taken over from Islam, thus completing the circle, described above, of borrowing an institution and handing it on in a modified form. Owing to its beautiful, solemn melody, this formula ("I am ready and prepared to fulfill the commandment of my Creator to do this or that") has become a very popular Hebrew folk song whose singers may hardly realize its long history.

Some such mutual relations may have existed also in regard to another institutional characteristic of Jewish and Muslim law, the custom of keeping Mondays and Thursdays both as fast days and as days for the sitting of the courts. Recommended, not obligatory, fasting on these two weekdays has obviously been taken over by Islam from Judaism, as Wensinck also showed. As the Geniza papers indicate, throughout the eleventh and twelfth centuries the sessions of the rabbinical court in Cairo were held invariably on Monday and Thursday, and only very rarely, under the pressure of business, again on another weekday. But—and this is very characteristic—I have never found so many entries in the casebook of the court than on an obligatory fast day (it was the 17th of *Tammuz*, or June, which must be rather hot in Cairo!). We know from Muslim sources that every Monday and Thursday the famous Saladin, the Egyptian Sultan, used to hold—as befitting a pious monarch—public sessions of justice, where he heard and decided in person cases brought before him. On the other hand, in Christian countries the Jewish courts did not adhere to this custom of holding their sessions on these two days. Thus it may be that the preservation of the ancient Jewish tradition in the earlier centuries of Islam was due to the fact that Islam itself regarded Mondays and Thursdays particularly fit for fast and judgment. These and many similar points of contact need further investigation.

It has been pointed out in chapter VI that from the middle of the eleventh century on, Jewish legal deeds in Muslim countries were principally written in Arabic, although they normally opened and concluded with Hebrew or Aramaic phrases. Quite a number of terms familiar from Muslim formularies are found in those documents. However, Jewish law was a far too highly developed system to be changed in basic principle through the influence of its younger sister. In addition, as far as legal terminology is concerned, one has to bear in mind that in those days it was already largely international in character. This was demonstrated by the editor of the very first Geniza document to be published, A. Merx, in his *Paléographie hébraique*, Heidelberg 1894 (he had acquired the documents from a Yemenite Jew in Cairo without even knowing of the existence of a Geniza). In his book, the Arabic terms found in the Jewish documents are illustrated by contemporary Greek parallels.

There exists, however, literary evidence of the influence of Muslim jurisprudence on the exposition of Jewish law. When Sa'adya Gaon wrote many of his legal treatises in Arabic, or when Samuel ben Hofni, another Head of a Babylonian academy, did the same in his *Introduction to the Talmud*, it is only natural that together with the language, Muslim ideas found their way into the writings of these authors. This was proved long ago with regard to Sa'adya's treatise on the law of inheritance and will become even more evident in D. H. Baneth's forthcoming edition of Samuel ben Hofni's work on the principles of law.

Even when writing in Hebrew, the Jewish scholars may sometimes have taken inspiration from their Muslim colleagues. Thus it has been assumed, perhaps correctly, that Maimonides followed in the arrangement of his huge codification of Jewish law to some extent the model of Muslim codes. He may have had an eye on them even with regard to details. As we pointed out in chapter III, there exists a fundamental difference between the Jewish and Muslim laws of contract, the former requiring symbolic acts for the transfer of property or other rights, the latter being thoroughly informal and satisfied with the merely verbal expression of the assent of the two parties to the transaction. Maimonides does not make any reference to Muslim law; but when he opens the section of his *Code* called "Buying and Selling" with the dictum, "By mere words, no rights of property can be transferred," he is certainly alluding to this difference between the two laws.

In the countries of Islam, as elsewhere, Jewish authorities had to fight for legal autonomy, at least for the application of Jewish law in civil cases and in those pertaining to personal status. This struggle is borne out by many of the Geniza papers. The parties agree not to turn to a non-Jewish court; fines are stipulated in the case that they do. The matter is often touched upon in Jewish legal writings and sometimes also referred to by Muslim lawyers. As a whole, it appears that Egyptian and most other Oriental Jewries during the Middle Ages, the Yemenite Jews up to the Turkish conquest of the country (1872), and those of Morocco almost to our own day were largely independent in legal matters, and that even transfers of immovable property were effected before the Jewish courts. Both from Geniza documents and from nineteenth-century deeds coming from Yemen we learn that the same cases were often taken simultaneously before a Jewish and a Muslim court, the one to make it religiously legal, the other to secure for it the protection of the authorities.

There is, however, one field in which Jewish law in Muslim countries early lost ground—the law of inheritance which is regarded as the special preserve of the various denominations inside Islam. In chapter III, the basic difference between the Jewish and Muslim laws of inheritance was explained: the former, that of an agricultural population, endeavors to preserve large portions for the few; the latter, that of an originally Bedouin and mercantile people, distributes small shares to the many. It was only human that those who stood to benefit from Muslim law brought their causes to a Muslim court—a fact deplored by rabbinical writers as early as the eleventh century. In order to avoid such occurrences, medieval Egyptian Jews wrote their wills according to the rules of the Muslim law of inheritance. The same thing was done in Yemen in our own time, with the effect that Jews became so versed in the intricate Muslim law of inheritance that in the villages they were sometimes asked by their Muslim friends to undertake for them the distribution of their estates in their wills.

It has been stressed in our discussion of the relationship between Jewish and Muslim mysticism (section 4) that Abraham, the son of Moses Maimonides, who was *Nagid* or Head of the Egyptian Jewry in the years 1204 to 1237, did not refrain from introducing Muslim practices even into Jewish worship. He did so, as he expressly stated, because those rites had been originally Jewish, but had fallen into disuse in the course of centuries. Like other reformers, Abraham Maimonides intended to restore what he believed was good old custom. As we shall presently see, in some respects he was right in this assumption, in others he was obviously wrong. In both he followed Muslim models.

He was right in the matter of worship by prostration. This was indeed an old Jewish custom, as many passages of the Bible indicate. As late as the second century A.D. it must have been quite common, for it was said of Rabbi Akiba, one of the most famous sages of that time, that at the beginning of prayer he was found in one corner of the synagogue and at the end in another, because of his incessant bowings and prostrations. Later on, however, prostrations were banned from the service of the synagogue, possibly because they had become so prominent in the practices of both the Christian monks and the Jewish sectarians, the latter calling their place of service an outright "House of Prostration." Muhammad, following either Christian or Jewish sectarian example, enthusiastically adopted bowings and prostrations; and subsequently the Muslim pietists adhered to this practice with particular fervor. Abraham Maimonides, lamenting the loss to Jews of this expression of utter human servitude to God, boldly reintroduced it, relying on the authority of Rabbi Akiba and other ancients.

He was on less firm ground, however, when he tried to give to the Jewish service in general the solemn, intense character of Muslim prayer. The very architecture of the synagogue militated against his endeavors; so did the highly developed, long-drawn-out Jewish ritual, which was so entirely different from the Muslim. Originally the synagogues—as we may still observe in the buildings of the Oriental communities—resembled an Arabic *liwan*, a hall, where those present sat along the four walls facing each other. Because the Jewish service, unlike the Muslim, lasted a number of hours, the congregation was comfortably seated on benches covered with cushions. All this was for Abraham Maimonides incompatible with the duties of "a servant standing in the presence of his Master"; seats and cushions should be removed from the synagogue; the congregation should sit in long rows facing the Holy Ark, the symbol of heavenly presence, and when seated at all should sit erect (as the Muslims do during the seconds they are required to sit during prayer).

Abraham Maimonides' reforms met with strong opposition, led by the family whose members had been the Heads of Egyptian Jewry before Moses Maimonides arrived from Spain and attained a position of unchallenged authority. Abraham's opponents did not refrain from bringing the case before the Sultan al-Malik al-Adil, Saladin's brother and successor. It may seem strange that the Muslim ruler was invoked against the "Islamistic" reforms of the synagogue, introduced by the religious Head of Egyptian Jewry. However, Saladin and his family were simple-minded Kurds and staunch supporters of conservatism in all religious matters. Therefore, Abraham Maimonides' opponents could rightly hope that the Sultan would give a ready ear to their complaints. In a highly interesting document, preserved in the University Library of Cambridge, England, it is reported that Abraham Maimonides, in a personal letter to the Sultan, explained that he, in his capacity as Head of the Egyptian Jewry, did not exercise any pressure on anybody in these matters and that his practices were but personal devotion, in which he was followed by worshippers of a similar inclination.

None of the "Islamistic" reforms advocated by Abraham Maimonides proved a success. The synagogues in Eastern countries continued to be built and arranged as they were before, and prostrations remained excluded from the service. Still, his preaching, and that of congenial religious men, was not in vain. The genuine Oriental service is of great decorum, more so than the average Jewish service in Christian countries. The Muslim prayer, which is of short duration and consequently of greater intensity, no doubt has something to do with this difference.

Abraham Maimonides' attempts to reform the synagogue service were not the only instances of Muslim influence on Jewish ceremonial. These relationships have been carefully discussed in an extensive study by N. Wieder, published first in *Melilah*, a Hebrew publication of the University of Manchester, 1946, and later as a separate book.

The impact of Muslim religion and society was certainly substantial with regard to the position of the Jewish woman in Eastern countries. Polygamy was prohibited by the Jewish rabbis in Europe, but remained legal in the countries of Islam. To be sure, the new Jewish *bourgeoisie* of the Middle East abolished polygamy in practice by inserting a clause in the marriage contract in which the husband undertook not to marry a second wife—a clause paralleled by the proviso found in Muslim papyri, by which the first wife has the right to dismiss the second, or to sell a slave-girl, should they behave unpleasantly. This clause prohibiting or fining a second marriage is found in many contracts preserved in the Geniza and has been in use in the Sefaradi Jewish community to the present day. In addition, the Geniza papers betray a degree of economic and social independence of the Jewish woman which is far higher than that foreseen by the doctors of the law.

Nevertheless, polygamy remained legal among the Jews inside Islam and in a thoroughly Arab country like Yemen it has been in vogue well into our own time. A number of immigrants from

Yemen to Israel arrived in the company of two or even three wives, quite a problem to the housing authorities since the laws of polygamous decency require each wife to have a separate hut or tent. Of course, even in a polygamous society only a small number of men can indulge in that luxury, as the quantities of males and females available for mating are approximately equal. The observation of anthropologists that in polygamous peoples, just as elsewhere, the wife is often the master in the house, applies also to Yemenites. And it is certainly true that in many cases the second wife is an ally of the first. Albeit, most of the Oriental Jews today regard polygamy as a disgrace, one of the degrading effects of their *Galuth,* or exile. Although the law of the State of Israel permits a man to keep the wives he has brought from abroad, many have separated since their arrival.

The position of women with reference to Jewish *ritual* deteriorated in the countries of Islam. This was especially conspicuous with regard to their participation in the synagogue service. The question of whether women should attend a public religious service was a controversial point in Islam itself, and here too the sects were, as a rule, less tolerant than orthodox Islam. Strong warnings against the attempts to exclude women from the synagogue were voiced in early Islamic times, but social prejudices became stronger than religious convictions. In a country like the highland of Yemen, which is ruled by a Muslim sect, women, as a rule, attended neither the mosque nor the synagogue.

Although in theory Islam made "the seeking of wisdom" obligatory for women as for men, in practice they were rigorously excluded from any kind of systematic education. The learned slavegirl was a highly priced plaything in early Islam—a phenomenon which obviously came to the Arabs from the Greeks through Byzantine mediation—but even the ladies of the high Muslim society remained, as a rule, illiterate, until Western influence slowly changed the situation. (Women should not be taught to write, some profound Muslim scholars argued, lest they send secret messages to their lovers.) The Jewish communities inside Islam, especially in a country like Yemen, which was far away from other

Jewish centers, closely followed the Muslim example. As a rule, no woman learned to read or write. Therefore, the witty Yemenites say: "He who reads to his mother never makes a mistake." Unlike the Jewish women of eastern Europe, the Jewish women of Yemen did not have books which told them in their own language the stories of the Bible or of the saints of later times. Therefore, the bulk of the Jewish women in Yemen were unacquainted with the contents of the Holy Scriptures—a fact mirrored in their names. While in Europe the names of biblical heroines were most common among Jews, almost all Jewish women in Yemen bore Arabic names, including Maryam, the Muslim equivalent for Mary, the mother of Jesus (who is, however, identified in the Koran with Miriam, the sister of Moses and Aaron).

Naturally, in Islam as well as in Jewish-Arab society, there were exceptions to the rule which excluded women from religious learning. A famous example of a learned Yemenite woman was Miriam, the daughter of the famous Hebrew scribe Benayahu (fourteenth century) from whose hand marvelous manuscripts have been preserved in the British Museum, and who herself was a scribe of renown; in the postscript to one book she asks for indulgence for her mistakes: she was nursing a child while copying the book. And there was Sham'ah, the daughter of the poet Shalom Shabazi, and herself a poet; some of her Hebrew compositions are still known. At the other end of the Muslim world we find the widow of Ibn Tarras, the propagator of Karaism in Spain, who bore the honorific title "The Teacher," because she continued the work of her husband after his death and became the main exponent of the new schism in that country. Among the immigrants from Yemen one can observe in each village one or two woman leaders, who, in addition to their capacity as poets—in Arabic, of course—are midwives, medical practitioners, and "wise women" in general (see the Second Book of Samuel 14:2 and 20:16). They know by heart many Hebrew quotations and Jewish stories, which they have learned from their husbands or picked up while listening to learned discussions. A man who had no son would teach his daughter all he knew, including ritual slaughtering, which is a complete science, the veterinary knowledge of the ancients. To find a woman officiating as a *Shohet*, or ritual slaughterer, perhaps even instructing men in the profession and issuing them Hebrew certificates, which testify to their proficiency, is very strange to anyone familiar with traditional Judaism. But there is nothing in the Law against it, and this and similar cases of learned women of official standing are recorded in the Yemenite and other Oriental Jewish communities. Even in Kurdistan, the most illiterate section of the Jewish world, at least one case of an excellent Hebrew woman scholar is known. This was the wife of Jacob Mizrahi, rabbi and head of a Yeshiva, or rabbinical college, in Amadiya in Kurdistan and afterwards in Mosul. Her father, himself a scholar, had given her a thorough education, and gave her in marriage only on condition that she should never be troubled with household work. Her husband kept his promise, but otherwise made good use of his wife's talents; for while he devoted his time to his private studies, he let her teach the students of his Yeshiva. When he died, she valiantly kept the Yeshiva running under the most difficult circumstances, until her son Samuel was old enough to take over. The story of this courageous sixteenth century woman is known to us from a collection of her Hebrew letters, and from those of her husband and son—and a Jewish visitor from Europe—which are preserved in the library of the Hebrew Union College, Cincinnati.

These exceptions, however, only confirm the general rule which confined the Jewish women in Islamic countries to the keeping of the religious ceremonials on the one hand and to the popular culture of oral vernacular traditions on the other.

C. POPULAR RELIGION AND CUSTOM

A favorite meeting ground for the cultures of peoples living together is popular religion and custom. This applies in particular to Jews and Arabs, who had largely the same cultural background.

Both were the heirs of the ancient, Hellenized East; both met on the higher levels of spiritual religion and theological thinking.

It was known to the Muslims of the ninth century that the Jews, if they could afford it, brought their dead to Palestine to be buried; for it was believed that the resurrection of the dead took place in the Holy Land. The Muslims soon followed suit and from the tenth century on the body of many a prominent Muslim was brought to Jerusalem to be buried.

According to Jewish folklore, the punishment of man was not postponed until "the World to Come" or the Day of Resurrection, but began as soon as the body was interred in the grave. This secret of "the tribulation of the tomb" was learned, according to an ancient Muslim tradition, by A'isha, Muhammad's favorite wife, from a Jewish woman in Medina, who taught her as well how to avoid the unpleasant experience by living an adequate life in this world. Later on, details about the first hours of the dead in the grave found their way back from Muslim to Jewish folklore.

The very center and pivot of popular religious life in Muslim countries lay in the pilgrimages to the tombs of the saints. In the ninth century, these were decried in Muslim circles as a Jewish abuse. However, in the following century, a Karaite writer of Jerusalem stigmatized pilgrimages as a sort of idolatry which the Jews had borrowed from the Muslims. The truth is, of course, that these pilgrimages represent the remnants of a more ancient civilization, a fact symbolized by the participation of adherents of different religions in visits to the tombs of the same saints. The other classical country of saint-veneration, besides Palestine, was North Africa. In his book, *Pélérinages judéo-musulmans du Maroc*, Paris 1948, L. Voinot describes Muslim tombs visited by Jews, Jewish tombs visited by Muslims, and no less than thirty-one which were claimed by the followers of the two religions simultaneously. Of those Muslim saints which attracted Jews, I should like to mention Lalla Jamila ("the Lady Beautiful") who, it is believed, made the barren pregnant, as did the ancient goddess of Fertility. Of the Jewish saints venerated by Muslims, a characteristic representative is Amram ben Dayyan, a messenger of the rabbinical college of Hebron in Palestine, who came to Morocco during the eighteenth century in order to raise funds. He was accompanied by his son, who fell ill and was on the verge of death when his father asked God to spare the life of the child and take his own instead. His prayer was accepted; his son recovered and he died. His tomb in the Moroccan town of Ouezzan is still venerated by Jews and Muslims as a place of miraculous cures.

Similarly in Yemen, the tomb of Shalom Shabazi, the seventeenth-century saint and poet, was the national shrine of the Jews of that country. However, from the many legends and stories about that sanctuary it is evident that Muslims, too, despairing of other saints, tried Shalom Shabazi with some success. It is interesting that among the Yemenites now in Israel there is a strong movement, headed by the most prominent Yemenite labor leader and a member of Israel's parliament, to transfer the bones of the saint to Israel. This movement was publicly opposed by only one Yemenite—a scholarly-minded young man, who had studied Arabic at the Hebrew University in Jerusalem.

It would be unjust to label these phenomena mere "pagan survivals." The interpretation of custom, given by the local people themselves, is what matters, and there could be no sterner monotheists than the Jews and Muslims of Yemen or North Africa. Everybody knows that it is not the saint, but his intercession with God which may work miracles. Historically, no doubt, the veneration of the tomb and its associated rites go back to pre-monotheistic layers, but all this has been brought under control within the framework of the ideas and institutions of both Judaism and Islam. The interested reader may find a discussion of this question from the pen of J. Berque in the new periodical *Studia Islamica*, edited by R. Brunschvig and J. Schacht, vol. I, Paris 1953.

The situation is similar with regard to what we would call superstitious practices—rain-making, the "averting" of locusts, or the curing of men and cattle by amulets and other magical means. The belief that the prayers of saints may bring rain is exemplified in the Talmud by many stories, quite a number of which have found their way into Islamic literature. In Yemen, in times of drought, the Jews, whose intercession was believed to be particularly effective, were almost compelled by their neighbors to hold fasts and assemble with their children at their cemeteries for rain prayers. On the other hand, when Muslims offered sacrifices to their local saints in order to secure rain, the Jews were asked to pay part of the expenses for the slaughtered animals, since they possessed fields which would benefit from the effects of the sacrifices.

A great concern of Middle-Eastern man is the invading hosts of locusts, which constitute a terrible threat to his fields and trees. Of many village rabbis in Yemen it was believed that they were able to "avert" the locusts by prayer and cabalistic practices. "Averting" locusts from one district meant, of course, driving them to another. There some other miracle-worker, possibly a Muslim, would be active. It was customary that in the magical battle between the two cabalists, the local Muslims sided with the rabbi of their own district against the Muslim functionary practicing in the other.

Almost every Jew in Muslim countries knew how to read—at least in Yemen—while the majority of the rural Muslims were illiterate. Since writing was one of the most popular means of magic, a Jew was often regarded as a sort of medicine man, capable of performing all kinds of miracles with the art of writing. In addition, the Jew was different in physical appearance from the Arabs who surrounded him in particular in his hairdress, his attire, his occupation, and his entire way of life; and it is only human to ascribe to the stranger mysterious capacities and traits. In talmudic times, when the Arabs were still a foreign minority in the frontier countries of Palestine and Iraq, they were famous among the Jews as masters of sorcery and witchcraft.

As an indication of the naive faith of the rural Arabs in the magical power of the literate Jew, two out of many examples may suffice. A Yemenite friend told me that while doing his work in the house of a Muslim villager, he was asked by the latter's wife to write her a charm; she was childless and had lost the attention of her husband. My friend, who belonged to a rationalist Jewish reform movement, which regarded such practices as an abomination, refused. The woman, however, had no doubt that he did so only out of feigned modesty (to refuse a dignity or a task is Jewish and Muslim etiquette; almost as imperative a custom as was once found in China). Therefore she repeated her demand so vehemently that he was forced to comply. Obviously fortified by the Hebrew charm, she regained the love of her husband and eventually bore him a son. My friend, however, had completely forgotten the whole affair. A year later, when he returned to the village, he was received "with drums and cries of joy" and showered with presents, which he had some misgivings about accepting.

I have been told of a well-known scribe who was engaged in copying out a Torah scroll, when an Arab tribesman burst into his house and demanded instantly an amulet for his sheep which were extremely sick. Angry at the interruption, the scribe wrote a juicy curse on a scrap of paper and handed it to the intruder. But the sheep recovered, and when the scribe, who was also a craftsman, sent his son during harvest time to collect the usual annual remuneration for these services, he got, in addition to his customary share of the crops, the fattest ram in the flock for his miraculous healing!

Close affinities between Arab Muslims and Oriental Jews are discernible also in the elaborate and extended ceremonies and meals connected with wedding and death. As the Yemenite proverb goes: "Man enjoys life only twice, when he marries and when he dies." The ceremonial grinding of the wheat, or *dhura*, for the feast days; the dyeing of the bride and the bridegroom with henna and other plants; the shaving of the bridegroom's head and the cutting of the bride's hair above the forehead; their ritual bath; the solemn dispatch of the dowry and the official presentation of the gifts by the guests; the bridal procession and the meal which the young couple takes in complete isolation; the gorgeous feast at the end of the mourning—all these, and many other ceremonies are found with variants in both Arab and Oriental Jewish communities. Similarly, they share common ideas and practices with regard to pregnancy, childbirth and childrearing, the first shaving of the boy's head, the children's play and education, the recreation of adults, their social prejudices and superstitions.

To many of the details discussed in this subsection, parallels could be found outside the Jewish and Arab worlds. It would appear that popular custom and religion are not so much an indication of cultural contact as they are of a common survival of previous stages of civilization. However, a very considerable portion of these ideas, customs, and patterns of behavior have found their way into Jewish and Muslim Oral Law; they have been incorporated into the literature of the Jewish Talmud and Midrash and into the Muslim *Hadith*, and in part have come into the official rituals of the two religions. They have, therefore, their proper place in any study of Jewish-Arab symbiosis.

d. FOLK LITERATURE AND ART

Scrutiny of the themes and artistic forms found in the medieval books of entertainment and edification, or in the oral traditions still alive among the Jews and the Arabs, reveals many international elements. One is struck by the similarities between the great treasure-house of genuine Jewish folklore, the Talmud and the Midrash, and their Arabic counterparts, the literature of the *Hadith* and the religious legend. However, as a rule the disparate elements have been related to, and tinged by, the central beliefs and the general outlook of the two peoples and are integrated in each culture. On the other hand, the very nature of popular literature makes imperative the utmost care in the search for mutual influence. One can only make assumptions where there are special indications that one culture has borrowed from the other. A few examples may illustrate this problem.

The brotherhood and mutual responsibility of all members of the Muslim community is emphasized in two famous similes ascribed to Muhammad. One is that of the living body which is sensitive to pain in any of its limbs; the other is the idea of "all

being in one boat." (The story goes that a passenger in a ship began to make a hole in its bottom. The other passengers cried,
"What are you doing?" The man replied, "What do you want? I
am making a hole only in my own place, which I hired for myself.") Azzam Pasha, a former secretary of the Arab League,
quotes these similes in his book *The Mission of Islam* and asks
whether there has been found anywhere in the world such a perfect expression of mutual responsibility in a community. However,
these two similes are far older than Islam. The first is commonplace in Greek philosophical writings and goes back to Plato. It
may have reached the Arabs in a thousand different ways. And
since the two similes are found together in the *Hadith*, as they are
in an old Midrash, it is highly probable, although by no means
sure, that they came to the Arabs from a Jewish source.

When one literature contains details which have their legitimate
place in the other, an interdependence may be assumed. On the
Jewish Feast of Tabernacles, branches of a palm tree, a myrtle,
and a willow are carried during the service, together with a citrus
fruit called *Ethrog* in Hebrew, for which the Arabic equivalent is
Utrunj. This strange combination of plants was explained by Jewish preachers as symbols of the various elements composing the
Jewish community: the citrus fruit which has both an agreeable
taste and a pleasant smell stands for a man who is both pious and
learned; the fruit of the date palm which is tasty but has no fragrance for a pious but unlearned man; the myrtle whose only distinction is its smell symbolizes the learned but wicked man; while
the willow exemplifies an ignoramus with no virtues. The implica-
tion is that everyone, even a man belonging to the last category,
has his place in the community. The same symbology of the
Utrunj, the date, and two other plants, carries the same application and is ascribed in the *Hadith* to the Prophet. Since this combination of plants has no place in Muslim ritual, it stands to reason
that the homily which makes use of them was borrowed from the
Midrash.

The case is different where a motif, although characteristic in
Jewish literature prior to Islam, does not appear within the two

literatures in circumstances which suggest borrowing. For example, it is sometimes told of the Ka'ba of Mecca, the holy shrine of Islam and the goal of pilgrimage for millions, that it leaves its place in order to meet a particularly godly person. The story goes that once Hasan Basri, the famous mystic, and other prominent Muslims, made the long and dangerous journey to Mecca but, to their dismay, the Ka'ba was not there when they arrived. It had gone away to meet Rabi'a, the woman saint, who was on her way to Mecca. The profound idea behind these stories is, of course, that the greatest sanctuary on earth is the human personality. Similarly, in an ancient homily on Genesis chapter 28, the story of Jacob's vision of the heavenly ladder, it is said that the house of God (verse 17), which is eternally fixed in Jerusalem, moved from its place and came to visit Jacob on his flight. However, the theme of the moving sanctuary is not confined to Jewish and Muslim literatures—it forms, for instance, the subject of a well-known poem by Goethe—and it offers no indication of mutual dependence.

The process operating in the higher spheres of the spiritual relations between Islam and Judaism is echoed in the absorption of considerable sections of the ancient Jewish popular literature into its Arab counterpart, which made the former ready to accept the influence of the latter. The Koran, the holy book of Islam, alludes to many Jewish stories, biblical and otherwise, but only rarely, as in the case of the Joseph story, does it tell them in full. Naturally, the Muslims wanted to know the details. Thus there arose in early Islam a class of professional story-tellers, whose subject was mainly the "prophets," i.e., the heroes of the Koran. These story-tellers freely borrowed from Jews and Christians, and in particular from the vast literature of the Midrash, the popular exposition of the Bible. Naturally, they added material from other sources and from their own imagination. In their turn, these "Stories of the Prophets" are echoed in some of the later Jewish Midrashim, which may contain even some Koranic material.

In a famous passage of the Joseph story in the Koran, the ladies of Egypt scold Potiphar's wife for making love to the Hebrew youth. The cunning woman invites the ladies to a party; while her guests are engaged in peeling fruits, she allows Joseph to enter. The ladies are so struck by his beauty that they inadvertently cut their fingers. This scene, which has been often depicted by Muslim painters, is found in Hebrew literature later than the Koran. It may have been told to Muhammad by a Jew, although it does not occur in the ancient Midrash, but it is more likely that the very un-Arab theme had come to the Arabs from some Persian romance and was introduced by Muhammad himself into the story of Joseph. Later on, it also found its way into Jewish popular literature.

Another branch of Muslim folk literature which belongs here is the "Israiliyyat," the stories which pretend to tell about the ancient Israelites often mentioned in the Koran. What were the special merits of those Children of Israel that they were the first to receive a heavenly book and the Muslims the last? And why, after such distinction, did their kingdom not endure? The answer to the first question gave rise to many beautiful legends of the pious men of the Children of Israel, some of which are found in talmudical literature. The answers to the second question reflect contemporary Muslim controversies rather than Jewish traditions. Thus we read that the ancient kingdom of the Israelites disappeared because the Jews decided religious questions according to logic and expediency rather than on the basis of their holy Scriptures; because they were continually engaged in civil wars (as were the Muslims); because they used to pray at the tombs of their saints (see the previous subsection); or even because their women wore wigs and high heels.

In addition to these fanciful "Israiliyyat," there were, however, others which were genuine Jewish stories. This applies particularly to Messianic material, i.e., imaginary descriptions of the cataclysm which would bring the history of the world to an end and inaugurate the Golden Age. This subject, which occupies so large a place in the Koran and which naturally interested the Muslims immensely, drew much material from Jewish folklore. This influence is felt not only in details, but in the whole framework of post-Koranic eschatology or teachings about the "End of the Days."

The Jews believed that the messianic age would be preceded by great world wars, a theme entirely absent from the Koran. Soon the Muslim story-tellers enlarged on these eschatological wars or *Malahim*, as they were called, an expression reminiscent of the Hebrew *Milhama*. These tales were eagerly received by their co-religionists, who wondered whether the incessant wars which they waged both among themselves and against non-Muslims were not themselves the predicted signs of the end of the world.

So much was the literary genre "Israiliyyat" connected with the idea of the Messianic age, that a modern Arab writer who translated into Arabic the title of a book called *Messianic Movements* (in Islam) rendered it as "Israiliyyat." However, some traits of the fully developed, eschatological fairy tales were incorporated into Jewish folklore from the Muslim.

In view of these close connections between Jewish and Muslim popular literatures it is not surprising that Jewish material has found its way also into the *Arabian Nights*, that treasure-house of Eastern narrative. About forty-five out of the roughly four hundred stories of the book have been identified as Jewish. The interested reader will find a list of these stories in the *Jewish Encyclopedia*, vol. 2, p. 45.

This popular literature, as a rule, never mentions the saints or scholars of the other denomination by name. Of course, biblical heroes were common to the two religions, but no post-biblical Jewish personality would be quoted in Muslim popular literature and no Muslim in Jewish. The stories or sayings taken over were either ascribed to an anonymous pious or wise man, to some legendary figure, or to a prominent person of one's own religion. Thus Rabbi Joshua says in the Talmud: "I have found a little girl being wiser than myself. I asked her, 'What do you carry under the cover of your basket?' Whereupon she answered: 'If I had wished everyone to know what was in it, I would not have covered it.' " In Muslim literature, this little story is ascribed to Amr Ibn As, the Arab conqueror of Egypt. The Talmud repeatedly quotes the following maxim: "It is not position which brings honor to a man, but a man who lends honor to his position." The Arabs ascribe this saying to one Arius (of whom they knew nothing), not, by the way, an inappropriate source, as the talmudic saying itself may go back to Greek popular philosophy. Many a saying attributed in Muslim literature to Muhammad appears also in Jewish literature, but a saying might be ascribed to anyone—even to Socrates—except to its reputed author. This procedure—irritating as it may be—indicates how thoroughly the foreign material has been absorbed.

Sometimes the form and not the contents was borrowed. This is applicable particularly to one of the most popular Jewish-Arabic compilations, *The Book of Comfort* of Nissim ben Jacob Ibn Shahin, an eleventh-century writer who lived in Tunisia. As his Persian by-name indicates, his family—as those of most Jews living in Africa (see chapter VI) came from the East. He was a great rabbinical scholar and author; this book, however, he intended only for entertainment. The title, arrangement, and language of the book are Arabic. Various Muslim authors before him had written books with the same name and which dealt with the same themes, but the content of Ibn Shahin's book is Jewish—stories selected from the Talmud and the Midrash. This was his professed aim, as he explained in his introduction, and he succeeded in carrying out his plan, as demonstrated first by D. H. Baneth and, recently, by H. Z. Hirschberg in the learned treatise which accompanies his new Hebrew translation (Jerusalem 1954). The Arabic original was edited by J. Obermann under the title *Studies in Islam and Judaism; The Arabic Original of Ibn Shahin's 'Book of Comfort'*, Yale University Press 1933.

Arabic was also the medium through which the treasures of Indian literature, fables, ethics, and fairy tales reached the Jews. Thus the famous Indian book *Kalila wa-Dimna* was translated in the eighth century from an ancient Persian version into Arabic. The translator, Ibn al-Muqaffa, was himself a Persian, but his Arabic was so superb that his translation became a classic of that language. However, the great Jewish scholar Abraham Ibn Ezra, in a general treatise on the translation of Indian books, asserts that *Kalila wa-Dimna* was translated directly from Indian into Arabic by a Jew at the request of the first Abbasid caliph (who was also

a contemporary of Ibn al-Muqaffa). The caliph gave that task to a
Jew; for never before in Islam had a secular book been studied,
and the caliph was afraid that the man who undertook such work
might die. If this story is true, that translation has not survived.
The two Hebrew translations in existence were made from Ibn
al-Muqaffa's version. A thirteenth-century baptized Jew from southern Italy translated one of the Hebrew versions into Latin under
the title A *Guide to Human Life,* which was printed as early as
1483. From this translation, all the European versions are derived
(except, of course, those made by modern scholars for scientific
purposes). Despite his fame, that southern Italian Jew must have
worked rather hastily, for in one story the word "fire" is used instead of "man," which, after all, has quite a different meaning. He
must have misread Hebrew *Ish* for *Esh.*

Another very famous Indian book which was translated into
Hebrew from Arabic is *Prince and Dervish,* the story of Buddha.
The translator was Abraham Ibn Hasdai, who lived in Spain in the
thirteenth century, but, as often happens with folk stories, some of
the material contained in his book had reached Hebrew literature
many centuries before. The Arabic version which served him as a
model has not yet been found, thus some scholars wrongly assumed that he had used Indian sources directly or intermediaries
other than Arabic.

Still greater uncertainty prevails about another popular book,
one much in vogue among Jews almost until our own times, *The
Tales of Sindabar* (in Arabic, Sindibad). This is the story of an
Indian prince, whose teacher Sindibad had imposed on him complete silence for seven days. A malevolent woman made use of his
disability to accuse him of a hideous crime, whereupon his father,
the king, ordered his execution. By telling every day a new group
of stories, particularly about the cunning of women, the seven
viziers of the king succeeded in postponing the execution until the
prince, at the end of his week of silence, was able to prove his
innocence.

Despite the setting, the Indian origin of the book is by no means
certain. Obviously, it also contains Hellenist elements. In any case,

whatever its origin, the Hebrew translation was made from an Arabic version, although here again the Hebrew book contains material unknown to Arabic sources. *The Tales of Sindabar* were so popular that they were re-translated from Hebrew into Arabic, this time into the colloquial Arabic spoken by the Jews of North Africa, and published in Leghorn, Italy, in 1868.

The nineteenth-century edition of *The Tales of Sindabar* was only one of a large number of story books printed in Judaeo-Arabic. From Calcutta and Bombay in the east, where Bagdadi and even Yemenite Jews had formed Arabic-speaking Jewish centers, to Tunisia, Algiers, and Morocco in the west, Jewish books of entertainment and edification were printed in Hebrew letters in the local Arabic vernaculars. One can still observe in Israel elderly people who come from these countries and read such books. Their content is variegated and ranges from ancient Jewish stories, such as "Hannah and Her Seven Sons," to purely Arabic romances of the heroes of the desert. A complete survey of that peculiar popular literature would be a useful contribution to the study of folklore in general and to the knowledge of Jewish life in Arab countries in particular.

Even more important would be the study and collection of the oral lore still alive among Arabic-speaking Jews, their local traditions, their prose and poetry, their wit and proverbs. A unique opportunity for such research is presented now by the fact that all these communities have moved to Israel in great numbers. The Jews of Yemen have almost wholly emigrated to Israel; the great majority of the Jews of Iraq and of Libya, and very sizeable sections from North Africa have also settled there. There have always been large contingents of Arabic-speaking Jews in Palestine, but their immigrations, naturally, had been selective and therefore not fully representative of the folklore of their communities in the countries of their origin. However, with the "Ingathering of the Exiles" after the birth of the State of Israel, when complete groups moved into the country and often remained almost intact after their arrival, new opportunities for the study of their social and cultural life were created. In a research report called "Portrait of a

Yemenite Weavers' Village," in *The Jewish Social Studies*, New York 1955, the present writer has tried to show what results may be expected from such a concentrated study. The amount of oral literature preserved in one single little village is indeed remarkable.

Four main branches of oral lore may be discerned. The first, and possibly the most valuable both for the knowledge of local life and for aesthetic value, are the "local traditions," i.e., stories of what actually happened in the village and its environment during the last 120 years, obviously the utmost limit of memory. Naturally, the accounts vary widely, the degree of truth is often relative and the quality of delivery differs sharply. Even the accounts of events which occurred quite recently are often artistically formed according to certain patterns, which the inquirer may easily discover by comparing eye-witness reports with the more elaborate versions of those who have heard the tale told as a story; in effect, molded it into an "oral tradition." In general, these stories reveal a fine standard of oral exposition, often compare favorably with the best examples of ancient Arabic story-telling, and have about them something of biblical lucidity and succinctness. Their ethos is an extremely significant blending of Jewish, Arab, and local concepts. The "life-story" given at the beginning of my *Tales from the Land of Sheba*, New York 1947, may give the interested reader some idea of this type of oral lore.

The second group comprises an enormous amount of "literary" stories, namely, stories which have not been developed by the narrator or other members of his village but were reproduced by him more or less as he heard them—more or less, because the story-teller always wants to present something new, and never tells the same story exactly in the same way. But the version, first heard in the village, and the version later recorded in the Hebrew University Laboratory in Jerusalem, resemble each other so closely that the strong "literary" tradition fully shines through. Naturally, the narrator sometimes mixes a modern Hebrew word into his Arabic account, but these words are easily distinguishable, both in pronunciation and character, from the traditional Hebrew words, which he would use while speaking in his local vernacular.

The "literary" stories fall into four categories: Arab general; Arab local; Jewish general; and Jewish local. The material of Jewish origin consists almost exclusively of legends, parables, and miracle tales—all of the greatest possible variety but all, nevertheless, with some religious or moral tendency. The narrators are normally women, but most, if not all of the Jewish stories must have been originally told by men to their women, for the material, as far as it is local, bears on it the stamp of male, not female, invention. Insofar as it is Jewish general, it almost certainly came to the country through books; as far as I am able to judge, not so much through Judaeo-Arabic tales published in the nineteenth or twentieth centuries but through older, Hebraic sources.

The Arabic lore, which is far more copious than the Jewish, comprises each and every species of folk narrative—fairy tales, histories, moral and humorous stories, linguistic jokes, puns on local habits and characteristics, riddles, etc. Here, the main tendency is entertainment, and the story often contains a moral completely at variance with both Islam and Judaism. Men, at least in public, refrain from telling spicy stories; women do so with gusto. This is one of the indications of their closer ties with the peasants' culture of their environment.

The stories of local origin, both Arabic and Jewish, are of higher interest than the general, although these, having behind them an older and greater tradition, are usually longer. The Arabic narratives from Lower Yemen, which were told to me recently by Jewish women, possess a particular charm, possibly caused by their being a blending of Arab and Indian morality. It does not seem that the narrators have made any tangible changes in the form or contents of their repertoire. The Jewish local stories largely reflect the occupations of their composers. There are many weavers' stories among them, including stories of the saint and poet Shalom Shabazi, whose tomb is found in this part of Yemen, and who himself was a weaver by profession.

The third branch of oral lore is poetry. Jewish men sing a great deal, exclusively religious songs, mostly those composed by classical or local Hebrew poets. Although many know the songs by heart, they normally use handwritten or printed books. These books, by the way, have an unusual oblong format (found also in some leaves of the Geniza), which has a practical purpose. The singer normally hides the book in his sleeve until required to use it. In any case, this poetry does not belong to *oral* lore. Such religious poems are still fabricated, mostly in Hebrew only, since the semi-classical Arabic style in which they were formulated is no longer mastered. On the other hand, men make up doggerels, either in the vernacular, or, even more frequently, in a particular type of Hebrew, in which they best express their disgust about the bad times (times, obviously, have always been bad). At present, such doggerels complain that boys play football instead of studying the Bible, or use knives and forks but forget to say the obligatory benedictions while taking food. Of late, some of these doggerels—all in Hebrew—have been published. One such collection was published by a Yemenite in Jerusalem over a generation ago.

Genuine poetry in the Arabic vernacular is the domain of the women. In former times a Jewish *headman* may have excelled in rhymed prose. Some of his creations, together with stories of the occasions which gave rise to them, may be repeated even a hundred years later. Some low-bred Jewish men even gain material profit by singing an encomium on an Arab notable or by amusing Arab women with farcical poems. But no self-respecting Yemenite Jewish man normally would sing a non-Jewish song, although, with their excellent memories, some would know by heart verses composed by Arabs in connection with local events.

However, in the female Jewish society of Yemen, poetry is one of the most popular pastimes. With the exception of formal wedding songs or songs in honor of guests, which seem to be traditionally Jewish, as they are found in districts far apart, and in towns as well as in villages, all poetry is either borrowed from the environment or composed—often extemporaneously—in the same pattern, or, most commonly, arranged as a mixture of quotation and original composition. In Arabia, the women produced what in a modern society is provided by newspaper editorials: comments on current events. The difficulty in understanding these women poets is that their creations—like those of the ancient Arab poets —refer at once to different times and are sometimes as unclear without a commentary as classical poetry. Such a poem would start with a verse or two of a poetical love song, then suddenly switch to a few lines which ridicule an Arab sheik in Lower Yemen who behaved in a cowardly manner during a British bombardment, and then return to what would seem to be the main topic—the ideal character of a true lover or the depravity of a man who is fickle. The song continues; without transition, pokes fun at contemporary conditions in Israel, where people take meat from the belly of a tin instead of the carcass of an animal, where girls join the army, and women vote in public elections. Immediately after such a departure into the present, the song hurls satirical curses at the head of the daughter of "the Vizier" (a family name), the rebel who was put to death after the murder of the King of Yemen in 1948, and concludes—if this may be called a conclusion—with the eloquent verses of a low-caste Muslim woman who had a love affair with a noble sheik. For this section even her own people had to ask for a commentary!

The Jewish women also recited songs of soldiers and other classes of people; these songs, however, were clearly marked off from the regular repertoire. All poetry is sung, and each type has its special melody. The relationships of these melodies to those used by the Jewish townswomen on the one hand and synagogue melodies on the other are being investigated by expert musicologists, who are at present engaged in a study of Yemenite and other Oriental Jewish folk music.

The miraculous transfer by air of the entire Jewish population of Yemen to Israel has found its expression, naturally, in Arabic, in the verses composed by Jewish women. According to the character of this poetry, there exists not a single complete poem which deals with the subject, only separate verses strewn into the general fabric of a poem. As I have heard the same verses with slight variations from women from all parts of Yemen, these creations obviously were the work of one poet and spread in transit camps near

Aden and in Israel. They are certainly a landmark in Jewish-Arabic symbiosis.

A fourth, but very significant, ingredient of the oral literature of the Arabic-speaking Jews, are their proverbs, their wit and wisdom. Of course proverbs exist everywhere, but in a society which is, on the one hand, largely illiterate (in Yemen no Jewish woman can read) and, on the other, follows very definite standards in all matters of life, possessing, in addition, a most expressive language, proverbs become a conspicuous part of common speech. They are quoted in the same way as a saying from the Bible and often help to make a long story short. It is interesting that one of the former chief rabbis of San'a, the capital of Yemen, made a collection of local sayings and proverbs and illustrated them with appropriate parallels from ancient Hebrew literature. As a matter of fact, in this he was preceded by the Talmud itself, where current Aramaic proverbs were compared with verses from the Bible (Tractate Baba Kamma 91–92).

In a study about "The Origins and Historical Significance of the Present-Day Arabic Proverb," in *Islamic Culture*, vol. 26 (Hyderabad, India, 1952), I have tried to prove that the proverbs in use today in the Arab world—as far as their origin can be ascertained at all—are not those known to us from the ancient Arabic literature, which depicts Bedouin life, but are translations and adaptions of the Aramaic proverb in vogue among the sedentary population of the ancient East. The proverbs of the Arabic-speaking Jews are, of course, no exception to this rule. On the other hand, only a fraction of the proverbs used by the Jews seem to be peculiar to them, e.g., those which refer to Jewish religion, handicraft, and social life, or those characterized as Jewish by the Hebrew words which occur in them. In a collection of over fourteen hundred proverbs, taken down directly from the Jews of central Yemen and published by the writer under the title *Jemenica* (Leipzig 1934), only a comparatively small number could be identified as specifically Jewish. A graduate of the School of Oriental Studies of the Hebrew University in Jerusalem, an immigrant from Iraq, is compiling a collection of Bagdadi proverbs, used respectively by Muslims, Jews and Christians. Among these, strangely enough, the dissimilarity between Jewish and Muslim usage seems to be greater than in Yemen. The Yemenite Jewish proverb, in its wittiness, its love for the pun, its predilection for pungency, seems more akin to the Yiddish proverb of the eastern European Jews than the Bagdadi Jewish proverb. However, a full appreciation of these relationships will be possible only after both the Muslim and the Jewish side of the question has been fully investigated.

The situation is similar with regard to the music of the Jewish communities in Arab lands. As we mentioned above, this problem forms at present the object of serious research. I would, therefore, like to content myself with some provisional remarks.

As many pages of the Bible testify, music played a very great role in the life of the ancient Israelites. When the Babylonians asked their Jewish captives to sing to them from the songs of Zion, they did not refer, of course, to the Hebrew text, which they did not understand, but to the music, which must have been famous all over the ancient East when "Zion" was a by-word for good music, just as Vienna was in the nineteenth century. But after the destruction of the Second Temple, and possibly also for certain moral and ascetic reasons, instrumental music was banned not only from the service of the synagogue but also from the Jewish home. In this prohibition, the Jewish rabbis were followed by their Muslim colleagues—because instrumental music normally was connected with the employment of slave-girls, who served additional purposes. However, the Muslim rigorists utterly failed to make their ruling stick. Instrumental music became a very prominent feature in Arab cultural and social life, and soon the Muslim philosophers, who found the subject copiously treated in the works of their Greek masters, made it the object of theoretical study. When the Jewish polyhistor Saʿadya Gaon wrote a treatise on music, he did so not because of any special Jewish tradition but because music was included in the regular curriculum of a course in general philosophy, as pursued by Greeks and Arabs.

Furthermore, it stands to reason that the melodies which accompanied the Arabic poems of the Jewish women were taken over together with the general patterns of these poems. Just how far this applies to special Jewish songs is a matter which requires further investigation. However, it is a well-known fact that even Hebrew poems often were composed according to the melodies of Arab, Turkish, Ladino, and other folk-songs. In the very popular book of Hebrew poems by the seventeenth-century Hebrew poet Israel Najjara of Damascus, often the name of the non-Hebrew melody, in which the poem was composed, is marked at the beginning. That Jewish players of Oriental music have become prominent in our own times is indicative of the talent of Jews for music, but it does not change the basic fact that no secular music of any importance was preserved or developed by Jews inside Islam.

The situation is somewhat different with the melodies in the synagogue service, and in particular in the canticles accompanying the recital of the various parts of the Bible, the Talmud and the Prayer Book. When the twelfth-century traveller Benjamin of Tudela visited Bagdad—he came from Christian Europe—he was told that the melodies he had heard chanted by the members of a clan which traced its pedigree back to the singers of biblical times were those once chanted in the Holy Temple of Jerusalem. (Of course, in all ages tourists get interesting bits of information.) However, Muslim sources ascribe to Muhammad the prohibition against singing the Koran in the same way that Jews and Christians chant their Holy Scriptures. This would seem to indicate that in Muslim canticles some of the traditions of the older denominations have been taken over. It is indeed made probable if one compares certain Koranic canticles with those of the Syriac church. Without wishing to anticipate the specialists in this field, my own impression from attending the services of oriental communities during the last thirty years is that, although their canticles are tinged by a general musical feeling which is "Arabic," they have retained traits which make them akin to certain traditional melodies of the European Jews. This impression, however, may have to be qualified in the light of subsequent research.

The opposition of the Jewish rabbis to art, in particular to sculpture, and during certain periods to painting, naturally was even stronger than their abhorrence of instrumental music; for the prohibition against making a graven image was one of the Ten Commandments. There were many fluctuations in this matter, and the Church Fathers were almost as strict about it as the teachers of the Jewish Oral Law. Those interested will find a readable and expert exposition of the whole subject in Boaz Cohen's article, "Art in Jewish Law," in *Judaism, A Quarterly Journal*, New York 1954.

It is well known that in later Roman times, synagogues were covered with mosaics and wall paintings representing biblical scenes and other subjects; similar decorations appear in churches. It is the considered view of the writer that the Prophet Muhammad was largely inspired by wall paintings of biblical stories and that the strange arrangement and interpretation of the biblical material in the Koran is partly to be explained by the visual origins of his first information.

Later Muslim sources ascribe to Muhammad the saying: "Whitewash your mosques and do not cover them with paintings, as is done in churches and synagogues." This saying cannot be authentic, for in the very early years of Islam, the Muslims did not as yet occupy themselves with these problems. Thus in a palace of an Umayyad caliph excavated near Jericho in Palestine, even sculptures abounded (sculptures of dancing girls, not of the caliph) and similar discoveries have been made in other ruins of that era. But it is significant for understanding of the close connection between Muslim and Jewish law that Islam later adopted Jewish abhorrence of graven images. The result was that in all Arabic-speaking countries the plastic reproduction of the human body completely disappeared. Painting, especially the illustration of manuscripts with scenes from human life, was not unknown, but it was never very common. The Arab Muslim spirit found its real artistic expression in the abstract ornament, in the arabesque, often combined with artistically developed Arabic script. Such ornaments can be found everywhere—on carpets, on vessels, in manuscripts or in stucco on the walls of buildings. The Arabs changed their style from period to period and from one country to another, but their non-human image of beauty was everywhere the same.

In this field, Jewish popular artists could borrow from the Arab Muslim tradition without scruples. The beautiful ornaments on the Bible and other manuscripts, preserved from the tenth century, testify to this trend. When one sees that Bible illustrations of that century used the same motifs as those found on ancient Jewish mosaics and coins, one may even assume that there did exist in this matter a Jewish tradition preceding Islam. However, there can be no doubt that, later, in their taste and style the Jewish artists followed closely contemporary and local models.

A tenth-century Egyptian cover of a Bible manuscript reminds one of Coptic linen with its patches of deep colors and robust patterns, dispersed over the white ground, while the thirteenth-century Yemenite manuscripts clearly have Ayyubid style, the whole page covered with delicate ornaments, even the Hebrew letter adapted to the light and elegant forms of a later time. That a Jewish scribe tried to imitate in Hebrew the creations of Ibn Muqla, the most famous of all Arab calligraphers, is stated expressly in a literary source.

The Hebrew letter, like the Arabic, was used also as a decoration for the interior of a building. This is the description given by Benjamin of Tudela in his *Travels* (or, *Itinerary*) of the great synagogue of Bagdad: "The great synagogue of the Head of the Diaspora has columns of marble of various colors overlaid with silver and gold, and on those columns are verses from the Psalms in golden letters. In front of the Ark are about ten steps of marble; on the topmost are the seats of the Head of the Diaspora and of the Princes of the House of David." Twelfth-century Bagdad has disappeared, but in Spain some synagogues of a slightly later time have been preserved. We find in the synagogue of Toledo, then the main city, the same forest of columns, the same covering of the interior with Hebrew script, together with other ornaments, carried out, of course, in the particular Moorish style of that time and place.

While the great synagogues of Bagdad and Toledo were certainly inspired by the examples of Muslim public places of worship, a synagogue normally—as we have seen above—was very different from a mosque both in its architecture and interior arrangement. The very function of the synagogue, so different from that of the mosque, and perhaps also the model of the traditional synagogue building, had the effect that, to the present day, the dissimilarity has remained. Thus a master mason from Reda', the second greatest Jewish community in Yemen, told me that he built the newest synagogue in the place (it was completed only a short time before the mass exodus of the Jewish community) exactly according to the plan of the oldest, which was reputed to have been erected immediately after the arrival of the Jews in Reda' from Palestine.

In Yemen, according to the German geographer Carl Rathjens, even the town houses of the Jews were different from the Muslim. Their main feature was an open court in the second floor, a characteristic which Rathjens explains both by its Mediterranean origin and by the fact that Jewish social life had its center inside the house.

The most important field of Jewish participation in the art of the Arab Muslim world were the small crafts, silver work, weaving, embroidery, and also many others. Jewish gold- and silversmiths had been active in Arabia before Islam and have been found in practically all Arab countries down to our own time. In a truly "Arabic" country like Yemen, the Jews were prominent everywhere as the craftsmen.

We learn a good deal about Jewish craftsmen from the Geniza, the fact that some of them were employed in the imperial workshops of the Fatimids; or that around 1140 three Jewish silversmiths—including two from North Africa—emigrated to Ceylon to pursue their livelihoods; or that a Tunisian Jew ran a factory in India, in which other Jews bearing Arabic names, possibly from Yemen, made brass vessels which are described to us in detail primarily for the sake of beauty.

An artisan depends on the taste of his customer. Even where we find, as once was the case in Yemen, certain arts almost exclusively in the hands of Jews, their creations must be regarded as a joint result of their own artistic tradition and the tastes of those who buy their products. Their creations are, therefore, in a most tangible way the outcome of a long-enduring symbiosis. Thus it may be true that certain traits of Yemenite Jewish folk art go back to Hellenistic patterns. We find the reason for this not only in the fact that the Jews emigrated to Yemen at a time when Palestine was within the orbit of Hellenistic civilization, but also in another fact, brought to light by recent excavations—that Yemen itself was completely flooded with the industrial and artistic products of the Hellenistic world. The inhabitants of Yemen appreciated the work of the Jewish silversmiths because they created objects reminiscent of those which they had learned to like.

In any case, the results of that common creation—as far as we are able to judge from the objects brought by the immigrants from Yemen to Israel—were by no means negligible. A good piece of Yemenite Jewish art, whether a necklace, a handwoven garment, or a piece of embroidery, leaves one with the impression of a perfectly integrated folk art, the expression of a secure culture.

For one all-embracing reason, Jewish handicraft in Islam countries has degenerated and, with few exceptions, can no longer be called an art. While in Damascus in 1924, I was shown by a Jewish coppersmith a brass ewer of perfect form made by his grandfather, while he and his colleagues fabricated only the cheap stuff sold in tourist shops. I asked him why he did not make the beautiful things his grandfather had. His reply was: "First, I can't; and, second: Nobody would buy." The real reason for this decline is that the great medieval civilization of the Middle East, which we are accustomed to calling by the misleading term "Islamic," has finally come to an end. Those who once belonged to it can no more create in the spirit of that civilization. The few Yemenites who still do are an anachronism, doomed soon to disappear. Any revival of the folk art of the Jewish communities in Arab countries—just as the revival of any other aspect of their cultural life—can be achieved only out of the clear knowledge that the profound changes in mind and matter, which have brought about the modern world, must necessarily affect and completely alter whatever is left of the ancient heritage of a great past.

8

THE NEW CONFRONTATION

1. *Arab Eclipse and Re-emergence.*

In the previous chapters, the common background and origins of the Jews and the Arabs, their earlier contacts and their prolonged and fertile symbiosis during the Middle Ages have been discussed. To all this a very important other affinity must be added: their common heritage of suffering.

In many respects the Arabs enjoyed happier fortune than the Jews. Israel had to fight, or to accept the yoke of the ancient Oriental Empires, Assyria, Babylon and Persia, when these were at the height of their power; the Arabs overran Sassanid Persia, when it was a decrepit, utterly weakened, feudal state.

The Jews braved Rome courageously but without any prospect of success, at a time when Rome was the lord of the world; the Arabs defeated its medieval heir, when it was emaciated by external wars and exhausted by inner friction.

The great majority of the Jewish people has been living in the Diaspora, that is, as minority groups, during the last 2,550 years, while the Arabs—by which word we denote here the populations speaking today an Arab vernacular—have in the past sometimes been forcibly displaced, but, as a whole, never have suffered *Galuth* (exile) as has the Jewish people.

In many other respects, however, these Arabs have fared worse even than the Jews. They have, so to speak, suffered "exile," while on their own soil.

This basic fact, requisite to a true appreciation of the present situation of the Middle East, needs some explanation.

When, about 1,320 years ago, the original Arabs came out of their homeland, the Arabian Peninsula, and conquered in successive wars lasting over three generations most of the countries between Spain and Central Asia, they accomplished a very great military feat, even though the kingdoms which they overran were worn out. They encountered in the whole Fertile Crescent not a single independent nation but only denationalized subject populations deprived of arms.

The empire of the Caliphs, which they erected on the ruins of the kingdoms destroyed by them was also a remarkable creation. However, the Arabs very soon lost their military prowess, and the state which they had erected disintegrated very rapidly; only nominal overlordship was conceded to the Caliphs of Bagdad by the successor states, and even then only by some of them.

Many causes seem to have contributed to this situation which was the source of great misfortune for the whole Middle East. Perhaps the very fact that the Arabs did not encounter any strong resistance on their march of conquest was in reality their disaster: they over-expanded and soon lost control over their vast realm. Perhaps they were by innate inclination more disposed to the cultural aspects of civilization, literature, art, science and religion, than toward the army and the state, those two pillars of society for which the Turkish peoples afterward showed such particular ability. Perhaps they were given too much to sensual pleasures.

In any case, less than a hundred years after the conclusion of the wars of conquest, the Arabs themselves were submerged in the large denationalized, subject population of the Middle East. They were no longer admitted to the regular army, which consisted mostly of slave soldiers imported from Central Asia or North Africa or other barbarian peoples, while in the administration men of Arab stock formed an insignificant minority. To be sure, Arabic meanwhile had become the language of the new medieval civilization of the Middle East and Islam its ruling religion. However, out of the Arab conquests no new nation emerged which was able either to defend or to rule itself, or to control its economic and social problems.

Thus, the Middle East was left unprotected and became prey to successive invasions from barbarian peoples, while later, from the thirteenth to the eighteenth century, it was ruled by castes of ruthless, foreign slave soldiers. The popular conception that the Arab countries were under foreign domination only during the four hundred years of Ottoman rule (1517–1917) is completely erroneous. The Mamelukes who ruled over Egypt, Palestine and Syria before the Ottomans (1250–1517) were called in Arab sources "The Turkish Government," because these slave soldiers were recruited from Turkish-speaking countries, and a similar system prevailed prior to the rule of the Mamelukes.

Thus, until the beginning of the nineteenth century the Arab countries were ruled by corps of slave-guards recruited invariably from foreign countries. These corps often were very efficient; for example, in September 1260, the Egyptian Mamelukes beat the Mongol hordes near *Ain Jalut* ("The Goliath's Spring"—in biblical and modern times called *Ain Harod*)—one of the decisive victories in Oriental history—one which largely accounts for the fact that, from that time to the present, Egypt has been economically and culturally far superior to Iraq and Syria, although these countries are very fertile by nature. On the other hand, that particular battle was not a very great military feat, for the main Mongol army was then occupied elsewhere. Nevertheless, it was these Egyptian Mamelukes who successfully withstood the Mongols as long as they were a menace to the Valley of the Nile.

These slave-guards mercilessly exploited the countries given to them; in addition, they often fought each other, so that civil war was the rule rather than the exception; they tended to deteriorate very rapidly. They were soon unable to protect the sedentary population against the rapacious Bedouins, who are always prone to penetrate into cultivated areas where there is a weak government. Being unable to protect himself against the rapacity of his various oppressors, the farmer limited production to the barest minimum. This decreased continuously, until that stage of under-nourishment was reached which is still prevalent in so many parts of the Middle East.

The reforms in the Sultan's Empire during the nineteenth century had some beneficial effect also on the Arab countries, but Ottoman rule as a whole remained foreign, oppressive and corrupt, and there was neither a Cavour nor a Herzl to fight for an Arab state—mainly because the idea of an Arab nation had not yet been born.

Not a single independent state with Arabic as its official language was in existence before World War I. If asked about his affiliations, an inhabitant of Arab Asia of that time would have described himself as a Muslim or a Christian, as a member of such-and-such a tribe or clan, an inhabitant of this-or-that town or village, or as a subject of the Ottoman Sultan, but it would hardly have occurred to him to call himself an Arab.

How far the world at large was unaware of the existence of a potential Arab nation, may be gathered, for example, from Sir Mark Sykes' book dealing with the future of the Ottoman Empire called *The Caliphs' Last Heritage*, which appeared as late as 1915—a bulky volume of 650 pages destined for expert readers. The author found it necessary to explain in his introduction that Turkey was not as Turkish as Scotland was Scottish, but comprised many peoples such as Greeks, Armenians, Kurds, Jews, Arabs, Turkomans, etc.

Whatever may be said about the precursors of contemporary Arab nationalism, the fact remains that the present state of the Arab world was mainly created by external factors, beginning with the "Young Turk" revolution of 1908 and particularly aided by the liberation of Arab Asia by the Allied armies in World War I.

Another consequence of World War I was that the proclamation of the principle of national autonomy by the victors gave the Arab peoples automatically a clear-cut aim: the erection of autonomous national states. Thirdly, during the first global war oil came into prominence as the world's most important fuel, and as the Arab East proved to be a particularly rich oil deposit, political liberation was coupled with bright prospects of almost unlimited economic possibilities.

The tensions preceding World War II and the events of the War itself highly favored the Arab claims. It may be said that, of the many peoples involved in the war, the Arabs were the only real winners.

To sum up: The great Arab conquests at the beginning of the Muslim era did not create an Arab nation; but they produced the elements, from which, after many, many hundreds of years of suffering and humiliation, Western ideas and, even more, Western politics could shape the foundations of modern Arab states. It remained for the Arabs of the present generation to take their destiny vigorously into their own hands. Considering their past, one must concede that they have not done badly at all.

2. *The Coming of Israel.*

Israel's revival, of course, came about in quite the opposite way. All outward factors were absolutely against it: a people dispersed over the four corners of the earth, with no soil beneath it, with no organized bodies of its own and lacking the social layers vital for the normal life of a people, in particular farmers and workers.

Israel's revival was, in fact, primarily the outcome of inner forces. The assiduous work of Jewish scholarship during the last one hundred and fifty years slowly created the idea and the material for a coherent history of the Jewish people in all countries and during all the ages; relief work for the more backward Jewish communities—which was not unconnected with research—gave rise to the creation of the first great Jewish organization; it is significant that the distinguished scholar Solomon Munk, in 1840, accompanied the philanthropist Sir Moses Montefiore and Adolphe Cremieux on their visit to Mehmet Ali, the Viceroy of Egypt, and gave, during his visit, the first impulse to the erection of modern Jewish schools in Alexandria.

Furthermore, the example of the revival of various European peoples gave momentum to the old Messianic hopes in the shape of modern, national resurgence.

A popular literature in Yiddish and another, connected with it, in Hebrew, gave articulate expression to the new self-assertion. Finally, social ideals, from various sources, paved the way for that occupational shuffle of considerable parts of the Jewish people, which alone made the creation of a Jewish state possible.

Nevertheless, without concomitant external factors the State of Israel would never have come into existence. World War I led to the establishment of the British Mandate over Palestine. The gruesome Nazi massacres made relief for the persecuted an international problem. The particular situation in the Middle East after World War II suggested bold solutions. Therefore it was not only the common inner rhythm of Jewish and Arab histories— a resurgence after long suffering—which made their revivals coincide, but also international factors which influenced the two peoples alike.

This coincidence is indeed remarkable. The year 1922, which saw the establishment of the first, great, independent, Arabic-speaking kingdom, Egypt, witnessed also the international endorsement of the Jewish National Home in Palestine. In 1925, both the University of Cairo and the Hebrew University, Jerusalem, were solemnly opened, both after preparations lasting for many years. Israel became an independent state only a few years after its northern neighbors, Lebanon and Syria, and had the opportunity to vote in the United Nations Assembly for the creation of another Arab state, Libya.

To these significant signposts of the new Jewish-Arab symbiosis, others of a less spectacular nature are to be added: the renaissance of the Hebrew and Arab languages and literatures, as well as the common discipleship of the two peoples to Western civilization.

3. *The Cultural Aspects of the Two Coinciding Revivals.*

We are now in a position to define with greater exactitude the similarities and the differences between the Jewish and Arab revivals in modern times.

The resurgence of the two peoples was effected after a prolonged period of suffering and humiliation, a period during which neither formed a nation in the ordinary sense of the word. The sufferings of Israel and the Arabs were of a very different nature and so were their revivals. Israel's birth was preceded by a long and vicissitudinous dawn and came into sight slowly and incompletely like a morning in the high North; the Arab revival broke out suddenly, like the glaring sunshine, which, in the South, comes so quickly after the darkness of the night.

Both revivals were achieved under the direct impact of the West. The Jews, the majority of whom had been living in Europe for many generations—indeed their forefathers may have been there prior to the peoples among whom they lived—naturally were affected by European culture earlier, to a larger extent, and more deeply than the Arabs; they have in fact become essentially a European people. On the other hand, it is true that until approximately 1750, the European Jews lived mainly in the East, so to speak, and shared only to a very limited extent the spiritual and social achievements of their neighbors.

At the same time, one should keep in mind that the Arab world has never been completely cut off from Europe. It formed with it in the past a certain unity of culture, based on the common heritage of the ancient East, Israel and Greece, and possibly also on a certain affinity in character and mentality. The latter point has been stressed by a number of European observers, such as Bertram Thomas in his book *The Arabs*. The former viewpoint—that of the common spiritual heritage—has been particularly emphasized by Dr. Taha Husain, one of the most prominent thinkers of contemporary Egypt, in his book *The Future of Civilization in Egypt* (1939), available in an English translation prepared by Sidney Glazer of New York.

Taha Husain confines his explanations to Egypt, but it applies, in different degrees, to the countries of Arab Asia. The real Orient begins in India, and there is no use throwing all the "Asiatics" into the same pot. On the other hand, the fact remains that modern science, the source of all great technical and social revolutions in our time, was the exclusive creation of Europe and America. All other peoples have been forced to find a synthesis of their own cultural tradition and that of Western science.

Because of the great affinity between Islam and Judaism, the tasks before Jews and Arabs are very similar. So far, Muslim Modernism has not produced impressive results as may be gathered from H. A. R. Gibbs' searching book *Modern Trends in Islam,* von Grunebaum's *Modern Islam* and similar publications.

However, it would not be fair to compare the Arab achievements in this field with the Jewish. They have not yet had modern religious thinkers of the quality of Nachman Krochmal or Hermann Cohen or Franz Rosenzweig, not to mention the countless others who have written on Judaism in the modern world, particularly those who are still with us. But it would be unfair to say that in comparison with the Jews the Arabs have given comparatively little toward a really scientific and critical appreciation of their history and literature, let alone that of others. True, they have not produced a Zunz, a Graetz, or a Solomon Schechter, let alone a Goldziher, a scholar who created an original interpretation of a foreign civilization. To be sure, many excellent editions of classical works, inspired by modern methods, have been brought out, especially in Egypt, and many well-written books and essays on historical and literary subjects, some even of a hypercritical character, have been published. Still, only a fraction of these can be regarded as original contributions to theology or history.

However, one must remember that the close connection of the Arabs with European science is not older than two generations. An Arab friend, with whom I discussed these matters a few years ago, rightly remarked: "We are just beginning."

There is no reason why these things should not change in the near future. Many young Arabs have the capacity, as well as the means, for prolonged, leisurely study at the best universities in the world, and quite a number of notable Ph.D. theses have already been published by these young men.

The problem is rather one of spiritual outlook: the question whether there will be released in the Arab world the moral forces which bring about a craving for objective research, for the seeking of truth, irrespective of merely utilitarian aims or propaganda.

In the past, the Arabic-speaking populations of the Middle East had a great tradition of scholarship. It will be very interesting to see whether this tradition will be revived under the impact of modern science and will lead ultimately to a renascence of scientific activity among the Arabs, comparable to that created a thousand years ago by the impulse of Greece.

With Israel, the intellectual relationship with the West is somewhat different from that of Islam. What the Jews have achieved in the way of modern interpretation of their history and spiritual heritage, or in science in general, they have achieved as a component of European culture. When *Al-Kitab*, one of the leading Egyptian monthlies, in a survey of the first fifty years of this century, mentioned two Jews—referring to them as Jews—among the twenty men who molded the twentieth century, it certainly did not intend to see in this a specific Jewish achievement.

The State of Israel is in this respect just a patch of Europe transplanted to the eastern shore of the Mediterranean. It has, of course, neither the human reservoir nor the natural wealth of the Arab countries. However, it can rely to some extent on the brains and the material resources of the Jewish people at large, and *Torah lishmah*, study for study's sake, is still a tangible ideal among many of its young men and women. Indeed, one of the most encouraging aspects of present-day Israel is the fact that the post-war generation of students, who have grown up in Palestine, do not fall short in zeal or intellectual capacity of the previous generation, recruited mainly from the old centers of Jewish learning in Eastern Europe.

All in all, it seems that the Middle East has excellent prospects for a revival of intellectual activity, comparable to the time when the famous seats of learning, Alexandria, Beirut and Antioch, flourished beside the Jewish academies of Palestine, or when, 600 years later, savants belonging to the three monotheistic religions could discuss in Bagdad in complete freedom the most delicate problems of Greek philosophy. The problems confronting the Middle East are so specific and so manifold—social, religious, agricultural, industrial, biological—that it is not far-fetched to assume that its contribution to science will bear to some extent a particular, regionally-inspired character.

In the field of literature, the impact of Western civilization on the revival of Jews and Arabs was not less complete than in the fields of science and philosophy. Not a single line of a really contemporary Hebrew or Arab author would have been written as it stands without that influence. The use of traditional literary forms, such as the Arab *Maqama* or the Hebrew *hasidic* story, does not change the picture, for these are used with modern application.

A really great writer, of course, achieves such perfect inner harmony that the reader may forget the sources of his inspiration. In the Hebrew writer S. Y. Agnon, for example, the European influence is veiled, but it is working subtly and is therefore the more real. European influence is present in every aspect of modern Hebrew and Arab literatures, their motifs, their forms, their whole approach, and last but not least, their language.

The linguistic aspect of the European impact is particularly significant. Here the common spiritual heritage of the Middle East and Europe, to which we have referred above, has left a strong imprint. Just as the "Eastern" biblical style was not without influence on the languages of Europe, thus—and in a far higher degree —Greek science and philosophy have enriched the Arabic language with countless abstract terms and expressions, a number of which have even entered into colloquial speech.

The medieval Jewish authors living in Muslim countries who wrote on philosophic or scientific subjects, as a rule used Arabic; however, as their writings were very much sought after by the

European Jews, who did not know any literary language save Hebrew, they were translated into this language almost immediately after their composition.

For this purpose, a new Hebrew style was formed congruent to the subject matter and modelled after Arabic. Thus, in some ways, Arabic did for Hebrew what Latin achieved for the European languages: it transmitted to it Greek terms and ways of expression, without which no abstract reasoning is possible. The general result of the whole process, however, was that Hebrew and Arabic, on the one hand, and the European languages on the other, came to possess a great common fund, even before the impact of modern Western literature on the two Semitic languages made the latter so thoroughly European in character.

This new westernized style is particularly prominent in the language of the newspapers. I often happen to read Hebrew, Arabic or English newspapers at a stretch; from the point of view of linguistic psychology, (leaving aside the outward aspects of script, vocabulary and grammar) the three languages are virtually one. As a curiosity I would like to mention that a number of biblical phrases have found their way into Arabic—through the medium of English or French.

Turning now to modern Arabic and Jewish literature, we naturally confine ourselves with regard to the latter to books written in Hebrew. The problem of Jewish authors writing in German or other European languages, such as Heine, Werfel, Kafka, Stefan Zweig,—all of whom, by the way, have found much attention among contemporary Arab literary critics—let alone the American Jewish writers, falls outside the scope of these pages.

Modern Hebrew literature which gives full expression and is a vehicle of actual life, came into being during the last third of the nineteenth century and is, therefore, fairly contemporary with modern Arabic literature—unlike modern Jewish thought and historical research, which preceded the Arab—as we have seen—by approximately three generations. Moreover, it would appear that modern Arabic literature is about to become an interpreter of Arab realities to a degree similar to that reached by Hebrew literature with regard to Jewish life.

Several contemporary Arab writers have attained universal recognition in the countries in which Arabic is read—and beyond. Of the older generation, one might mention the following: Tewfik al-Hakim, equally fluent in French and Arabic (his *Mace of Justice* has recently been translated into English by Mr. Abba Eban); Mahmud Taimur, many of whose short stories, written partly in classical and partly in colloquial Arabic, have been published in European translations; Mikhail Nu'aima, a Lebanese-American writer of short stories and essays; Salama Musa, a Copt, whose recently published autobiography deserves an English translation; and, of course, Taha Husain, whose sincere sketches of the life of the Egyptian countryside constitute only a small fraction of his immense literary production.

In general, it is a most characteristic feature of contemporary Arabic literature that many of its leading men do not specialize in a definite field of creation but are poets, writers of short stories, novelists, playwrights, essayists, journalists, scholars engaged in research work, and sometimes also politicians, in one person.

The literary output of a man like the Egyptian al-Aqqad is simply stupendous, and so is that of quite a number of other Egyptian writers who have all died recently, within the last ten years — Muhammad Husain Haikal (like Taha Husain a former Minister of Education), or the poet Abu Shadi, or Ahmed Amin (a former Dean of Cairo University). A serious and prolific scholar like Abderrahman Badawi is at the same time a fertile poet and the same is to be said of some Syrian and Lebanese authors who have successfully written about literary and historical subjects. However, if we take narrative prose as the representative form of artistic expression of modern man, the younger post-World War II generation of novelists, who specialize in this field, must be regarded as the avant-guard of Arab letters.

It cannot be said, of course, that all aspects of Jewish life have already found adequate expression in modern Hebrew literature. There exists quite a number of novels on life in the *Kibbutzim*, the communal settlements, but despite considerable merit they cannot be regarded as doing full justice to this greatest of all Palestinian social experiments.

On the other hand, I believe it is fair to say that contemporary Arab letters have not yet produced anything which could compare in rank with the twelve volumes of novels and stories of S. Y. Agnon, which represent a complete world in themselves, with a distinctive style, have a philosophy of life, delicate artistry and, at the same time, offer a reliable guide to various periods and aspects of the life which they describe or symbolize.

In addition to the "Classics" of modern Hebrew literature, there are many other authors of various merit who have written attractively and instructively about the groups or classes to which they belonged, or which they had special opportunity to study thoroughly. Such are Y. Burla (*Sefaradim* and Oriental communities) or Moshe Smilanski (the old Jewish colonies in Palestine). These two, as well as the late Y. Shami, a native of Hebron, have written as well many fine stories on the life of the Arab *Fellahin*, Bedouins and townsmen, many of which—as far as I am able to judge—compare favorably with Arabic material on the same subject.

The working class of the second generation Yemenites is well represented by one of their own, M. Tabib, while H. Hazzaz, an author of great distinction, has devoted five of his twelve published volumes to the old Yemenites. The war years produced a worthy crop of plays and stories, of which the most impressive possibly are the short novels of S. Yizhar, which represent the heart-searching, almost militant, pacifism prevailing among the best boys of the *Palmach*, the "Commandos" of the *Haganah*.

The Jewish people underwent a deep social and cultural rebirth, before it achieved its political independence; to the Arab countries the first half of the twentieth century brought nationhood and political autonomy; however, their social integration has still to come. There is little doubt that these future social changes—whether achieved by planned reforms or by violent upheavals—will not fail to bring about new ventures also in Arabic letters.

SELECTED BIBLIOGRAPHY

1. Arabs and Islam

LEWIS, BERNARD, *The Arabs in History*. London-New York 1954. The most recent short history of the Arabs, written by a competent historian. Brings the story down to the present times.

HITTI, PHILLIP K., *History of the Arabs*. London-New York 1953. Stresses cultural history.

BROCKELMANN, CARL, *History of the Islamic Peoples*, with a review of events 1939–1947 by Moshe Perlmann. New York 1947. Concentrates on facts and political history.

POLIAK, ABRAHAM N., *A History of the Arabs*. Jerusalem 1945 (in Hebrew). Emphasizes social and economic developments. An original contribution.

V. GRUNEBAUM, GUSTAVE E., *Medieval Islam*. Chicago 1947. Stimulating study of the medieval civilization of the Middle East and its relation to Hellenism.

MEZ, ADAM, *The Renaissance of Islam*. London 1937. Detailed picture of Muslim society in the tenth century.

GOLDZIHER, IGNAZ, *Vorlesungen über den Islam*. Heidelberg 1925. This German book of the Hungarian Jewish scholar still is the most authoritative account of the development of Muslim religion.

GUILLAUME, ALFRED, *Islam* (Pelican Books A 311). London 1954. The latest popular presentation of Islam, written by a theologian and veteran Arabist.

GIBB, H. A. R., *Modern Trends in Islam*. Chicago 1946. Searching study of the nature of Modernism in Islam.

VON GRUNEBAUM, G. E., *Modern Islam: The Search for Cultural Identity*. Berkeley and Los Angeles 1962. An outstanding collection of studies by the author, illustrating various aspects of contemporary developments.

SMITH, WILFRED CANTWELL, *Islam in Modern History*. Princeton 1957. Specifically devoted to a discussion of the state of Islamic religion today.

BERGER, MORROE, *The Arab World Today*. New York 1962. A comprehensive picture of contemporary Arab social life and institutions.

HOTTINGER, ARNOLD, *The Arabs: Their History, Culture and Place in the Modern World*. Berkeley and Los Angeles 1963. Brings the story down to May 1963.

For current events and developments:

Middle Eastern Affairs, A Monthly. New York.
Middle East Journal, A Quarterly. Washington.
Hamizrah Hehadash (The New East), A Quarterly (in Hebrew, with summaries in English). Jerusalem.

2. Jews and Judaism

ROTH, CECIL, A *Short History of the Jews*. Illustrated Edition. London 1953.

GRAYZEL, SOLOMON, A *History of the Jews*, Revised Edition. Philadelphia 1952.
The two latest shorter histories of the Jewish people, each with its own merits, the first representing a European approach, the second an American.

BARON, SALO WITTMAYER, A *Social and Religious History of the Jews*. Second edition. Philadelphia 1952 (in the course of publication.) The contemporary standard work on Jewish history.

FINKELSTEIN, LOUIS (Editor), *The Jews, Their History, Culture and Religion*. Philadelphia 1949. Four volumes. Many important contributions; note especially Halkin, Abraham S., Judaeo-Arabic Literature.

ROTH, LEON, *Judaism: A Portrait*. New York 1961. "My purpose in this volume is to promote fresh thinking on the nature of Judaism, and, since Judaism is the prototype of the monotheistic religion, to offer material for reflection on the nature of religion in general."

MOORE, GEORGE FOOT, *Judaism*. Harvard University Press, 1927. 3 volumes. A fair Christian account of talmudic Judaism.

GUTTMAN, JULIUS, *The Philosophies of Judaism*. New York-Philadelphia 1963. A history of Jewish theological thinking.

HESCHEL, ABRAHAM JOSHUA, *God in Search of Man: A Philosophy of Judaism*. Paperback, New York-Philadelphia 1959. A personal approach by a creative religious mind.

BENTWICH, NORMAN, *Israel Resurgent*. New York 1960. A sober account, emphasizing external relations.

For current events and developments:

Jewish Agency Digest.
American Jewish Yearbook.

3. Relations between the Arab and the Jewish peoples and between Islam and Judaism

The present book would not have been written, if a survey covering the whole field were on the market. The following books touch on various special aspects of the subject.

GEIGER, ABRAHAM, *Was hat Mohammed aus dem Judenthum aufgenommen?* Published first in 1833. Translated into English by F. M. Young under the title Judaism and Islam. Madras 1898. Still valuable.

HOROVITZ, JOSEPH, *"Islam"* in *Encyclopedia Judaica*, vol. 8, 566-588. Important summary with still useful bibliography.

TORREY, CHARLES CUTLER, *The Jewish Foundations of Islam*. New York 1933. Stimulating, but partly unfounded.

MONTGOMERY, JAMES A., *Arabia and the Bible*. Philadelphia 1934. The basic thesis of the book that the Israelites were an essentially Arabian people is based on unclear definition. See above ch. 2 and 3.

MARGOLIOUTH, DAVID S., *The Relations between Arabs and Israelites Prior to the Rise of Islam*. London 1924.

See note to preceding item.

GUILLAUME, ALFRED, "The Influence of Judaism on Islam," *The Legacy of Israel*, Oxford 1927, pp. 129–171. The subject as viewed by a Christian theologian.

HIRSCHBERG, W. H., *Israel in Arabia*. Jerusalem 1947 (in Hebrew). The latest detailed history of the Jews in Arabia down to the time of Muhammad.

KATCH, ABRAHAM I., *Judaism in Islam*. New York 1954. A commentary, with an introduction, on the three first chapters of the Koran based on Jewish sources.

VAJDA, GEORGE, *Introduction à la Pensée Juive au Moyen Age*. Paris 1947. Stresses the Islamic background of Medieval Jewish thinking. Meanwhile Vajda has made important contributions in this field.

MANN, JACOB, *The Jews in Egypt and in Palestine under the Fatimid Caliphs*, a contribution to their political and communal history based chiefly on Geniza material. Oxford 1920–1922. Somewhat incoherent, but revealing new aspects of Jewish life under Islam.

FISCHEL, WALTER JOSEPH, *The Jews in the Political and Economic Life of Mediaeval Islam*. London 1937. Deals with some especially dramatic episodes of Jewish participation in the life of various Muslim states.

GOITEIN, S. D., *Jewish Education in Muslim Countries, Based on Records from the Cairo Geniza*. Jerusalem 1962 (in Hebrew). Illustrates an important aspect of Judeo-Arabic symbiosis with the aid of newly identified source material.

STRAUSS, ELI, *The Jews of Egypt and Syria under the Mamluks*. Jerusalem 1944. 2 volumes (in Hebrew). Detailed and well-documented picture of some medieval Jewish communities under Muslim rule.

LANDSHUT, SIEGFRIED, *Jewish Communities in the Muslim Countries of the Middle East*. London 1950. A valuable survey despite some inaccuracies.

The Jewish Observer and Middle East Review, a London weekly, edited by Jon Kimche. A reasonably impartial and usually well-informed commentary on current Jewish-Arab relations.

CHRONOLOGICAL TABLES OF JEWISH

AND ARABIC HISTORY

The Jews

B.C.

1. ca. 1500. The forefathers of the Jewish people (Abraham and his house) emigrate from Iraq and Northern Syria to Palestine. Later on, some clans branch off and emigrate from there to Arabia.

2. ca. 1250. After a prolonged stay in Egypt, the main stock of the Israelite tribes is united by Moses into a confederation with a national religion and reoccupies Palestine.

3. ca. 1000. An Israelite state with a central Temple in Jerusalem is formed.

4. 853. Battle of Karkar. Ahab, king of Israel, and Gindibu, an Arab chieftain, take part in a coalition against an Assyrian invader.

The Arabs

B.C.

1. ca. 1500. See opposite column.

2. ca. 1250. The final domestication of the camel in North Arabia has farreaching results: 1. The desert becomes habitable for human beings, known as Bedouins or "Arabs"; 2. The transportation by land of heavy merchandise to distant countries becomes comparatively easy.

3. ca. 1000. The Bedouins, using camel warfare, begin to form larger political units.

4. See opposite column.

5. ca. 500. After the destruction of the first Temple and the first Jewish state, a new Jewish commonwealth is formed and the second Temple is erected. The collection of Hebrew religious and national literature known as the Bible is taking shape.

6. ca. 330. Alexander's conquest of the East. Hence, for about a thousand years, Jews and Arabs are under direct Greek (Hellenistic) influence.

7. ca. 165. The Jewish revolt, lead by the Maccabeans, against their Hellenistic overlords safeguards the existence of Monotheism and prepares the ground for the rise of Christianity and Islam.

A.D.

8. ca. 50. Jews "in every town in the inhabited world." Greatest expansion of the Hellenized Jewish Diaspora. Rise of Christianity both out of the soil of genuine Palestinian Judaism and out of Hellenistic Jewry.

9. 70. Destruction of the Second Temple. Judea a Roman province.

10. ca. 200. Full development of a new Jewish culture, which is subsequently condensed in the vast literature of the Talmud and the Midrashim. Its main characteristics: the sanctification of daily life by innumerable religious injunctions and general adult education by the fostering of study as worship. This strongly anti-hellenistic

5. ca. 500. Arabs begin to settle in the borderlands around the North Arabian desert, taking to local civilization and to the Aramaic language, which then was spoken in all those countries.

6. ca. 330. See opposite column.

7. ca. 165. The Nabataeans, an Aramaic speaking Arab people, form in parts of Syria, Transjordan and Northern Arabia the first enduring Arab kingdom.

A.D.

8. ca. 50. Rising importance of Arabia as a producer of incense—a commodity needed then as much as oil in modern times—and as a participant in international trade.

9. 105. Destruction of the Arabic Nabataean kingdom and its conversion into several Roman provinces.

10. ca. 200. The "Arabs," i.e. the Bedouins of Northern Arabia, begin to occupy the mountainous, agricultural and highly civilized countries of Southern Arabia and to absorb linguistically and socially their ancient populations. Through this process, the physical and spiritual manpower is created which will be needed for

culture becomes the main inspiration of Islam in the early and decisive stages of its development.

11. ca. 550. The Piyyut, the Hebrew religious poetry which is related to Byzantine poetry in full blossom.

12. ca. 600. Flourishing Jewish communities all over Arabia, especially in Hejaz, the future cradle of Islam, and in Yemen in South Arabia.

13. 622. See opposite column.

14. 635–715. The Jews, especially in Palestine and in Syria, and later on in Spain, hail the Arabs as their liberators from the persecutions of the church and side actively with the conquerors. They share, however, the rather precarious lot of the subject population as a whole.

15. 750–950. The fact that Iraq, which for many centuries had

the subsequent Arab conquest of the Middle East.

11. ca. 550. Full development of a "literary" Arabic language and a high standing, entirely secular, poetry, which forms a cultural unit for the linguistically and physiologically widely differing Arab tribes.

12. ca. 600. Arab traders regularly reach Egypt, Palestine, Syria, Iraq and Southern Persia.

13. 622. Muhammad, the founder of Islam, emigrates from his home town, the merchants' city of Mecca, where he is persecuted, to the agricultural settlement of Medina, where the presence of a large Jewish population has prepared the ground for the acceptance of a monotheisitic religion. For various reasons, mainly inner-Jewish, the Jews are unable to recognize Muhammad as a prophet and are subsequently driven out of most of North Arabia. They remain, however, in Yemen in South Arabia.

14. 632–752. During a hundred and twenty years of wars the Arabs conquer and partly colonize the countries between Spain and Central Asia.

15. 762. Foundation of Bagdad. Although originally conceived as

been the main center of Jewish life, becomes also the center of the Muslim Empire is of great importance and facilitates mutual influence. As one of the results of the rise of capitalism in the Middle East (see opposite column), the Jewish people, which up to that time had been largely agricultural, is transformed into one predominantly commercial.

16. ca. 900. As from that time, Jews emigrating from Iraq, Persia and other Asiatic countries, take prominently part in the economic opening up of Egypt and the Muslim West. Egypt, Tunisia, Morocco and in particular Spain are soon to rival with Iraq as centers of Jewish life and literary activity.

17. 942. Death of Saʿadya Gaon, an Egyptian Jew, who became spiritual leader of the Iraqi Jewish community. His death marks an epoch. By that time, the urban upper Jewish classes had become thoroughly arabized. Therefore, Saʿadya translates the Bible into Arabic, comments it and expounds the beliefs and ideals, and even the laws, of Judaism, as well as the rules of Hebrew grammar, in that language. He uses Hebrew, while writing religious poetry or polemics, or while addressing less assimilated Jewish communities.

18. ca. 1000–1141. The so-called "Golden Age" of the Jewish dias-

the seat of Government and imperial garrison, Bagdad becomes immediately a great commercial center and symbolizes the new mercantile civilization, which is largely due to the economic, social and spiritual forces set moving by the Arab conquests.

16. ca. 900. The Arabs are definitely replaced by the Turks and other races in their role as military rulers of the Muslim world. They are not to regain independence until modern times. This loss, however, is made good by the Arabization of most of the Middle East and of North Africa.

17. 956. Death of Masʿudi, a manysided, typical Muslim scholar and personal acquaintance of Saʿadya. Possessed by an inquisitive and receptive mind and a predilection for schematization, the Arabs take comparatively quickly to Greek philosophy and science transmitted to them by Christian and pagan scholars. A complete set of sciences, dealing with all aspects of human life, comes into being. Although most of the scholars engaged in those sciences were of non-Arabic extraction (some of them being of Jewish stock), this early Muslim civilization certainly is to be regarded as a creation of the Arab genius.

18. 1111. Death of Ghazzali, "the renewer of Muslim religion".

pora in Muslim Spain and Morocco. Its economic base is large-scale commerce with the other Mediterranean Muslim countries, as well as with South Arabia and India. Its finest product is perhaps the Neo-Hebraic poetry, which develops under Arabic influence. The invasion, from North Africa, of the Almohads, Berbers forming a dissident Muslim sect, puts an end to the flourishing state of the Jews in Muslim Spain and Morocco. The death, in 1141, of Yehuda Halevi, the Hebrew poet and thinker, appropriately denotes the termination of this period.

19. 1204. Death, in Cairo, of Maimonides, born 1135 in Cordova, Spain. Unlike Ghazzali, who was a professor of theology and opposed to philosophy, Maimonides is a doctor by profession and bases his exposition of the Jewish faith entirely on the then modern philosophy, which he himself helps to develop considerably. At the same time, corresponding to Ghazzali's role in Islam, he is the codificator of Jewish law. His philosophical and medical works are written in Arabic, his huge Code in Hebrew.

20. 1237. Death of Abraham, the son and follower of Maimonides as head of the Egyptian Jewry. He and his descendants were considerably attracted by Muslim mysticism. In this and the following centuries, many Jewish intellectuals, including members of the royal house of David, defect to

He brought about a synthesis between genuine Islam, which has its roots largely in Judaism, and Muslim ecstatic mysticism, which is a blend of inner-Islamic developments and Christian, Greek, Buddhist and other influences. Although a Persian by origin and mother tongue, he writes most of his works in Arabic. He marks the climax of medieval Islam.

19. 1193. Death of Saladin, the Kurdish hero, who temporarily united Egypt and Syria and broke the power of the Crusaders. Although personally a man of high qualities, his reign denotes the beginning of that Muslim orthodox reaction, which dominated the history of the Middle East down to the 20th century and possibly was one of the causes of its decline.

20. 1260. Battle of Ain Jalut or Ain Harod in Palestine. The Mamluks, a caste of soldier-slaves ruling Egypt and a part of Syria, defeat the remnants of the retreating Mongol army. While Iraq and Northern Syria never fully recover from the devastations wrought by the Mongols and other invaders,

Islam. The Jews participate in the general decline of the Arab Muslim world.

Egypt remains the center of the Arab-Muslim world. But here too, owing to the rapacious character of the military rulers and due to other reasons, general decline sets in.

21. 1492. Expulsion of the Jews and of the Moors (Muslims) from Spain. Many of these Spanish speaking Jews settle in Ottoman Turkey and contribute towards the revival of the Jewries in that great Muslim Empire.

21. 1517. The Ottoman Turks conquer Syria, Palestine and Egypt. Temporary revival of those countries as a consequence of their inclusion into a vigorous and expanding state.

22. 1572. Death of Isaac Lurya, the great Jewish mystic. The spiritual movement connected with his name rejuvenates Judaism in the countries of the Middle East.

22. 1565. Death of Sha'rani, paramount Muslim mystic. Unlike his compatriot and contemporary Isaac Lurya, who never wrote a book, Sha'rani's literary output was immense.

23. 1666. The Pseudo-Messiah Sabbatai Zevi of Smyrna, Turkey, in whom, for a short period, most of the Jews all over the world believe. His initial success demonstrates the prominence still enjoyed by the Jews of the East. His failure initiates a new period of decline and stagnation.

23. 1683. The unsuccessful siege of Vienna by the Ottoman Turks marks on the one hand the enormous extension of their Empire and at the same time signals its eclipse, which was particularly felt in the Arabic speaking countries.

24. 1789. The French Revolution inaugurates an era of gradual emancipation of the Jews from their civil disabilities.

24. 1798. Napoleon's conquest of Egypt marks the opening up of the Middle East by Western power politics and civilization.

25. 1840. The mission to Mehmet Ali, viceroy of Egypt and Syria, of Moses Montefiore (England) and Adolphe Cremieux (France), who were accompanied by the eminent scholar Solomon Munk, marks the beginning of the philanthropic and cultural activities of the Jews of the West for

25. 1805–1848. Mehmet Ali, an Albanian Turk, who created an Egyptian Empire, by organizing the army and economy of the country on European lines.

their underprivileged brethren in the East.

26. 1882. The "Biluim." Beginning of the agricultural colonization of Palestine by immigrants from Europe and Yemen.

27. 1897. First Zionist Congress in Basle, Switzerland, which adopts Theodore Herzl's program of the erection of a Jewish National Home in Palestine.

28. 1922. The League of Nations endorses the Brish mandate over Palestine.

29. 1925. Official Opening of the Hebrew University in Jerusalem.

30. 1948. Erection of the State of Israel. Increasing importance of the Jewish community of the United States for the welfare of Jews all over the world and in particular in Israel.

31. Ingathering to Israel of about half a million Jews from Muslim countries.

32. 1956–1964. The Sinai campaign and its aftermath. Consolidation of Israel's society. Rising importance and integration of the oriental communities.

26. 1882. Revolt of Arabi Pasha, a local Egyptian, against the rotten government of his country and subsequent occupation of Egypt by the British.

27. 1916. Husain, the Sherif of Mecca (and great-grandfather of the present ruler of Jordan) etc. revolts against the Turks and joins the Allies.

28. 1922. Egypt, although still occupied by British troops, is declared a sovereign kingdom.

29. 1925. Official opening (in fact: re-opening) of the University of Cairo.

30. 1941/1946/1951. Independence, respectively of Syria and Lebanon, Jordan and Libya. Growing economic and political involvement of the United States in the Middle East.

31. The revolt of the "young officers" in Egypt in July, 1952, possibly marks a new phase in the social history of the Middle East.

32. 1956–1964. The Suez crisis. "Arab Socialism." Sino-Russian rivalry for primacy in the Arab world.

INDEX